RANGER MOSBY

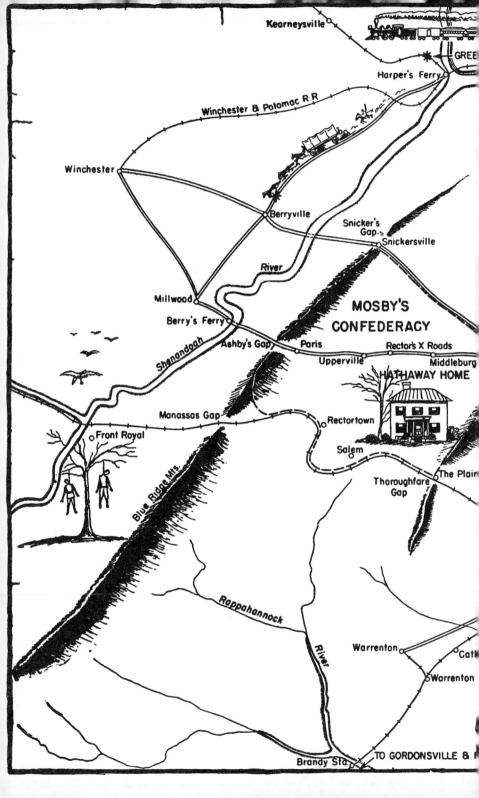

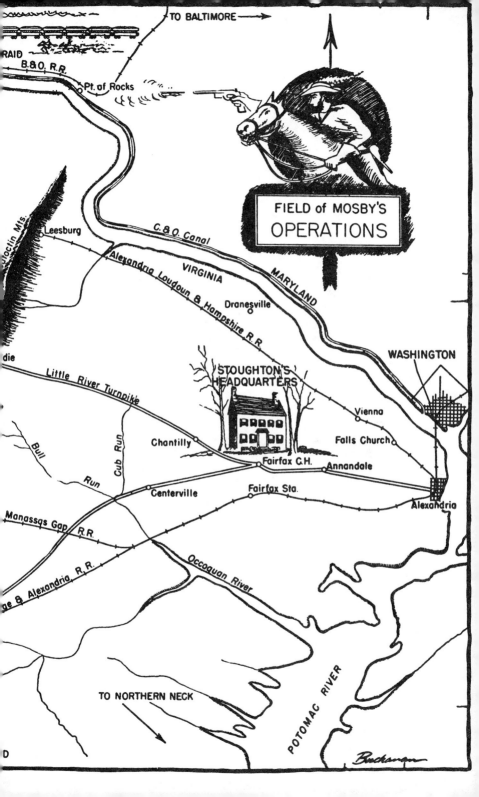

TO BALTIMORE →

RAID

B.&O. R.R.

Pt. of Rocks

Bull Mts.

Leesburg

C.&O. Canal

Alexandria Loudoun & Hampshire R.R.

VIRGINIA

MARYLAND

Dranesville

WASHINGTON

die

Little River Turnpike

STOUGHTON'S HEADQUARTERS

Vienna

Cub Run

Chantilly

Falls Church

Bull

Run

Fairfax C.H.

Annandale

Centerville

Fairfax Sta.

Manassas Gap R.R.

Alexandria

ge & Alexandria, R.R.

Occoquan River

FIELD of MOSBY'S OPERATIONS

TO NORTHERN NECK

POTOMAC RIVER

D

Buchanan

PORTRAIT OF MOSBY

From a painting by L. M. D. Gillaume.

RANGER MOSBY

Virgil Carrington Jones

EPM PUBLICATIONS, INC.
McLEAN, VIRGINIA

Library of Congress Cataloging-in-Publication Data

Jones, Virgil Carrington, 1906-
    Ranger Mosby.

    Reprint. Originally published: Chapel Hill, N.C.:
University of North Carolina Press, ©1944.
    Bibliography: p.
    Includes index.
    1. Mosby, John Singleton, 1833-1916.
2. Guerrillas—Southern States—Biography. 3. Soldiers
—Southern States—Biography. 4. Diplomats—United
States—Biography. 5. United States—History—Civil War,
1861-1865—Underground movements. I. Title.
E467.1.M87J6   1987   973.'45'0924   87-5059
ISBN 0-939009-01-3 (pbk.)

EPM Publications, Inc., 1003 Turkey Run Road
    McLean, Virginia 22101

Printed in the United States of America

Cover and book design by Tom Huestis
Portrait of Mosby is reproduced from the collections of the
    Library of Congress

TO MY MOTHER

PREFACE

THIS BOOK can be traced back to a conversation I had in Richmond one night early in 1938. It was with Richard V. Carter of *The Times-Dispatch*, who was convinced America had overlooked one of its greatest heroes. With his words in mind, I have been working for nearly six years, putting together a story told me in bits since childhood—at night beside the stove in my great-aunt's bedroom, around the banquet tables at Confederate reunions, often in the corner-store gatherings of my home town. My most recent informants have been the old folks who remembered and the younger folks who had heard—for members of the Forty-third Battalion, Partisan Rangers, were virtually extinct before I began my research. The glorious days when veterans narrowed their fading eyes and relived the past at mention of "Mosby's Men" could happen again only in the memory of succeeding generations.

My thanks for assistance go to many persons. Mosby's own family—his daughters, Mrs. Stuart Mosby Coleman and Miss Pauline Mosby of Warrenton, and his son, Mr. Beverly C. Mosby of Washington, D. C.—has been overly generous. Mr. H. I. Hutton of Warrenton, Mr. J. W. Slaughter of The Plains, and Mr. Curtis Chappelear and Mrs. Sadie Jeffries of Delaplane, all were of great help to me. So were attendants at the University of Virginia, the Virginia State Library, the Library of Congress and at other centers to which the trail of Mosby records led me. I am indebted also to that great historian, Dr. Douglas Southall Freeman, who gave me counsel when sorely needed.

Perhaps my greatest inspiration to finish this book has come from the present war in Europe. Almost daily I read in the newspapers of the amazing activities of the Commandos. Feats

vii

described were those of Mosby, moved up three-quarters of a century. The Confederates about whom I was writing were a fearless and visionary counterpart of the modern independent, paced by a Spartan who led his charges to what seemed impossible feats. Throughout the war their movements gave enemy officers their greatest embarrassment. Some high in command were cashiered, others court-martialed, because blame for the successful raids of Mosby's Rangers lay heaviest upon them. Reports of his activities did not sound reasonable, and it was downright waste of time to attempt an explanation. Thwarted in their efforts to dispose of the battalion, Union troops frequently prescribed for it a tragic fate. No less a figure than Federal General Joseph E. Hooker averred that, "if the reports of the newspapers were to be believed, this whole party was killed two or three times" during one winter. One of the major tributes to its leader came in later years when it was discovered that General Robert E. Lee had complimented and commended him oftener in his official papers than he had any other subordinate.

Mosby built his command to 800 before the end of the war, but the largest force he ever assembled for a raid scarcely exceeded 350. Usually his forays were accomplished with from a dozen to eighty, a number he preferred because a small party could be concealed or moved about quickly as necessity demanded. All were well equipped. They lived wherever they found lodging and assembled whenever their leader gave the word.

While not recognized as a cavalry leader in the same class perhaps with Stuart or Forrest or Morgan, Mosby carved his own niche in the hall of fame. He was a master of prompt and skillful use of cavalry. Unlike his prototypes—the legendary Robin Hood, who hid deep in the shadows of Sherwood Forest, and Marion, the fox who took refuge in inaccessible Carolina swamps—he gathered his men along the rolling open country of Loudoun, Fauquier and Fairfax Counties in Northern Virginia and there set up his realm, known unofficially as Mosby's Confederacy. It was a quadrilateral whose boundaries were roughly between the present landmarks of Bluemont (then

Snickersville), Ashby's Gap, Marshall (then Salem) and Aldie. In this confederacy, Mosby became a law unto himself. With their civil law wiped out by the invading Blue columns, citizens came more and more to look on him as the dictator of that part of Virginia. Horse stealing and other forms of thievery were brought to his attention and he dealt with the culprits severely.

Partisan warfare was a serious practice with this man who put aside his law books to defend the South. Mosby believed that, by assuming the aggressive, he could compel his adversary to guard against a hundred points while he waited to attack any he chose. His scouts went everywhere and often kept him better posted concerning enemy movements than were the Federals themselves.

Federal correspondence and newspapers almost invariably described him as a guerrilla. This he never resented. But he pointed out in behalf of his men that they were enrolled properly in the regular army and subjected to customary military control, yet without the tiresome routine of drill.

Mosby took orders from no one, although his immediate superior was golden-voiced, bronze-bearded Jeb Stuart. They had mutual understanding of warfare, mutual sympathies. Little is assumed in the belief that, when the Partisan chieftain, a year the junior, trotted away in the dawn to take up his operations inside the Federal lines, Stuart's heart went with him. So also is there little assumption in the conviction that war was never hell to Mosby. He lived and operated with the freedom of an independent commander, believing that the fierce hostility the Federals displayed toward him was more on account of the sleep he made them lose than the number he killed and captured.

V. C. Jones

Washington, D. C.,
January, 1944.

CONTENTS

ILLUSTRATIONS

RANGER MOSBY

CHAPTER

1

The Fox of Fauquier

TWENTY MILES NORTH OF THE FEDERAL LINES along the Rappahannock River the little Virginia town of Warrenton stirred restlessly in the discomfort of a hot June day. All morning soldiers in blue had combed the place for a Confederate major. Citizens watching them gallop back and forth, peering, searching, shouting, noted with individual amusement that there was frequent repetition of effort. But this easily was understood. The United States Government wanted John Singleton Mosby, dead or alive.

In the shade of a tree on the lawn of the Warren-Green Hotel two spectators hid their interest behind a somnolence that verged on slumber. For half an hour no word had passed between them, one a silver-haired patriarch in worn alpaca, the other a young parolee whose crutches explained his absence from the Confederate army.

Not a leaf stirred overhead, and off toward the back of the grassy sweep of hillside, a cicada split the heavy quiet with a wide cadence of shrill notes. Except for the tireless clatter of cavalry in neighboring streets, the day might have been nature's peace offering after two years of bloody civil strife, her bait to lure blue-uniformed men from the North and gray-uniformed men from the South again into each other's good graces.

But the odds against her were hopeless. Never before had this town been so full of activity and yet so shorn of its natural beauty. Private lawns, once as neat and well manicured as a plantation owner's daughter, now lay overgrown with weeds. This was true from the outskirts up to the point where five inroads put their heads together on the crest of a hill near the business center. Everywhere the story was the same. Walkways down which in bygone days had twinkled dainty slippers were ragged and unkempt. Fences were missing or fallen, some fed to campfires, others damaged by the weight of soldiers resting on the march.

For months, ever since hostilities had been resumed in the spring, the town had been under Federal control. Union cavalry filled her streets, took over her homes, spread out monotonous lines of tents across the rich pasture meant as grazing land for thoroughbreds. Peaceful days were forgotten. Her residents—women, children and war-exempts—now lay awake at night and listened to the thunder of horses' hoofs, the rumble of guns rolling toward more lively scenes of action, the blaring notes of bugles and the sound of Mosby's wild raiders on the roads at night.

A ray of sun burst through the branches and flashed blindingly in the tiny, narrow eyes of the alpaca-clad individual. He took off his deteriorated straw, cupped the brim in his withered old hands and gave it a sharper slant across the bridge of his nose. With both hands he hitched his chair to give it better tilt against the tree and stared squintingly toward greenish-gray ramparts of the Bull Run Mountains.

Somewhere out there was Mosby.

There had been surprising reports lately on the activities of this mysterious Rebel who struck in the dark, from behind, or however he best could employ the element of surprise. He had snatched a Federal brigadier-general out of bed at Fairfax Court House, twenty miles inside the Union picket lines, and only a few days past he had derailed and destroyed a train on the main line to Alexandria. Since then the enemy had spent frantic days of speculation as to his next move. And today he was even reported to have slipped into the midst of the Federal ranks at Warrenton.

Sound of cavalry came from a side street and a band of horsemen rode out behind a heavily-moustached captain. They formed a cordon around the courthouse and, automatically, some got down and followed the leader into the building.

The two citizens watched these movements through half-closed lids.

"A party just searched that building not an hour ago," whined the old man.

"Let 'em hunt," said his companion. "As long as they're wasting their time like that they can't be off shooting at Lee."

Five minutes later the two men saw the searchers emerge and remount. The captain, reining in his horse, stared about. He looked toward the loiterers under the tree and spurred his charger through the gate and across the lawn to within a few feet.

"You men seen anything of the guerrilla Mosby?"

The old man reached into his pocket for a scarred black pipe and began to pack it with tobacco crumbs.

"Don't believe I'd know him if I saw him."

The captain leaned forward in the saddle.

"Have you seen anyone you thought was Mosby?"

The old fellow glanced slyly off toward the distant mountains.

"Reckon not," he said.

The horseman looked at the young man.

"How about you?"

"I ain't sayin'."

The officer sat his horse in silence, studying the pair. Then he turned and rode toward the gate.

"We'll catch that damn horse thief," he threw back. "And if we find you've had anything to do with hiding him, we'll hang the three of you to the same tree."

The old man waited until the officer had disappeared. "Mosby sure makes those fellows mad," he said.

"That's because he's too smart for 'em. Don't care about anything." The young man's eyes narrowed as he spoke. "Just soon ride all night as eat. He's a hellcat, too. When I rode with him at Miskel Farm I saw him fight six Yankees at one time, shooting with a gun in each hand. But he won't send his men any place he won't go himself."

The old fellow pressed the ashes of his pipe.

"I don't believe Mosby's comin' in town this morning," he said. "He's too smart for that. He ain't gonna throw hisself into the lion's den."

"He's done it before," his companion reminded. "Remember when he took Stoughton out of Fairfax."

"That was at night. This place is running over with Yanks. They'd have him 'fore he set foot in town. Look yonder."

The old fellow pointed with a bony finger. Far down the street half a hundred horsemen waited patiently, separated by a narrow lane for vehicles.

"They've got every entrance to the town blocked. How could he expect to get through such a guard?"

The young man studied the horsemen before he answered. "That won't keep him away if he makes up his mind to come through."

A smile lit the speaker's face.

"Pop, you don't understand Mosby's system," he said. "The four thousand Yankees around here wouldn't stop him if he had any reason to come to town. They think he won't come, and that's just the reason he will. He figures his safety lies in doing those things the enemy considers impossible. He got Stoughton that way."

The younger man turned a rock over with the tip of his crutch.

"I first saw Mosby last January when he passed through on his way to start his operations. A bunch of us was gathered around the fireplace in the hotel swapping yarns. It was cold and rainy and sleety, and we weren't paying much attention to anything outdoors until we heard a passel of horses. There must have been fifteen or twenty of 'em.

"Pretty soon the door opened and in walked Mosby. He was so slim and frail none of us picked him to be the leader until we saw he was the only one with a feather in his hat. He had a gun on each hip—I can see those six-shooters now. They seemed almost as big as he was. When the fellows all got in, Mosby said they wanted something to eat. The clerk told him he must be crazy, that he had nothing prepared, and Mosby answered quiet like that they'd wait until he did have something. That food was ready in a jiffy."

A dust-covered victoria, drawn by two scraggly horses, rolled around the courthouse. High in the driver's seat perched a stately, gray-haired man in silk hat, black cutaway coat, black satin waistcoat and stock. Behind him sat a pretty young woman, full-breasted, erect, in a gray bonnet and a flowing dress of pink poplin. The vehicle and its passengers seemed a vision out of another world, a sacrilege against the background of war material around the streets—broken howitzers, wheelless caissons, spent shells.

The two men stared curiously. Seeing them, the gray-haired driver lifted his high silk and bowed courteously. There was no tension about his act, nothing unusual, and the woman scarcely glanced in the direction of his nod, scarcely noticed the equally polite bows of the pair on the lawn.

The victoria rolled on, lonesomely, apart from all the madness and destruction. It took the street toward the wagon yard.

"What you think of that?" muttered the young man.

The old man looked up. "What's the matter? Ain't it Old-Jim Hathaway from over at The Plains? He drives in here every now and then. Saw him here last week."

"Yeah, but you know who that is with him?"

"His daughter, ain't it?"

"No—it's Mosby's wife. She's come here to see him, I'll bet."

"But why don't she pick somewhere else—where there ain't so many Yankees?" asked the patriarch.

"Maybe she's got to pick crowded places," the young man suggested. "The Yankees keep guards on all sides of the Hathaway house and they don't let a vehicle leave that they don't follow."

Toward midday the two men left the shade of the lawn and walked a short distance down the street to the barber shop, an institution of serious intent. It had a lever-controlled swivel chair and a table with the usual assortment of bottles, both in front of a wall mirror just large enough for customers to view their tonsorial metamorphosis. But there was little in the way of furniture—a few straight chairs and near the front window a small, square table on which newspapers bleached in the morning sun.

All except the barber watched the newcomers move the papers and edge the table farther into the corner opposite the swivel chair. From a wooden box used as a seat they took a dirty checkerboard and sorted the red and black pieces. Then they settled down to serious study. Two Federal soldiers sitting against the wall waiting turn stared interestedly.

"What's all the stir round town today?" asked the barber, raising his clippers from the neck of a sandy-haired patron.

"Soldiers searchin' for Mosby," replied the veteran of the alpaca coat. "They got a notion he's in town."

"Yeah? They got the same notion little more'n a month ago, but they never could find him. He was here, though. I saw him."

"How short?" he asked the patron.

"Like the last time."

"It was kinda long—longer than usual," observed the barber.

"I've been busy."

Footsteps sounded at the front of the shop and the battered screen door creaked back. The barber looked up, dropped his clippers on the table with the bottles, and straightened.

"Come in, Mr. Hathaway."

"No, thank you," said the stately old man from The Plains. "I have a young lady here who wants to see you."

The barber walked to the door, beyond which waited the woman in pink poplin. She handed him a small package.

"This is just a little raspberry shrub for your wife," she explained.

The barber thanked her.

"Have you seen my husband lately?" she asked.

The barber hesitated. On the inside, the sandy-haired man coughed, and the woman continued before turning away. "Tell him we are all well and anxious to see him."

A few minutes later heavy tramping sounded in front of the shop. Blue uniforms blocked the doors and windows. The barber kicked the pedal on the swivel chair as a lieutenant and two privates entered, their weapons clicking. The chair collapsed into a horizontal table, and the barber smoothed out the neck apron almost to the sandy-haired man's feet. Then he took up a dripping brush from a large china mug and spread lather generously over the customer's face.

The officer halted beside the chair. "You seen Mosby?"

"Me?" asked the barber, turning slowly.

The officer snorted impatiently and clicked his heels.

"Come on, man," he said. "We got word Mosby came into town today. Have you seen him?"

"Mosby'd never come in here with you fellows hanging around."

"We heard his wife stopped in to see you a few minutes ago."

"Yes, she brought some shrub for my sick wife," explained the barber, motioning toward the package he had placed on the table.

The lieutenant leaned over the sandy-haired man.

"What's your name?"

"Johnson."

"Soldier?"

"Parolee."

"Where your papers?"

"Home."

"Where you live?"

"Five miles west."

The officer looked up at the barber.

"You know this man?"

"Sure—Hiram Johnson—known him all my life. He used to butcher my hogs."

The officer turned and walked from the shop, trailed by his escort. The barber went back to his trade, working feverishly, silently. In a few more minutes the sandy-haired man was shorn, shaved and shampooed. He got up, paid his bill and walked out. No one but the barber noticed that the package went with him.

Futile search for Mosby, like this at Warrenton, went on unbroken in Northern Virginia for two and a half years. One night a party of New York cavalry turned off the main highway and followed a winding trail down through the woods to the Hathaway home, that place whence had come the victoria and its passengers. Since 10 A.M. the day previous these Union soldiers had been beating bush. They had been on a wide circuit and finally had been put on what they considered a hot trail.

In the darkness the horsemen formed a circle around the tall old mansion, and a captain and two privates dismounted. Steeling their ears to a confusion of barking dogs, they walked cautiously toward the front door. Upstairs, Mosby stirred from his sleep and raised on one elbow. He waited for evidence that members of the Hathaway family had been awakened and then gently shook his wife.

As he had done on other occasions, Old Man Hathaway pulled back the door, lamp in hand, and faced the intruders. The Yankee captain pushed into the wide hallway, directed one of the privates to go toward the back of the house and the other to stand guard at the front. Then began a careful search. From one room to another the captain moved, looking in closets, under furniture, tapping walls and floors for hidden recesses as he went. In an upstairs chamber he found a white-faced young woman in robe and nightdress, trying impatiently to calm the fears of two sleepy youngsters. Parts of a gray uniform lay near the bed, rumpled, but neither the owner nor his boots could be located.

Half an hour later the captain abandoned the search and left the house, much disgruntled. Slowly up the woodland path toward the main road he walked his horse, trailed by his companions. Near the edge of the woods he halted to stare back over the cleared land at the lights gleaming from the mansion. One by one they winked out, drawing an inky curtain over their secret. The command to ride on was given. At that moment the agile Mosby swung lightly from the limb of a tree to his bedroom window, pulled himself through and felt for the bed in the dark.

2

Mosby's Tam O'Shanter Rebels

NARROW ESCAPES AND THRILLING INCIDENTS in the career of Mosby created one of the most picturesque characters of the American rebellion. This slim little man brushed shoulders with the enemy on numerous occasions and twice was their prisoner. But in each instance their recognition of him came too late, and he was allowed to make his way back to his confederates.

Over Virginia and eventually over the nation during the last years of the war spread his name. It was a synonym in the South for brave deeds and daring escapades; a byword in the North for fear and hatred and chagrin, and now and then an arched eyebrow, for frequently the tireless legion for which it was a countersign performed deeds that strained human belief. Wagon trains were raided. Bridges were burned. Ammunition and arms and supplies were captured. Pickets, scouts and stragglers were gobbled up as if the earth had opened and swallowed them.

Far ahead of his time, Mosby employed cavalry as it is being employed today. To him it was no weapon of strong offense, but a scouting and pestering arm designed to upset and delay the enemy's plans. The value of Partisan warfare was questioned then because military tactics had no place for it in its manuals. Generations were to pass before it received general recognition—in the daring and amazingly effective thrusts of the Commandos against the Nazis. But a few leaders, even three-quarters of a century ago, saw its worth. Sheridan was

among them. In his campaign against General Early in the
Shenandoah Valley in '64, he had 94,000 men to Early's not
quite 20,000. He writes in his memoirs that "the difference of
strength between the two armies at this date was considerably
in my favor, but the conditions attending my situation in a
hostile region necessitated so much detached service to protect
trains, and to secure Maryland and Pennsylvania from raids,
that my excess in numbers was almost canceled by these inci-
dental demands. . . ." [1]

Grant, who knew the force of Mosby's surprises and sanctioned hanging his men without trial, instructed Sheridan before he started after Early to detach "a sufficient force to look
after the raiders and drive them to their homes." [2] The detachments necessary undoubtedly were largely responsible for pro-
longing the war until the spring of '65. If Sheridan could have
joined forces with Grant around Petersburg sooner, Lee's lines
may have crumbled months before they did. But threats from
Early and Mosby prevented the junction. Sheridan was kept
busy in Northern Virginia. He first defeated Early, after which he
set to work on the insurmountable task of eliminating Mosby.
His greatest problem was that of finding the raider, and he
finally concluded that destruction of Mosby's band would be
"well nigh impossible" because of its intimate knowledge of
the region in which it operated. [3]

While Mosby was successful in creating a diversion that un-
questionably delayed the end at Appomattox, his greatest importance grew out of his reconnaissance reports. He was of
untold value to the Confederacy in keeping a watch on enemy
movements. Intelligence brought in by him figured in several
of the major campaigns. His ability in this respect received
early appraisal and was relied on increasingly as the war
advanced. [4]

Mosby's elusiveness was a matter of constant worry to the
enemy. Time and again he slipped through Federal clutches
and struck from behind, sometimes after false report of his capture had spread to headquarters. A bounty, never claimed, was
placed on his head. And the picture he made as he dashed
across hilltops with flaming coat was passed on as familiarly

to the man in the ranks as to the officer behind the lines. Story after story came of his cunning, of his escape from traps that could not fail, of his death in a fusillade of bullets. As they increased, the veil of mystery about him expanded until it reached the bedtime talk of children and there grew rife, swelling him by youthful reverence into a godly figure that dashed out of the wind.

To one young Fairfax County girl he was "the greatest hero and the star of the Confederacy." [5] Children of her neighborhood recognized him by the brisk trot that marked his riding. One morning she begged her brother to take her with him to look at rabbit traps. They went across an old field, cutting paths in a light snow that had fallen during the night, and entered pine woods where the trees were small and close together. Among the first traps they found a broken trigger and stopped to repair it. "As we arose to our feet," she related, "we were astonished to behold Mosby sitting on his horse right behind us. Such a place for a horse, a horse with velvet slippers, for we never heard his footsteps. 'Good morning,' he said, 'have you seen any Rebels in these parts lately?' He was evidently thinking his disguise was complete. 'No,' replied Brother, 'none but Mosby's men.' 'Ah, indeed,' he exclaimed with a drawl, and repeated it. He was taken by surprise and tried not to show it, and turning his fine horse, he casually remarked, 'Nice morning for rabbits,' and disappeared into the pines."

Mosby's cape was turned back always in a flow of scarlet. A curling ostrich plume extended over his shoulder from a gray felt hat, and at each side hung a large Colt revolver, suspended in holsters well studded with brass. Once people got over the fantasy that his size matched his reputation, they could more easily identify him. But they never could figure out what lay beneath his exterior. He could lead his men into the jaws of death one moment and talk of birds and books and poetry the next. His slight frame of medium height was muscular, supple, vigorous, capable of great activity. His hair was sandy, his face clean cut, his lips firm like a cameo. He had features that were large and youthful. His eyes did not glance; they pierced. And here doubtless lay a part of the credit for his success. One raider wrote in recording the first time he saw Mosby: "He turned upon me suddenly, meeting my full glance. At that instant the secret of his power over his men was disclosed. It was in his eyes, which were deep blue, luminous, clear, piercing; when he spoke they flashed the punctuations of his sentence." [6]

Clean-shaven except when he wore a full beard during the latter part of the war, he was quick and agile and rode at 125 pounds. But even with his beard he could never assume the fierce, story-book appearance that mythical praise gave him. A slight stoop that developed in his shoulders during youth took away most of his military air, outweighing the effect of a uniform.

Around him Mosby gathered what was by and large a motley crew. Some of its members deserved the enemy charge that they were cutthroats and freebooters. Still, for all that could be said against them, far more could be said in their favor. They were fighters not held together by the desire for booty, as universally charged, so much as by the strong personality of their leaders. [7] They had more fear than love for this strange man almost any of them could have bent double in a physical test. It was his iron nerve, his utter disregard for death, his reputation as a scrapper, that banded them into a fraternity of fighters.

Men frequently, without justification, claimed his banner, forcing him at one time to issue certificates of identification to his bona fide confederates. These membership tags went out to boys with pink cheeks, to men with gray hair; to the planter's son and the overseer's son; to the banker in richly-trimmed officer's gray and the adventurer in clothes gleaned from the litter of the chase. It was a conglomeration of ages and classes that followed his leadership, serenading the forests of Northern Virginia with the strains of their war ballads—

> When I can shoot my rifle clear
> At Yankees on the roads,
> I'll bid farewell to rags and tags
> And live on sutlers' loads.

Rough riders all of them, they preserved their organization for two and a half years within a few miles of the enemy capital, inside armies bristling with vicious guns. Artists pictured them with bridle reins in their teeth, spurs sunk deep into the flanks of their horses, blazing revolvers in each hand. Fifty miles a day was no unusual jaunt. The same party that prowled through Federal camps in Fairfax one night broke up Sheridan's wagon trains in the valley the next. They struck quickly, according to their code and their leader's belief that surprise was one of the greatest weapons of offense. And they retired with the same rapidity with which they had come, scattering to the four winds of the earth, to meet again in a few minutes, a few hours, or a few days.

Mosby called them his "Tam O'Shanter Rebels."

3

To Virginia a Fighter Is Born

WHAT A PITY THE WORLD CANNOT EVALUATE BIRTH with the same astuteness it appraises death. More than three decades—decades in which valuable biographical detail was lost—passed before some special significance was attached to the infant's cries that rang through the McLaurine household early on the morning of December 6, 1833. They sounded strong and impatient and carried far through the century-old house on the outskirts of Edgemont, in Powhatan County, forty miles west of Richmond, Virginia. They traveled along the wide hallways and into crannies of small-paned windows, even to the hearths of a five-sided chimney that served rooms upstairs and down in a long wing off to the right. And where the sound did not reach—out to the storeroom with its rows of preserves, pickles and catsups, its mortars, pestles, rolling pins and sifters, back to the kitchen where plum puddings, pound cakes, citron tarts and real calf's foot jelly were concocted—tongues of excited servants carried the message.

"Miss Virginny done had her baby!"

Late that afternoon, vehicles arriving without schedule rolled up the woodland lane to the homestead on the crest of a hill. Some of the carriages were shiny and clean except for rich loam clinging to their wheels or damp clods flecked against the dashboard by high-spirited horses. They came at intervals, from one to three or four at a time. James McLaurine had given ample notice that his daughter, wife of Alfred Daniel Mosby of Nelson County, Virginia, Hampden-Sydney College graduate, had come home to give birth to what the family hoped would be a boy. It would be her second, but now her only, child: the first had died in infancy.

McLaurine was in his glory, an old man hobbling about with the aid of a long, polished stick, flushed with the thought that another branch had been added to the family tree. Occasionally a racking cough shook his bent frame and caused him to halt. It was a discomfort that had been with him many years, from the time he had gone down of exposure and smallpox as a soldier in the Revolution.

Cheerful talk came from the friends and relatives. Tongues of light from the giant old fireplace nudged in between them, and unbroken rows of books stared out from quaint, built-in, glass-doored cupboards on each side of the hearth. Some of these volumes were of the old masters, some on subjects strictly religious. Many had come from The Glebe a few miles to the east, for years the home of James' father, Robert McLaurine, Scotch immigrant and Episcopal minister who had come to America in 1750.[1] For more than two decades the solemn old cleric had ministered over Southam Parish, preaching to his flock on Sunday and going out into the fields to help, spiritually and physically, during the week.

Behind many of those who thronged the McLaurine hearthstone that day in 1833 was proud and worthy ancestry. This and more had generated the infant that Virginia McLaurine described to the wife of her husband's brother, John, a month and one week after his birth:

"I have seated myself to write you a few lines as I know you have been expecting for me to write to you for a long time and I am much ashamed of not answering your last, but I know you will readily forgive me when you know I had neither news or opportunity. I suppose you have heard before this of my being confined and of the birth of my son. I suffered greatly during my confinement, being threatened with the milk leg and would have had it dreadfully if I had not have had a Tomsonian attendance. I never got out of my room until my month was out. I am now very well and fat and I have one of the finest children I ever saw at its age. He is a remarkably fine child larger now than my dear little Cornelia was at her death. I have named him John Singleton after your old man and his grandpapa. He claims a present from both for his name. . . .

"I suppose I must give you a description of my boy. He has fair skin and hair and very dark blue eyes. Some say it will be black though I don't think so myself. He is right pretty, but not as much so as my other baby was. . . ." [2]

Little that is known of Mosby's life before he reached manhood sets him apart from other young Virginians who came up during those turbulent years before the war. Despite a frail body, the dominant trait in his physical and spiritual makeup was a tendency to fight, whether his antagonist was his own size or a towering force above him. He was a battler by instinct, and he graduated from fist to firearms with the same easy evolution that the Southland swung from a haven of mint juleps and honey to a battlefield of rotting bodies.

Mosby started his education at a small country school near a postoffice in the backwoods of Nelson County called Murrell's Shop. With him each morning and back for him each afternoon, as a bodyguard to soothe a mother's fears, went a young Negro boy. Once John begged his escort to stay all day and for potent allure patted the side of his lunch basket. The Negro succumbed. At recess, when the liberated children swarmed into the open to play, some of the older boys spied the ebony-skinned visitor and at once set about a new game. He was hoisted to a stump, frightened and screaming, and struck off at auction to the highest bidder. It was a touching scene. While the amateur auctioneer called for bids his juvenile audience was given a fine display of sobbing and chest-beating from the outskirts of the circle. The young master, thinking the sale bona fide, howled until the Negro once more stood beside him. That was the last time the future Partisan leader came to school with an escort.

While enrolled in this woodland lyceum, Mosby got his first glimpse of a drunken man—the schoolmaster. It was a sight that upset an important world in a childish mind. There, lying beside the road, as blotto as the dirt on his face, stretched one of the great figures of the boy's experience, waiting to be picked up by his pupils. Mosby kept the memory always; in later years he gave it as the principal reason why he never took more freely to strong drink. From it, as well as from his realization that the laxity of alcohol would not mix with the precision of his style of fighting, came his ironclad rule that spiritous liquors had no place in the ranks of the Forty-third Battalion of Partisan Rangers.

Around 1840, at a time when John was just learning to spell, his father left Nelson and moved across into the adjoining county of Albemarle. Their new home was tucked back under an eave of the Blue Ridge Mountains, four miles from Charlottesville, on a shelf that resembled an inverted oyster shell. Around it were 395 acres of rich farm land and tall timber. A small body of oaks, throwing spotted shade over the circular drive looping to the high front porch, earned for the mansion the name of Tudor Grove.[3] The countryside in front rolled over red hills toward Carter's Mountain, high on which sat Monticello, home of the venerable democrat, Thomas Jefferson. Many a night the lonely yellow glow from its windows in the distance was the only assurance the Mosbys had that there were other people in the world.

At this new location, John was sent to a school conducted by a widow in a forested area known as Fry's Woods. He studied from Peter Parley books in which there were impressionable pictures of General Wolfe dying on the battlefield in the arms of a soldier, of Israel Putnam riding down the stone steps at Horseneck in flight from Governor Tryon's dragoons. And one day, in the shady quiet of a woodland spring, the country classroom's source of water supply, he learned the flowing words of "Ben Bolt."

At ten he was transferred from the limited instruction of Fry's Woods to the broader curriculum of a Charlottesville school. Sometimes he traveled this greater distance to classes by horse and sometimes by foot, rarely missing a day. He had become enthusiastic over the avenues of learning opened to him by the change. Among his new instructors were James White, master of Latin and Greek, a man of strong influence, and Aleck Nelson, mathematician, both of whom later served

on the faculty of Washington College during the presidency of
General Robert E. Lee.

As John grew older he continued delicate in appearance, yet
there was something hardy and virile in his nature. Seldom a
Saturday passed that he did not slip down in the darkness for
a sip of coffee before starting out afoot over the mountains for
a day of hunting.

It was during these years that Miss Abby Southwick, young
abolitionist from Massachusetts, came to serve as governess
for Mosby's sisters. She was an outspoken woman, a friend of
William Lloyd Garrison and Wendell Phillips, and she frequently expounded her opinions on slavery and other political
subjects around the Mosby fireside. The family took her in as a
friend. Her words were carefully heeded and were associated
later with some of the weighty developments then troubling
the nation.

Mosby learned rapidly at school. He showed distinct literary
taste and strong proficiency in Greek. He could recite generously from Tacitus and Thucydides, and there was no great
exaggeration in the assertion that he was a walking dictionary
of the classics. So it was with a fine background that he enrolled at the University of Virginia October 3, 1850, signing his
name "John S. Mosby" and listing himself as a non-resident.[4]
By alphabetical order, the name directly above his was that
of Aristides Monteiro, medical student from Goochland Court
House, Virginia, and the seventh son of Francis Xavier Monteiro de Barros, Castilian of great learning who had been forced
to flee to America after taking part in an unsuccessful attempt
to establish a republic in Portugal. Their paths would merge
at another period of their lives.

Mosby's standing was good in subjects he preferred, but he
met with difficulty in others. He distinguished himself the first
year, for instance, in Latin and Greek and passed the examina-
tion of a special class in English in May, a month ahead of
schedule. Balancing these fine marks on the other side of the
ledger was mathematics, a science he failed in utterly.

Mosby was a deep thinker and naturally quiet except for
frequent discussions with the professors. These outbursts gave

ample evidence of a strong mentality. Among faculty members with whom he conversed liberally was Dr. Gesner Harrison, who was convinced the student was a clever young man and that he would earn a prominent place in life.

His second year at the university began October 15, 1851. On that date he enrolled as "Jno. Singleton Mosby" and, because of the heavy curriculum he had chosen—ancient and modern languages, mathematics and natural philosophy— moved his trunk from Tudor Grove to the Brock Boarding House near the campus. He studied hard, earning honors in Latin, and was graduated from the school of Greek languages and literature. During his third and final session, his classes were devoted mainly to courses prescribed by his professors to round out his education. They included chemistry, moral philosophy and mathematics.

With much lighter studies during his last year in college, he took part more freely in the social life of the campus. He was now on the verge of manhood and had begun to develop his own philosophy of the world. Many hours throughout the fall and winter he spent at parties or talking shop and swapping yarns with his circle of friends in their rooms. Amid this levity he found much enjoyment and, as spring opened and the red mud that bogged down vehicles on the road to Tudor Grove began to dry, he announced plans for a party at his home.

The gun shot that came in a hollow echo from the hallway of the Brock Boarding House shortly after noon March 29 brought a circle of curious onlookers to the scene. The blast was discord in a peaceful but lively setting. Students had been having their noon meal. They had been talking and bantering and joking around the table as they ate. In none of this had there been slightest indication of disagreement anywhere on the campus. Local harmony from all appearances was at a peak.

But those who crowded up the narrow stairway leading from the dining room in the basement, those who rushed from other rooms of the building, those who hurried in from the street, found ample evidence of disruption that verged on tragedy. Prone on the floor, shot in the neck, lay George R. Turpin, medical student. Above him, smoking pistol in hand, stood the slim, youthful Mosby, calm and unaffected. Charles Brock, fellow student, had been a witness to the shooting.

It was one of those merciless blows fate can deal and only brave mothers can bear that came to Virginia McLaurine at Tudor Grove that afternoon. Her son, her first boy, was a prisoner, held fast in a dank cell of the little jail overlooking the main business street of Charlottesville, small red-dirt town that knelt in the valley and prayed to the white-fronted totem left by Jefferson on Carter Mountain. The scion of Scottish ecclesiastic was charged with unlawful and malicious shooting.

For days campus life at the university was disrupted. The town, too, reacted to the commotion. From its street corners, gatherings signaled that something was amiss. A student had been shot by another and might die. But this was an extremely pessimistic outlook. Already the wound in Turpin's jaw and throat had begun to heal, and there was ample reason to believe he soon would be fully recovered.

Gossip went the rounds meanwhile. There were all kinds of rumors as to why Mosby, far inferior in size, had attacked the more robust Turpin. The blustering medical student had a reputation of his own on the campus. He had stabbed one fellow with a pocket knife and had almost killed another with a rock. But Mosby, on the other hand, also had a record that warranted investigation. There had been a previous offense. Two years earlier, during his first session in college, he had leapt on George Slaughter, clumsy town policeman, and had thrashed the officer soundly. Some folks took this case as a portent of ungovernable temper. Each day brought new talk. It was said a girl was involved. Brock, the eyewitness, kept his tongue. Only a few on the campus knew the true story.

Classes gradually went back to normal, shy one member. Spring came on in full, freshed the countryside, softened the air, sprinkled it with perfume of lilac and violet. Up in the stinking little jail meantime waited the delicate culprit, under grand jury indictment. As time went on, the public clamor for full vengeance grew stronger. The university faculty acted at its next regular business session. In the minutes along with routine record on delinquencies and unexcused absences was written the simple statement that, in view of the recent shoot-ing affair between Turpin and Mosby, it was resolved that "the said Mosby be expelled."

This drastic action brought another blow to the parents at Tudor Grove. They had talked for months of moving from Albemarle. Now they put their thoughts into action. While John bided the time behind bars until the May term of court, they packed up and went by wagon to a farm in Amherst County, at McIvor's, fifteen miles from Lynchburg. Their new home was deeper in the mountains. Still more important, it was farther from the thoughts of disgrace which haunted them when they appeared at Charlottesville.

Only Mosby's family and his immediate friends still saw him as a slim, studious youth of stooping shoulders, and they were not in the majority on May 16 when he was brought to trial.[5] At 10 o'clock that morning the jailor of the Albemarle Circuit Court escorted him to a place in front of the bench of Judge Richard H. Field, presiding. The charge was read. The judge looked down at the defendant. "Not guilty," answered the youth in a clear voice without turning in the direction of his counsel, two prominent local attorneys. The arraignment was over in a few minutes.

Four days later the jailor again brought the accused before the bar. Much of the day was taken up with selection of the jury. After this routine was completed, evidence was opened by the prosecution. It proceeded slowly and was scarcely well under way when, toward night, the jury was entrusted to the care of the sheriff and the prisoner was returned to his cell.

More evidence was given next morning, a Saturday, and again on Monday. Late the afternoon of that day, one week after the arraignment, testimony was completed and counsel began their arguments. It was Tuesday before the case was placed in the hands of the jury. Late in the day the jurors filed into court: they had been unable to reach a verdict. Judge Field sent them back to reconsider.

More hours of waiting passed next day. Conjecture kept the throng in the courtroom occupied. To all appearances the jury was deadlocked, and in a way this could be understood. There had been considerable conflict in the testimony as to which of the principals had been the first to advance on the other in the boarding house hallway. Even the sole eyewitness was unable to clear up this point. But what actually was going on in the jury room was not revealed to the public for months.

At last the jurors emerged. Their foreman announced they had reached a verdict. It was that Mosby "is not guilty of malicious shooting as in the first count of the indictment against him is alleged, but that he is guilty of unlawful shooting in manner and form as in the second count of said indictment is alleged, and they do ascertain the term of his imprisonment in the county jail to be twelve months, and assess his fine to be $500." [6] Five days later the youth was sentenced formally.

As ready as Albemarle residents had been to punish Mosby, equally as ready were they after his quiet demeanor in court to help him gain his freedom. Scarcely had the jail door clicked behind him before a movement was under way to have him pardoned. And as unexpected acceleration to this drive came the sudden news that the prisoner and the Commonwealth's attorney who had prosecuted him had struck up a friendship.

This had come about surprisingly through the defendant's affability.[7] The attorney, William J. Robertson, later a justice of the Virginia Supreme Court of Appeals and first president of the Virginia State Bar Association, stopped by the jail one day to discuss business with the jailor. While they talked a voice sounded behind them. They turned to find Mosby, smiling through the bars, a book under one arm and the other extended toward Robertson.

The attorney was dumbfounded. He had expected only animosity from this youth to whom his vigorous prosecution had brought punishment.

"What are you reading?" Robertson asked as he took the proffered hand.

"Milton's 'Paradise Lost' and I hope soon to enjoy 'Paradise Regained.'"

If Mosby intended a pun in reminder of his captivity, the attorney ignored it. "You should do some writing. John Bunyan, you know, wrote 'The Pilgrim's Progress' in a prison cell."

"No," said Mosby, seriously, "I have determined to study law." His firm, cameo lips twisted into a smile. "The law has made a great deal out of me; I am now going to make something out of law."

The prosecutor stared into the youth's eyes.

"Fine!" he encouraged. "You may have the use of my library whenever you want it."

Later that day a package was handed through the bars. It contained a copy of Blackstone's "Commentaries" and a volume of Greenleaf on evidence. On the flyleaf of both was inscribed the name of William J. Robertson.

On December 23, 1853, the jail door swung back and Mosby walked out, free. The Governor had granted him a pardon as a Christmas present.

There was still more leniency in store for the prisoner. At the next session of the State Legislature a few weeks later, Senator Benjamin F. Randolph went to work on a successful campaign to have the $500 fine rescinded. In his behalf, Governor Joseph Johnson communicated his reasons for pardoning the youth:

"It appears that Mosby had invited some of his fellow students to a social entertainment at his father's. A short time afterwards he was told that a young man by the name of Turpin had said that two of his guests had been invited to the entertainment not as guests, but as fiddlers; seeking an explanation of this accusation, he addressed Turpin a respectful note, which was carried by a friend. Instead of replying to the note, Turpin used towards Mosby insulting and contemptuous epithets, and threatened to thrash him if he came about him with any of his impertinence. This being communicated to Mosby, he determined to seek a personal interview, and as Turpin was larger and more athletic than himself, and had threatened violence, he was advised to take with him a pistol which he accordingly did.

"On the same day Turpin went to the house at which Mosby boarded to dine, as he said, with a friend. As he came up from dinner, he was accosted by Mosby with the remark, 'I understand you have been making some assertions'—when Turpin without waiting for him to finish the sentence, 'sprang upon him.' As he did so, Mosby drew his pistol and instantly fired, wounding Turpin in the jaw and throat. From the evidence of Turpin, Mosby drew his pistol before Turpin attempted to seize him. Upon this point there is a conflict of testimony. The wound inflicted upon Turpin proved to be slight, and in a short time he entirely recovered.

"In this case I received a petition, signed by nine of the jury who rendered the verdict. They state that the circumstances attending the shooting went far to palliate if not to justify the act; that four of the jury were in favor of an entire acquittal; that six were for a confinement in the jail of the county for a short period, and the other two insisted on a verdict which should consign the accused to the Penitentiary; that one of these avowed in the jury room feelings of the strongest dislike and prejudice towards the father of the accused; that a failure to render a verdict would of itself have been equivalent to a sentence of confinement in jail from the spring to the fall term of court; but as two of them would consent to nothing less than imprisonment in jail for the longest period, and the infliction of the highest fine prescribed by law, they reluctantly consented to the verdict." [8]

There were other reasons why the Governor had pardoned the youth. To the executive had come a petition signed by 300 citizens and asking his interposition because of the youth and usual good disposition of the accused. Also forwarded to him were certificates from several respectable physicians. Each medical man gave it as his professional opinion that Mosby was constitutionally consumptive, that he was in a precarious state of health, and that imprisonment for a year would incur the risk of his life. [9]

A Lawyer "Jines the Cavalry"

BRISTOL, VIRGINIA, MADE LITTLE NOTE of the day a sandy-haired young stranger spread a few law books in one room of James King's corner lot building, Fourth and Cumberland Streets.[1] The community's growth had been too rapid in late years for much attention to be given to newcomers, particularly those who, like this fellow, were frail and apparently delicate. It had been only a short time past that a progressive real estate agent had come down into the Holston country from Pennsylvania. He had sold the scattered inhabitants on the idea that their little town, hanging over the edge of Virginia into Tennessee and divided in a choice of names between Bristol and Goodson, by rights should be the center of a large trade area. Swelling to the dream, people went to work. Hotels and stores sprang up. Residences, some large, some small, some of brick, rose rapidly along Main Street and along the rolling ground stretching off to the northern and southern forks of the Holston River. Local government soon was organized and a charter to incorporate was obtained. In the fall of 1856, two railroad tracks came together there and a gilded spike was driven to mark the first rail connection between the North and South. Then it was that the stagecoach bugle gave way to the cry of "wood up!" From that day on engines panted impatiently at Bristol while passengers and crew tossed up logs to carry the huge monster along another lap of its journey. Settlers came into town by wagon and horse, some wild and lawless, some God-fearing and thrifty. There was hope, faith, and a sort of rough independence characteristic of men of big muscles, strong backs and unlimited energy.

So meager acknowledgment was the lot at first of the owner of the law books. But the welcome was more cordial a day or two later when a shingle, engraved by red-hot poker and fastened above the front door with a huge square nail, supplied the modest identification: "John S. Mosby—Lawyer." The fact that he was the first member of his profession to stop in the community made little difference. Law to some extent still was dealt from the hip, and there had been meager opportunity in the past to reason the right and wrong of things.

But the activity of the place promised Mosby a bright future. It had been Bristol's air of thrift, coupled with an unanticipated influence, that led him to tack up his shingle in the town in November, 1858.[2] His release from prison had been followed by months of study in William J. Robertson's law office. After being admitted to the bar, he had established himself in the little Albemarle County town of Howardsville, James River settlement separated only by the stream from Nelson and Buckingham Counties. There the unexpected influence had appeared —in the form of a girl visitor to the neighborhood who caught and held his interest. She was Pauline Clarke, daughter of Beverly J. Clarke of Franklin, Kentucky. Her home was much nearer Bristol than Howardsville.

On December 30, 1857, they were married, in a hotel at Nashville, Tennessee, just across the state line from Franklin. History does not tell much about this wedding, but it is related that Tennessee's prominent United States senator, Andrew Johnson, was among the guests.[3]

The Clarkes were substantial people, all of the Catholic faith. Beverly had been born in Chesterfield County, Virginia, in 1809 and had gone with his family to Kentucky while a young boy. He learned law from the books he could find and became a criminal attorney of great distinction. He served for years in the United States Congress and for a time as minister to Central America. And he reared a daughter who was pretty and spirited and full of life, a devout woman who worked her way into the heart of a quiet, steel-nerved young man and impelled him to lay siege to her affections with the same persistence he later used on the Yankees. She was the type he needed, fine of figure, handsome of face, calm, brave, fitted for the uncertain, nerve-racking hours which are the lot of a raider's wife. Their religious faiths made no difference between them. Mosby had been baptized a Methodist,[4] but he was not a religious fanatic and permitted his wife to dominate this phase of their life together.

At Bristol John and Pauline set up house in a modest way. They had a small retinue of slaves, as was the wont of that day, and the most valued of these was old Aaron, nappy-headed servant said to be part Indian.[5] He had been included among Mosby's wedding gifts from home.

It is to the extent of his ambition that a man enters into his work, and Mosby was ambitious. He drilled into the Bristolites that the court was the place to settle disputes and his demonstration of this in one or two instances, forensically portrayed before the bar·of the county seat at Abingdon, brought clients in increasing numbers. Many of them based their conviction that he was a great propounder of the law not so much on his quotations from Blackstone as on his ready store of classical and poetical citations. These came rarely enough to be doubly appreciated, for Mosby still was governed by a reluctance to engage in idle conversation just for the love of it. Manhood and his months in prison had not changed this characteristic, nor had they done much to alter him physically.

He worked quickly into the life of Bristol. There was not much in the way of civic activity and there were no other lawyers with whom he could share his problems. But he made a friend of the newspaper, almost as new an addition to the town as he, and this and other things added to his prestige. His fellow inhabitants saw him as a happy young husband and in time as a happy young father. The first child, a daughter, May, was born May 10, 1859, and in a few months the parents were talking confidently of others.

But in the midst of their happiness, national sentiment reached high heat and exploded in the very face of politicians and sectional patriots. A fever of argument swept over the nation, and its irrationality vaccinated the people with madness. All through the South militia companies were drilling, with corn stalks and sticks, and with guns that dated far back into American history. It was a romantic experience for poor and rich alike, a taste of the thing that had given their fathers and their grandfathers something to talk about, and they swarmed to their choice of the neighborhood gonfalons.

More and more, conversation turned to discussion of States' rights and slavery and the invasion expected from the North. Mosby was a listener to it all, so carefully keeping his political leanings to himself that few of his neighbors knew with which of the several parties he sided. Then came the campaign of 1860, and in the midst of the haranguing the young lawyer suddenly spoke up as a staunch supporter of the Douglas ticket. It was an abrupt transformation that had come over him, this sudden willingness to engage in argument, one that was to disappear after the excitement died down, but to flare up again later in life. Now that he would talk, folks dropped in oftener at his office. Many of them came not so much to participate in discussion as to hear his argument against the growing sentiment for the South to withdraw from the Union.

Mosby was almost the only Douglas Democrat in town. He was openly against dividing the Union. He argued that any state or territory of the United States should have the right to vote for or against slavery within its own borders. As he watched developments, he became convinced that William L. Yancey was doing more than any other man in the South to bring on the war. Yancey had been a strong advocate of slavery in the territories. He wanted secession, a league of united Southerners, and repeal of the laws making the African slave trade piracy. He walked out of the Charleston convention of the Democratic Party in April, 1860, championed the nomination of John C. Breckinridge and even went so far as to stump the country in the Kentuckian's behalf. It was while on this tour that he stopped in Southwest Virginia and put up as a guest at the Abingdon home of former Governor John B. Floyd, Secretary of War.

Mosby harbored ill feeling against Yancey for his political

sentiments. He recalled with bitterness the charge the secessionist had made that Virginia was a breeding ground for slaves
to be sold to the Cotton States and that her opposition to the
African slave trade was based on her desire for a monopoly of
the market. So when a few Douglas men of Washington County
delegated Mosby to call on the visitor and invite him to engage
in joint debate with Tim Rives, Virginia orator, he jumped at
the chance.

Yancey was arrogant and contemptuous to the lawyer's approach. He declined the invitation and talked so sharply
that Mosby left the Floyd home with the politician's words
ringing in his ears. Later in the day he stood on the outskirts
of a crowd and listened to a speech by the Southern "fire-
eater." It seemed to the young attorney a strong argument for
the Breckinridge supporters. But he noticed that Yancey, realizing Virginians had not yet been worked up to the secession
point, was careful to veil his disunion purposes. That night the
Douglas Democrats put up Tim Rives to answer Yancey. Mosby
thought it a great reply, furnishing an excellent picture of dis-
unionism and war, and he wrote an account of it for a Richmond paper.

A few weeks later, while attending court at Abingdon, Mosby
met William Blackford, classmate at the University of Virginia.
Blackford had news. He and others of the town were trying to
raise a cavalry company, of which he expected to be lieutenant,
and he wanted the lawyer to join. Just a precaution, in line with
the movement all over the South, he argued, and a possible
step to bring the North into compromise. Mosby consented: it
would indicate a lack of patriotism to refuse and he had talked
several times with Pauline about joining up. But he was so
indifferent over an introduction to the field of military that he
was among the absent when the company was organized a short
time afterward.

Just before the presidential election, Mosby stopped on the
streets of Bristol to listen to a meeting of the Bell and Everett
ticket, political faction that avoided issues in the campaign and
appealed solely for preservation of the Union. Someone, knowing the lawyer's opposition to secession, asked him to speak.

He shook his head. He was no orator, he said. But the crowd insisted and lifted him to the stand. He stood there, coolly surveying the throng. Then he spoke in measured tone.

"I see no reason for me to make a Union speech at a Bell and Everett meeting. It's my purpose to call not the righteous but the sinners to repentance."

That was all he said. The crowd was disappointed at the brevity of his remarks, but it drowned out its dissatisfaction with wild cheers as he leaped to the ground.

December came, and with it the secession of South Carolina. The situation grew taut. Other states prepared to follow.

One morning early in January, '61, Mosby met J. Austin Sperry, editor of the town's newspaper, the *Bristol News*, a secession sheet. They stopped to talk.[6]

"I believe you are a secessionist per se," the attorney remarked.

"What has led you to that conclusion?" asked the editor.

"The editorial in your paper today."

Journalist Sperry protested. "You have not read it carefully," he said. "There is nothing in it to justify such a charge. In summing up the events of the week I find that several sovereign states have formally severed their connection with the Union. We are confronted with the accomplished fact of secession. I have expressed no opinion either of the right or the expediency of the movement. I am not a secessionist per se, if I understand the term, but a secessionist by the logic of events."

"I'm glad to hear it," Mosby replied. "I have never coveted the office of Jack Ketch,[7] but I would cheerfully fill it for one day for the pleasure of hanging a disunionist per se. Do you know what secession means? It means bloody war, followed by feuds between the border states which a century may not see the end of."

"I do not agree with you," said Sperry. "I see no reason why secession should not be peaceable. But in the event of the dreadful war you predict, which side will you take?"

"I shall fight for the Union, sir—for the Union, of course. And you?"

"Oh, I don't apprehend any such extremity," replied the editor. "But if I am forced into the struggle, I shall fight for my mother section. Should we meet upon the field of battle, as Yancey said to Brownlow the other day, I would run a bayonet through you."

"Very well, we'll meet at Philippi," Mosby threw back as he walked away.

The newly-formed military company Mosby had joined met for its first drill on January court day. The lawyer borrowed a horse and rode up to Abingdon to attend. His initial lesson in the art of warfare was a novel experience for the man who later envisaged a use of cavalry popularized in a coming century. Many other young men were in the temporary drill hall on the third floor of the courthouse when he arrived. They stamped about importantly, chests bulging, and stopped occasionally to talk with a rugged individual dressed in blue jeans, hickory shirt and old homespun coat with soldier straps unevenly attached to the sleeves. Mosby was curious over his identity, and someone explained that he was William E. Jones, their commander, an experienced soldier.

Jones already had given the company a name, calling it the Washington Mounted Rifles, both after the county and after his old regular army unit in Texas. He was a peculiar man, only a week or two short of his thirty-seventh birthday, eccentric, stubborn, irascible. He was warm-hearted, but profane. Curse words, gushing too fast to come from memory, rolled off his tongue like corn from a sheller. He cracked them harshly in the ears of his listeners, and picked neither time nor place to loose the flow. Native of Washington County, he came out of Emory and Henry College in 1844 at the youthful age of twenty, was graduated with honors from West Point and started military service in Oregon. About this time he married. En route back to his post in the West, his young bride was drowned. There was considerable talk back home about the mysteriousness of her death. Folks recalled Jones' army reputation as a hard, cruel fighter, but there the matter dropped. In 1857 he resigned from the army, took a brief tour of the ancient spots of Europe, and then came back to live the life of a hermit up in the mountains near Glade Spring. The exile was self-imposed, never explained. But when the bugle blew over the South this strange fighter buckled on his sword and returned to public eye, bringing with him his old army nickname, "Grumble" Jones.

After the drill Mosby went to hear a discussion of current conditions by John B. Floyd. This statesman's recent resignation from the United States Cabinet as Secretary of War had been requested, President Buchanan said, because of a questionable practice in handling drafts, but there were rumors that Floyd's secession sympathies had been the actual reason. In his speech that day at Abingdon, the ex-Secretary made a strong appeal for the people to prepare for the coming conflict, which he warned was imminent. Near him on the platform as he spoke sat Mosby, much impressed by the speaker's appearance and manner, and mentally noting how much they confirmed the report that the Floyd family was part Indian.[8]

Early in February delegates of the first six states to secede met at Montgomery, Alabama. They took four days to prepare a provisional constitution. Then they elected Jefferson Davis to the presidency of the Confederate States of America.

March was a nightmare. April saw the storm break.

When the tragic message came over the wires that Lincoln had called for 75,000 volunteers to put down the uprising that three days before had burst at Fort Sumter, Mosby again was attending court at Abingdon. He hurried directly from the telegraph office to the home of Floyd and told him the news.

"It'll be the bloodiest war the world has ever seen," predicted the statesman in grave tones. "The men who prevented the secession of Virginia three months ago and those at Montgomery who have fooled away the season of preparations will be responsible for the tears of every widow and orphan."

Late that night Virginia seceded.

Happenings of the next few weeks were hard to remember in later years. Everything was a maelstrom of excitement, of maddening, unsystematic activity as men left their routine life and made ready for what they thought would be only a short spell of fighting. To the recruiting offices flocked sons of planters and sons of field hands who never before had manifested patriotic interest. They signed up for three months' service, the length of time the Confederate Congress estimated it would take to drive the invaders from the North back across the Potomac.

The Washington Mounted Rifles, along with other companies of cavalry and infantry, went into camp in a half-finished building of the Martha Washington College on the edge of Abingdon. Mosby was granted time off from the first days of intensive training to wind up his law business and to get a horse from his father's farm. He found debt collections amid the excitement of the times not easy, abandoned hope of obtaining many fees due him, and finally made his last court appearance at Blountsville, Tennessee.

Before taking leave of his family, which now included a baby son named Beverly Clarke after its maternal grandfather, he stopped by the office of Editor Sperry. The journalist was bent over his desk and did not see the visitor until he was at his elbow.

"How do you like my uniform?" asked Mosby.

"Why, Mosby!" exclaimed the editor. "This isn't Philippi—nor is that a Federal uniform."

"No more of that," replied Mosby. "When I talked in such a manner, Virginia had not seceded. She is out of the Union now. Virginia is my mother, God bless her. I can't fight against my mother, can I?"

Editor Sperry embraced him.

The scent of lilacs was in the air around the Abingdon camp late that afternoon. Mosby breathed deeply. His eyes, those roving eyes of the scout, took in all around him. Everything was activity, most of it centered about the headquarters of Circuit Judge Fulkerson, Mexican War veteran and commanding officer in view of his recent appointment as colonel of Virginia Volunteers. Over toward the temporary stables horses neighed and stamped in their stalls, impatient for the freedom of the green fields. Darkies curried sleek haunches and sang songs of the corn rows, while young masters gathered in little groups and boasted of the merits of their steeds. Off another

way several squads of raw recruits stumbled over one another
in great confusion, occasionally sprinkling their military efforts
with choruses of laughter. And somewhere in the distance two
long-winded buglers struggled with the notes of Reveille.

Mosby thrilled at the scene and touched his horse gently
with his heel.

But scarcely had the attorney found his billet in a corner of the
college building when a sergeant brought word to the newcomer that he had been assigned to guard duty. For hours that
night while chilly stars twinkled overhead and a bitter wind
slapped at his bob-tail coat, he walked post. This was his first
experience at a routine that was to be his lot three times a
week. It was an embarrassing misfit with the self-conceit and
cockiness he had acquired from law practice. Moreover, he was
reminded of the uncomfortable months in the Charlottesville
jail. It cooled his enthusiasm and sent him to his pallet in the
pre-dawn chill with his ardor for military life at the zero point.

Mosby's 125 pounds made him the smallest and frailest man
in his company. But there was no mercy for him or his size
when he lined up before Grumble Jones next morning. The
West Pointer had two companies to drill, his own and another
from Marion, and to each of them his lessons were equally
rigid. He took good care of both men and horses. He had
patience where patience was deserved. But a generous helping of profanity awaited the man who appeared at inspection
with an improperly groomed animal. Some of the neophyte
soldiers thought he was too strict. Few realized the same instructions he meted out were being given at the identical
moment by Jeb Stuart and other Confederate cavalry officers
who had attended the Academy.

All day long it went. Stand to horse! The men rapidly learned
to snap their heels together, left hand hanging naturally at the
side, body erect, right hand grasping the reins at regulated distance from the bit, head and eyes to the front. In and out
among them moved the instructor, punching a man's belly
here, straightening a back there. Now all was pleasing to his
eye. Prepare to mount! The men pivoted on the heel, half face
to right. Mount! The riders, some new to horseback, struggled

to climb into their saddles. "Ragged! Ragged!" roared the captain. "It must be smooth! Some of you damned farm hands haven't gotten out of the bulrushes!" Over and over they tried, again and again, until their muscles rebelled at the effort. Grumble Jones had his faults, but Grumble Jones was master of the Trooper's Manual.

Mosby grew to like the rough veteran, even though Jones hounded him because of the stoop to his shoulders. Frequently the recruit stopped at the commander's tent at night to hear him talk about his experiences at West Point; about Stonewall Jackson, in charge of defenses at Harper's Ferry; about his military career and about things a cavalryman should know. The future Partisan leader later attributed much of his success to the knowledge he gained from these conversations.

Forgetting his law books and the chill of that first night's guard duty, Mosby took enthusiastically to his occupation as a soldier. The more he learned of the cavalry manual, the more he wanted to put it into practice. But it was not long before his zeal received a sudden chill. Seeing a troop go out to drill one day, he saddled his horse and went along. In a near-by field they were put through the paces, Mosby showing up to shame some of those in the line. Then two men with muskets came up and arrested him. At headquarters he was told he was doing double duty without assignment, a breach of the discipline demanded by the army.

Early in May Governor John Letcher issued an official proclamation calling Virginia to war. "The sovereignty of the Commonwealth of Virginia having been denied, her territorial rights assailed, her soil threatened with invasion by the authorities at Washington, and every artifice employed which could inflame the people of the Northern states and misrepresent our purposes and wishes," he stated, "it becomes the solemn duty of every citizen of this state to prepare for the impending conflict."

This formal action by the governor was followed a week later by Grumble Jones' notice from General Robert E. Lee, commander of military and naval forces in the state, that he had been commissioned major in the Virginia Volunteers. He was instructed to call out and muster into service at a rendezvous at Abingdon not more than two mounted companies and eight companies of infantry and riflemen from the counties of Washington, Russell, Scott and Lee. Much of this the busy Grumble already had done. In a few days the camp at Abingdon was moved to a new location, where there were plank sheds for shelter and larger grounds for drilling. Instruction became intense: it lasted for hours at a time, a merciless grind in the heat and dust. As another spur to activity, word came that the Yankee nation was preparing to move southward. Still more alarming developments followed. Federal troops, fully armed against their Rebel brethren, made a thrust across the Potomac.

Meantime Mosby was becoming dissatisfied. While he liked Grumble Jones and his strict and efficient military instruction, he found too little congeniality in the company in which he was enrolled. Most of his Bristol friends were in an infantry unit that later became a part of Stonewall Jackson's immortal brigade, and he wanted to join them. Jones was sympathetic and advised him to apply to Governor Letcher. The day Mosby wrote, the Abingdon troops were ordered by telegraph to move to Richmond. Mosby never heard from his transfer request. Perhaps it was better so. The individuality that later came to him as he streaked with flaming cloak across Loudoun and Fauquier might have been smothered in the ranks of Jackson's "foot cavalry."

5

First Smell of Powder

A BINGDON WAS A JUMBLE OF FACES Thursday afternoon, May 30, when Grumble Jones set out for Richmond with his cavalry. Colonel Fulkerson and the infantry had gone by rail, leaving the mounted troops to follow more slowly by road in a drizzling rain. But dampness was no hindrance. Impatient horsemen strung out along the narrow, winding highway. Up front were the Mounted Rifles, 102 strong, parading behind their crude company flag, gift of a young lady who had sententiously reminded them that "cowards die many times before their deaths; the valiant men taste of death but once." At the rear moved the body servants, an odd-looking entourage of black faces forgotten until time for feeding horses or making and breaking camp. Among them was Mosby's servant, Aaron.

Ten miles they moved the first day, accompanied a part of the way by several old men whose enthusiasm carried them along. But one by one these fell off until only the recruits remained. As they pushed on, songs grew louder and turned oftener to the Union President. "If Abraham Lincoln could have been sung out of the South as James the Second was out of England," Mosby observed, "our company would have done it and saved the country all the fighting." [1] One ditty they sang became more popular with each mile:

> "He who has good buttermilk aplenty
> And gives the soldiers none,
> He shan't have any of our buttermilk
> When his buttermilk is gone."

That night Jones called a halt at Glade Spring, divided his
men into squads and directed them to homes in the neighborhood. Mosby was assigned to a group under command of
Orderly Sergeant James King, West Point cadet who later fell
at Kernstown. They were quartered at the hospitable dwelling
of Major Ab Beattie, landed gentleman who opened up smokehouse and pantry in a generous effort to make them feel at
home. But there was no comfort for Mosby. Recent developments had drained him of legal and political argument and he
once more was the silent person who talked only when occasion
demanded. Underneath his stoic front, he was lonesome, thinking often of the young wife and two children he had left at
Bristol.

When the recruits gathered next morning at the Glade Spring
Church, not a man was missing. There was much excitement.
Just a week prior, the enemy had occupied Alexandria, and
they were afraid the war would end before they could get
within hearing distance of the guns. Despite this enthusiasm,
Jones made easy marches. Towns along the way gave them
ovations. Young ladies bombarded them frequently with bou-
quets and bashfully blew kisses as they passed. Mosby noticed
that one man who rode at the head of the column and enjoyed
the richest of this acclaim was conspicuously absent at their
first battle a few weeks later.

They approached Richmond Monday afternoon, June 17,
tired, dirty, but still full of spirit. Their column closed up as
they neared the city, and they drew rein on the south side of
the muddy James River to stare at a vast encampment that
recalled to most of them only the story-book drawings of their
childhood. There on the nearest slopes of the capital's series
of hills was bustle of ant variety. Figures were everywhere,
moving about, some aimlessly, some intently, and all creating a
babble that came clearly to the horsemen across the water.
Tents poked up on vacant lots and out of the trees to the west.
From the historic state building, massive on the horizon,
flapped the Stars and Bars, a flag noticeably larger than those
topping other buildings. Streets were a beehive of humanity.

cluttered by more people than some of the husky Southwest Virginians ever before had seen.

Already troops, newly tutored by cadets from the Virginia Military Institute, were marching. They were on a parade ground to the left, at the edge of the city, some in the gaily-colored uniforms which young wealthy planters brought so proudly out of the deep South, others in the new hand-stitched, Confederate-gray outfits Richmond women had made in church basements since the order to mobilize had been given. Into the hands of many had been placed some of the thousands of flint-lock rifles taken out of storage and percussioned in the old armory at the foot of Ninth Street.

Filing into Richmond, the cavalrymen took ample notice of the general activity, intensified a few days before by the arrival of President Jefferson Davis. They were halted momentarily while Jones got his bearings and then they advanced up the hill toward the capitol. Along the sidewalks civilians and even soldiers of other commands remarked on the appearance of the Rifles. They had a more seasoned air than most troops, it was noted, and they sat and managed their horses with few exceptions like seasoned veterans. These chance admirers were unaware that credit for this excellence was due the hard-boiled fanaticism and West Point ideals of the rugged individual in homespun coat near the front of the column. Because of the home-team spirit the arrival of these men engendered, Grumble's troopers were cheered as their mounts pranced along the cobblestones. Pistol shots were fired into the air at one corner, and at another a woman in gaudy costume yelled in a voice unbecoming a lady. Behind her a drunken sergeant reeled out of swinging doors.

After camp routine next morning, Mosby made his way to the store of George S. Palmer, his father's friend, and wrote, among other letters, the following to his mother:

Richmond, June 18, '61.

Dear Ma: I reached this place yesterday evening. We had been eighteen days on the road. We generally slept on the ground at night, and I never before had such luxurious sleeping. I had no sign of a cold, although it rained a good deal of the time. I fattened every day. Our march was a perfect ovation. The people threw open their doors to us. I don't know how long we will stay here, about a week, I think, and from this place to Ashland eighteen miles from here to the Camp of Instruction. Virginius and McKendrie Jeffries are there in a co. (company). The first person I met was Dick Wyatt—belongs to the Goochland Artillery. Wilby Eppes treated the company. He introduced me to his family and said he knew you very well. I sent all of my clothes on here by railroad and have not been able to find them. I did not have even a change with me, though a soldier looking dirty is nothing thought of. I stayed one night with Aunt Polly, as we camped near her. They were very kind and gave me a good many nice things to bring with me to eat. A whole roasted ham. I wish you would send me something to eat. The fare here is very rough—nothing but fat salt meat and cold, hard bread. You can send it to the care of Peter Woods. I will write often to you all. My love to all.

Yours affectionately,
John S. Mosby.

Added was this postscript:

"I am writing in Mr. Palmer's store—he is very anxious for me to go with him home, but I have on nothing but dirty clothing—a blue jeans hunting shirt over a blue flannel one.

"Always address me: Captain Jones, Washington Mounted Rifles.

"Mr. Palmer says ours is the finest company that has come to Richmond. Not in dress (for I can tell you we look like ———) but in fighting qualities . . ." [2]

Richmond was experiencing the greatest chapter of its history. More troops were arriving on every train. Every state in the Confederacy was represented. They filled the camps, vacant buildings, stores and streets. Bugle calls and drum rolls were familiar sounds at all hours of day and night. The mayor and Council started plans to build defenses around the city, and penitentiary convicts harvested a crop of hay from Capitol Square to make way for dress parades.

Editors were impatient. They found thousands of men loitering about or lying down in the tents and under the shade trees at the camps, and "enough to spare of fair women and brave men not in uniform." "This morning's paper," commented one journalist, "tells us of the fighting on the Seaboard, and makes us quite dissatisfied to remain so inactive in our camps. I mean so inactive in relation to fighting. True we are drilling twice daily . . . but it is too tame a life for us. We either want to pick them off with our carbines on the northern border or rush impetuously upon their opening batteries."

One newspaper item in particular caught Mosby's attention.[3] It stated that Colonel J. J. Daniel and Lieutenant Thomas W. Upshur were raising for immediate service in General Wise's brigade a corps of mounted guerrilla rangers. "This movement is sanctioned by Colonel Davis (the President)," the paper added. "Guerrilla fighting will help us out wonderfully." Mosby read it a second time. It reminded him of Francis Marion.

A few days after he reached Richmond, the young attorney encountered on the street one of his political friends of the preceding year—Tim Rives, the orator. Rives was unusually cordial, perhaps because he had liked the newspaper account the younger man had written of his Abingdon speech. "You have no business in the ranks," he said, sizing up the cavalryman. "You ought to be an officer. Come with me to Governor Letcher and I'll get you a commission. He was a Douglas supporter, you know." But Mosby protested. He reminded the orator that he had had no previous military training and that it would be much better for him to serve as a private under such an able commander as Jones.

True to the prediction made in the letter to his mother, the Washington Rifles soon were transferred from the Fairgrounds to the camp of instruction at Ashland. Training became more intensified. From early morning until late at night they drilled, they practiced, they studied. The Trooper's Manual was fingered constantly. Grumble Jones had heard people were saying his Rifles were the best looking outfit to come into Richmond.

One thing worried Jones: his men had only their sidearms and horses—no uniforms, no rifles. He made requisition on the

quartermaster department for the missing items and his order
a few days later came back partially filled. A small number of
Sharp's carbines were issued and these were distributed as far
as they would go. Mosby was among the few who got them.
But the uniforms almost caused a mutiny. They were ugly and
ill-cut, of a dingy, coarse, drab-colored cloth made on the looms
at the state penitentiary. The high-minded gentlemen from
Southwest Virginia would have none of them and piled them
with scorn in a heap in front of the captain's tent—all except
two privates—Mosby and his close companion since they had
left Abingdon, Fountain Beattie. These two dressed in the
"penitentiary cloth," as their derisive comrades called it, and
rode into Richmond to Palmer's store, where they found one of
their officers busy about the purchase of a neater, less durable
outfit. In a few months, Mosby noted, the entire company
would have been glad to get the discarded clothes.

Since the first of June, General McDowell, commanding Fed-
eral forces in the field, had been planning an offensive move
from Washington. This was to be made in coöperation with an
army under General Patterson, lying with its base at Frederick
City, Maryland, and its eyes upon Harper's Ferry, held by
General Joseph E. Johnston with 11,000 Confederates. Mc-
Dowell's aim was to engage General Beauregard at Manassas
Junction and bar him from sending reinforcements to Harper's
Ferry. But an unexpected move on the part of Johnston broke
up this plan. He retired in the face of the advancing Patterson
and fell back to Winchester to cover the Manassas Gap rail-
way, running from Manassas Junction to Strasburg in the
Shenandoah Valley. Following this voluntary withdrawal of
the enemy, Patterson curled up his army in the valley to wait.

Such was the situation at the close of June. At one end of
the Confederate defense line lay Johnston and, at the other,
sixty miles southeast, Beauregard and his 20,000-man army, its
outposts pushed forward to Falls Church and Annandale, almost on the outskirts of Washington. Now McDowell came
forward with another plan: if Patterson could keep Johnston
busy, he would take 30,000 men and drive Beauregard back
behind the Rappahannock.

Early in July, more activity was started. The impulsive Colonel Thomas Jonathan Jackson, with his Virginia brigade and Lieutenant-Colonel J. E. B. Stuart's cavalry regiment, had a small fight with Patterson's advance guard above Harper's Ferry at Falling Waters. Johnston was proud of what happened and recommended both Jackson and Stuart for promotion.

Now the area around Manassas became a no-man's land, and the armies on both sides stirred restlessly. Up from Richmond marched and rode more of the 65,000 Confederates under arms in Virginia, among them Grumble Jones' Rifles, by this time a crack outfit except for experience under fire. Straight to Winchester the Abingdon company moved, halted a day near Johnston's headquarters, then set out to join Stuart as a part of the First Virginia Cavalry. At Bunker Hill, Mosby saw for the first time the young, bearded leader he was to follow. While only a year his senior, Jeb Stuart had something that awed the future Partisan leader. Maybe it was his strength, his ruddiness, his flaming beard and wide, brown moustaches; or maybe it was the white buckskin gauntlets and golden silk sash. They seemed as much a part of the cavalryman as the great ostrich feather and the gold star that adorned his hat. Mosby wondered if the day would come when he would meet face to face this dashing horseman. Perhaps that moment an ideal was formed in the mind of the frail man who later fostered plans that brought great renown to Stuart.

After another day of rest, during which nearly everyone wrote home, Jones, who had relinquished his state commission for a captaincy in the Confederate service, was ordered to take his company on a scout toward Martinsburg. The men were intensely excited, and the fact that the first enemy they had advanced upon lay many miles to the fore in no way abated their enthusiasm. But slight benefit was gained from this initial outing. They moved to within a mile of Patterson's army, stared at it for some time and returned to their bivouac. It had been a day of little adventure. Yet there were some extremely proud hearts among the tired soldiers. A handful of men had surprised two of the enemy foraging at Snodgrass Spring, had chased them across a field and had captured them without firing a shot. As a member of this group, Mosby received out of the loot taken from the captives the first canteen he ever had seen. He put it into service immediately.

While they waited in the valley, a number of cavalry pistols were distributed by Stuart. Jones got six for his company and issued them personally, explaining as he did so: "I shall always put these men in front. I shall always place them in the post of greatest danger." Mosby was surprised to find himself among the chosen few.

The clamor for action became stronger at Washington. Politicians wanted McDowell to move before the three-month enlistment of the militia expired. So McDowell advanced from Alexandria July 16. The Confederates retired from Centerville the next day and took position behind Bull Run, four miles back. Beauregard wired Jefferson Davis that the enemy was moving on him and that he was heavily outnumbered. Johnston prepared to come to his aid. He sent Stuart at 1 A.M. on the 18th to get as near Patterson's lines as he could and to assume threatening attitudes in plain view of the Federals. Out under the stars rode the First Virginia Cavalry, at the same time Jackson and his infantry started in the direction of Manassas. The horsemen moved for miles through darkness and then, as dawn broke, began to harass the enemy outposts. All day there was vigorous activity in Patterson's front. He wired Washington that Johnston was preparing to attack him with 35,000 men.

During the day the Rifles, included in the detail from Stuart's horse, kept almost constantly on the move. At one time, while the men lay in a field holding the bridles of their horses, a battery appeared on a distant hill and opened fire.[4] A shell burst near Jones. The West Pointer lazily arose, ordered his men to mount and rode off, in no bigger hurry than if he had been bossing a gang of field hands. His recruits were much calmer after that.

Stuart, satisfied as the sun sank that he had bluffed the enemy, divided his command, leaving a part of it as a screen before Patterson. With the remainder he moved to join Beauregard. The 20th found him going into bivouac at Ball's Ford, near the left center of the Confederate line. He had traveled more than sixty miles in two days. In the bushes on the other side of the Bull Run lay the enemy. The Blue and Gray armies were in close contact. As tired horsemen stretched in their blankets under the stars, rifles of pickets along the slopes of the stream kept up an intermittent rattle, twinkling like fireflies in the dark and driving away sleep.

Long before sunup, Stuart's men were astir, fully awake. They drank coffee and stared off at the growing paleness to the east. It was predicted that the day would be hot, and already there was sultriness in the air. When the Rifles counted off, Mosby was No. 1 man in the first set of fours and rode at the head of the squadron. Nothing afterwards in his military career gave him more satisfaction to remember.[5]

Stuart soon ordered Jones to make a reconnaissance. It was light now, and lively firing could be heard in the direction of Stone Bridge, up where Colonel Nathan G. Evans with the Fourth South Carolina Infantry and Wheat's Louisiana Battalion was trying to check an awkward turning movement. Across open country rode Jones' men. They crossed Bull Run with caution and halted near a wooded section in which the commander suspected the enemy might be lurking. He called for the six men with the cavalry pistols and sent them to reconnoiter. They were filled with pride at the distinction. All eyes were on them as they disappeared in the woods, strung out like bloodhounds. But the Federals were not there, fortunately, and they came back presently after much trampling of underbrush.

Cannonading grew louder. It was mightier than the great roar of falling forests and continued as the morning wore along. At one time shells fell dangerously near Stuart's cavalrymen, but no one seemed to be hurt. Stuart divided his regiment. A part was sent to protect the flank of the infantry farther upstream; the remainder, including the Washington Mounted Rifles, was held in reserve under command of Major Swan, a Marylander. The men left behind waited impatiently and wondered what was taking place off where the big guns were belching forth their tons of death.

Most of the afternoon, the reserve sat still. Up near Henry Hill, their comrades and Beckham's guns flanked Jubal Early's brigade, moving up from Union Mills, and the knockout blow was delivered. Blue lines gave way before the shock and fell back in confusion toward Washington.

Late in the day, when word came that the enemy was in retreat, the men under Swan were halted in a field near a battery busily firing at the fleeing troops. Jones chafed at their inactivity. At last, raising in his stirrups, he yelled: "Major Swan, you can't be too bold in pursuing a flying enemy!" But Swan was unmoved. He could not see the wisdom of supporting the battery. After dark, he ordered the disappointed soldiers to the rear. Jones was furious. That night, in a rich flow of profanity, he earned, if never before, the sobriquet of Grumble.[6]

Heavy clouds came up in the darkness after nightfall. They spread in a solid heaven above the Manassas plains, and a warm July rain began to fall. Too much taken up with the day's experience to prepare for such weather, the recruits scurried for the best cover at hand. Mosby bivouacked under an oilcloth in a fence corner. Rain was spattering in a downpour when he fell asleep and it was still falling when dawn crept under the cloth and awakened him. Everything seemed soaked. But safe in his bag he found some writing paper that was only slightly damp. Curling up under his temporary shelter, he scribbled to his wife the following hurried note in which he purloined perhaps a few of the glories of battle:

> Monday, July 22d,
> Battlefield of Manassas.

My dearest Pauline: There was a great battle yesterday. The Yankees are overwhelmingly routed. Thousands of them killed. I was in the fight. We at one time stood for two hours under a perfect storm of shot and shell—it was a miracle that none of our company was killed. We took all of their cannon from them; among the batteries captured was Sherman's—battle lasted about seven hours—about 90,000 Yankees, 45,000 of our men. The cavalry pursued them until dark—followed six or seven miles. General Scott commanded them. I just snatch this moment to write—am out of doors in a rain—will write you all particulars when I get a chance. We start just as soon as we can get our breakfast to follow them to Alexandria. We made a forced march to get here to the battle—traveled about sixty-five miles without stopping. My love to all of you. In haste.

Yours devotedly,

John S. Mosby.[7]

The expected pursuit to Alexandria did not develop. All day long they lay still, and only once did Mosby move out of camp. He was ordered then to take a dispatch to Stuart at Sudley Spring. This greatly pleased him and gave him opportunity to look over the battlefield. Frequently he stopped to engrave on his memory the sight of the dead, dying and wounded still lying in the rain. At places a wheelbarrow could not have been rolled between them, and around the cannon they were piled waist high. Next day, Stuart moved to Fairfax Court House and camped on each side of the Alexandria highway. To Mosby the country seemed "like Egypt after a flood of the Nile." Dead bodies littered the roadside; baggage wagons, guns, trunks, clothes were scattered widespread.

Somewhere along the route he found stationery left behind by a company of Zouaves. The following morning he used it to write "the particulars" of the battle to his wife. "There was scarcely a minute during the battle that I did not think of you and my sweet babes," he concluded. "I had a picture of May [his daughter] which I took out once and looked at. For a moment the remembrance of her prattling innocence almost unfitted me for the stern duties of a soldier—but a truce to such thoughts. We are now marching on to bombard Washington City."

Mosby's first battle was in the past. At its close, he was as much a nonentity as thousands of other men in the ranks. He had not fired a shot. He scarcely had been in danger. He had not even witnessed the front-line fighting.

But the war was just three months old.

A Scout Turns Raider

AFTER MANASSAS, THE FEDERALS WITHDREW into Washington to attend their wounds and to recover from the shock. Waiting across the Potomac, in plain view of the city's church spires, were the Confederates. Their picket lines were spread in a huge semicircle. Up front on outpost duty was Stuart's First Virginia Regiment, and not the least conspicuous of its figures was Captain Grumble Jones. He was delighted to be in the open, surrounded only by men, where he could swear until the trees rocked with his rhythm. His blasphemous flow was noticeably unstinted these days. At headquarters one day, he offered to "cuss out" a soldier for the pious Stonewall Jackson.

Mosby's admiration for the rough, untidy Jones became a controlling influence with the lawyer. Nights in succession he stopped to hear the veteran's discussion of warfare and a recitation of the errors committed during the opening battle between the North and South. Then the younger man would hurry to compare notes with Noland's "Employment of Cavalry," Mahan's "Outpost Duty," Marmont's "Institutes" and Napoleon's "Maxims of War." Once he overstayed in the commander's tent and it cost him extra hours on patrol next morning. But his dislike for guard duty gradually waned. It was more exciting out here in the bramble thickets of Fairfax County, where he could stretch beneath the stars and stare toward Washington. The scurry of a rabbit, the hoot of an owl, and the constant danger that an enemy bullet might come plowing out of the dark drove away sleep. Twenty-four hours at a

The Hathaway home near The Plains, Virginia, at which Mosby's wife stayed during the war. Below is shown the huge walnut tree at the back of the house, with a long limb extending to the bedroom window. Onto this the raider leaped one night, to elude a Federal search party.

Mosby on a Moonlight Raid

stretch, three times a week, the cavalrymen were posted in trios to swap turns with one another at watching.

One night, not long after they had gone into this siege of waiting, Jones moved with a patrol to station them on picket duty. Suddenly a volley was poured out of a thick clump of pines, and Grumble's horse went down, shot through the head. "We were perfectly helpless, as it was dark and they were concealed in the bushes," Mosby wrote his wife. "The best of it was that the Yankees shot three of their own men—thought they were ours."

Around the middle of August, Mosby and nine others rode rapidly down a road. All at once, above the clatter of their horses, came the noise of approaching cavalry, and a moment later a column of Federals appeared on a hill in front. "We fired on them and, of course, retreated before such superior numbers," Mosby recorded in more of his frequent correspondence to his wife at this period. "We jumped into the bushes to reload and give it to them again when they came up, but instead of pursuing us, they put back to their own camp." In this same letter he recorded that while last on picket he had been so close to the enemy that he could hear the morning drum beat, that some of the Federals had come to his post under flag of truce, eaten supper and spent the night. "We treated each other with as much courtesy as did Richard and Saladin when they met by the Diamond of the Desert," he added.

Late in August Mosby was stationed with two others in a drizzling rain on the road leading from Falls Church to Lewinsville, seven miles west of Washington. About dusk Jones had ridden to the post and informed them there were no troops outside their lines, to fire on anything that approached from the enemy's direction. Then down over Fairfax came a blackness that shut out even the trees. Mosby finished his turn of duty eventually and stretched out beneath oilcloth and blankets. Scarcely had he dozed when the man on duty shook him: "Cavalry coming." Mosby jumped up, half asleep, and threw himself into the saddle. Nearer out of the darkness, from down the lonely, sopping road toward the enemy, came the thunder of hoofs. Jones had said fire on anything that ap-

proached from that direction. So Mosby fired. At the flare of
the carbine, his horse, the one he had brought from his father's
farm, whirled and galloped off uncontrollably. The rider held
on, struggling, pulling frantically. Branches slapped him painfully in the face, forcing him to bow his head. His horse stumbled ... rolled ... and that was the last he remembered.

When he regained consciousness, he found himself lying on
a bed at a tollgate keeper's house near Lewinsville. In the room
stood Jones and several others, and it was between the sand-
wiched curse words of his commander that he learned what
had happened. The cavalry at which he had fired had been
from his own command, riding contrary to orders. He wrote
Pauline the details, concluding: "Our troops are gradually en-
croaching on the Federals,—now occupying a position in full
view of Washington,—a brush is looked for here today.... I
rode out one day about a week ago with our wagon after hay,
came to where our pickets were stationed—they were in full
view of the Yankees, a few hundred yards off on the opposite
hill. The Yankees were firing at our men with long-range guns,
but ours could not return it, as they have only old muskets.
I have a splendid Sharp's carbine, which will kill at a thousand
yards. I dismounted ... and turned loose on them ... I had to
fire at them most of the time in a thick field of corn—of
course, could not tell the effect—but once, when a fellow ran
out into the road (in which I stood) to shoot at me, it took several men to carry him back."

Though Mosby frequently saw Jeb Stuart during his rounds
these days, he still had not come in personal contact with the
bearded officer or in any way drawn attention to his own presence in the army. The opportunity came September 11. That
day, Stuart rounded up 305 men from the Thirteenth Virginia
Infantry, took Grumble Jones' and another company of the
First Virginia, as well as a section of Rosser's battery, and went
to meet the enemy. Near Lewinsville he picked three men at
random, one of them Mosby, and rode forward to reconnoiter.
They moved slowly, stopping often. Out of the woods across a
field, within easy shooting distance, a force appeared. Mosby
dropped from his horse and took aim with carbine at a gayly-

dressed officer. But Stuart stopped him. "They might be our men," he cautioned. Mosby wrote his wife about it: "I never regretted anything so much in my life as the glorious opportunity I missed of winging their colonel. We went back and brought up our artillery, which scattered them at the first shot."

In a letter that followed quickly on this, he displayed a touch of sentiment that would have seemed a dissonance in the light of his reputation in the North two years later:

> Camp near Fairfax Court House,
> September 14, 1861.

My dearest Pauline: ... Today we go on picket at the Big Falls on the Potomac. One hill we occupy commands a full view of the Capitol. I went to take a view.... We could see it distinctly, with all their fortifications and the Stars and Stripes floating over it. I thought of the last time I had seen it, for you were there with me, and I could not but feel some regrets that it was no longer the Capitol of my country, but that of a foreign foe.

> Devotedly,
> John S. Mosby.

The day this note was written, General Johnston sent a letter to Richmond suggesting that a cavalry brigade be formed with Stuart at its head. He urged also that Jones be made colonel in Stuart's place and that Fitzhugh Lee be promoted to lieutenant-colonel. These changes came through in due time.

Now the weather grew cold and the roads bad, and the men thickened their blankets in readiness for winter. Many of them received ample supplies of bedclothing from home and those whose families neglected them made up for the deficiency from the large store left by the Federals who had fled back across the Potomac in July.

On November 18, Mosby was one of eighty men sent under command of Fitzhugh Lee to drive back a company of Federals who had approached near enough for attack. In the skirmish that followed, he and Fount Beattie got separated from the main body and had a duel with two Union soldiers in the woods. "We ordered them to surrender," Mosby related to Pauline, "but they replied by firing on us. One of the Yankees jumped behind a tree and was taking aim at Fount when I leveled my pistol at him, but missed him. He also fired, but missed Fount, though within a few feet of him. I then jumped down from my horse and, when the fellow turned to me, I rested my carbine against a tree and shot him dead. He never knew what struck him. Fount fired at one with his pistol, but missed. A South Carolinian came up and killed the other. The man I killed had a letter in his pocket from his sweetheart Clara. ... They were of the Brooklyn Zouaves and fought at Manassas."

Mosby had little chance for action during the next two months. Many of his comforts as the wintry weather fastened down over Northern Virginia came from the faithful Aaron. The darky was respectful, boasted a certain degree of popularity among the Mounted Rifles and talked of the soldiers as "his boys." Mosby accused him of feeling next in command to the captain.

New Year's came and the icy first days of '62 rolled along. On January 21, Mosby asked a six-day furlough to visit his "sick family in the County of Nelson." [1] The request was granted, mainly perhaps on the strength of such an indorsement as this from Grumble Jones: "Private Mosby left home a lawyer in good practice as a private in the ranks and has always been ready in the most active and dangerous duty, rendering brilliant service. If any is entitled to consideration, surely he is. His application is most cordially and urgently recommended." Mosby found his family shut in by the wintry conditions, but suffering from no more than the vicissitudes of the season. He ate heartily, refurbished his wardrobe and soon was back on the picket line.

Now fate took hold of the young lawyer and pushed him forward with the same guardian angel care it later maintained over him in battle. Early on February 12, the guard detail at Fairfax Court House was surprised to see Stuart ride into the little village trailed by an empty carriage. The morning was raw and cold, and the weather-wise cocked their heads at the leaden skies and decreed there would be snow—lots of it. A few minutes after Stuart rode by, the carriage reappeared, this time with occupants, and went rapidly off toward Centerville. On the front seat perched the 125-pound Mosby, whip in hand; behind him, two young ladies. The surprise of the pickets was no greater than had been that of the man with the whip. It was a high honor to a man of the ranks to be selected to drive pretty girls of Jeb Stuart's favor farther inside the Confederate lines.

Stuart's headquarters, for the time being, were at the Grigsby home in Centerville. He had returned early from Fairfax Court House that day and was seated with General Johnston and General G. W. Smith when the frail soldier he had watched ride off with the fair cargo during the morning was ushered into his presence. Mosby had two things in mind—to report and to get a pass for his return to camp. But Stuart motioned to a seat after returning his salute. "The weather is too bad for you to walk to camp tonight. Stay here until morning."

Mosby set out for camp a few minutes after breakfast. Only the most gentlemanly courtesy and consideration had been shown him by the three military leaders whose names were household words. He had sat at table with them in the evening and again in the morning, and once had engaged in brief conversation with Johnston.

At camp, before he had had time to remove his coat, he was summoned to Grumble Jones' tent. The veteran was waiting. Without ceremony, he gruffly announced that Mosby had been made first lieutenant and adjutant, a promotion that was to take effect immediately.

As spring approached, signs came that the South was feeling the weight of superior numbers and better equipment. Not since a battle at Ball's Bluff in October had there been a Confederate success of any importance. Fort Henry and Fort Donelson had fallen into the hands of the Federals. Powder was nearly exhausted, guns were scarce. Moreover, McClellan was moving troops down the Potomac toward the Peninsula and it was evident he planned to advance on Richmond from that direction. So in early March, while the buds were be-

ginning to peep through along the ridges of the Bull Run
Mountains, Johnston closed the ranks of his army and gradually fell back from the line of the Rappahannock. There was
much discussion of what was happening.

A few days later, Mosby wrote home: "Nobody here is the
least discouraged at our late reverses. That they will prolong
the war I have no doubt. But they have not made the first step
toward subjugation. Nothing can reverse my own decision to
stay in the foremost ranks, 'where life is lost or freedom won.'
I want to see in Southern women some of that Spartan heroism
of the mother who said to her son, when she buckled on his
armor: 'Return with your shield or return upon it.' Our army is
now falling back from Centerville, but whether to Manassas
or Gordonsville, I don't know. We haven't moved our camp."

Johnston retired leisurely, with Stuart following as a rear
guard. In time a large column of the enemy was reported coming up on his rear. Grumble Jones' cavalry fell back to observe.
Next morning the Federals advanced toward Bealeton Station,
forming line of battle within a mile of the place. Stuart made
proper dispositions and then fell to observing with his glasses.
"General Johnston wants to know if McClellan's army is trailing us or whether this is just a feint," he said to officers around
him. A strange voice spoke up. "Give me a guide and I'll find
out for you." Stuart turned. It was Mosby, standing near Grumble Jones.

As daylight forced its way down into the bottoms along the
Rapidan River the following morning, a gray-clad soldier,
muddy and wet, appeared out of the mist and strode toward a
point where Stuart, waiting for the Federals to attempt a crossing, conversed with Ewell. The cavalry chief was slow to
recognize the bedraggled figure as that of the man who had
volunteered for scout duty the day before. Mosby reported the
enemy was feinting with an isolated body and kept up no communication with Washington. Stuart gave orders that promptly
sent Jones on a flying pursuit toward Warrenton Junction that
soon dispersed the column.

In his report to Johnston next day Stuart wrote with elation,
giving the future Partisan his first mention in Confederate rec-

ords: "Adjutant Mosby . . . of the First Virginia Cavalry volunteered to perform the most hazardous service, and accomplished it in the most satisfactory and creditable manner. (He is) worthy of promotion and should be so rewarded." This was the initial development toward Mosby's career. It was the first official recognition of his ability as a scout.

Federal transports were moving rapidly down the Potomac now, so Johnston increased the pace of his army as it swung around through the capital and went on along the Peninsula to support Magruder's force waiting in front of McClellan at Yorktown. On April 16, the First Virginia reached Richmond and was recognized in the *Dispatch* with a brief item: "This regiment will pass through the city this morning en route to another field of action. The First Virginia has been in the war for the last twelve months and has seen very hard service."

A week later, the Confederate army was upset by one of the most stupid laws ever passed by a legislative body. Exercising a right granted them in the military bill enacted by Congress the preceding January, soldiers walked from picket post and bivouac to ballot on who should be their commanding officers. In the shuffle, leaders were picked on a basis of popularity rather than military ability, and the efficient Grumble Jones gave way to Fitzhugh Lee. Change of commanders in some instances brought new faces to minor stations. Mosby, for instance, resigned his commission immediately after the election, and Fitz Lee accepted it. "The President has commissioned me for the war, but I would not be adjutant of a colonel against his wishes or if I were not his first choice," he explained to Pauline, and added that General Stuart had promised to see that he got a commission.

In this letter to his wife, Mosby's dislike for Fitzhugh Lee is hinted for the first time. It grew during the next three years of the war until it became almost an obsession. Perhaps it was due to Fitz Lee's lack of humor. This had come out on one occasion especially.[2] As a lawyer, Mosby had shown some gift at affecting the drawl and peculiarities of clients. One day when Jones was absent and Lee was in command, Mosby came up and announced in the vernacular of the Southwest Virginian:

"Colonel, the horn has blowed for dress parade." Lee paled with anger. "Sir," he exploded, "if I ever again hear you call that bugle a horn, I will put you under arrest."

The election may have been a lucky development for the Bristol lawyer. He had learned much during the year he had been under Grumble Jones, and now, with different leadership, he was to learn more. Stuart did not want to lose him. The dashing cavalryman knew this frail man's coolness and his flair for scouting, so he stationed him, sans commission for the moment, with his couriers to serve more as a scout than a dispatch bearer.

Things took on a more serious slant during May. Johnston, slashing at the Federals twice along the way, backed up from Yorktown and squatted inside the Richmond defenses. There he waited while McClellan moved up with 100,000 men and straddled the Chickahominy, a muddy, swamp-infested stream winding southeastward along the Peninsula from a point north of the Confederate capital. But on the 31st, with the newspapers jeering at his inactivity, he struck at the invaders with confused, disconnected fighting at Seven Pines. Much blood was shed. The church steeples of the capital rocked with the heavy firing. And toward nightfall, Johnston lay wounded, leaving his command open to Robert E. Lee, a general about whose capabilities people had their doubts.

A few days after taking command, General Lee began to work on an offensive to drive back this foe that had withstood the South's second angry protest against invasion. The Federal right, composed of 25,000 men, lay north of the Chickahominy and was fed by a line of communication extending across the Peninsula to White House on the Pamunkey, at the head of York River. It was the new commander's plan to bring Stonewall Jackson secretly from the Valley of Virginia and to let the "foot cavalry" pounce suddenly upon the right wing from behind, while the main body of Confederates attacked the front and flank. But he needed more exact information about the enemy's position and, for this, he called upon his trusty aide, Jeb Stuart. The cavalry leader in turn looked to Mosby. At breakfast on the morning of June 10, he explained what Lee wanted to know and hurried the scout away.

Heat of summer had driven Stuart to the shade of a tree in the yard at headquarters when the tired, dusty Mosby returned the following day and stretched out on the grass to rest. The scout had met with little success. While his route had not taken him far from Richmond, it had led through country thick with Federals, and they had chased him back at every point.

"I couldn't get through, General," he told Stuart, "but I saw enough to convince me McClellan's right is made up mostly of cavalry pickets. For miles, all the way back to the base at the White House, his line of communications is protected only by a screen of men."

Mosby raised on one elbow.

"Look, General," he said enthusiastically, sketching with his finger on the grass. "Here's McClellan's right lying along here. Here's Ashland. Here's Hanover Court House. The road is clear along the Pamunkey until you strike a few pickets here. Then you cross the York River railroad here and cut on around back across the Chickahominy."

He made a wide sweep with his finger.

"There's nothing to stop you," he said, looking into the general's eyes.[3]

Stuart was stirred. "Go to the adjutant's office and put that down on paper," he said, and a few minutes later, with the plan in his pocket, rode off at a gallop toward the Dobbs farm to talk with Lee. He came back hours afterward in fine spirits. The commander-in-chief had approved.

On the morning of June 12, a body of 1,200 picked officers and men from the First, Fourth and Ninth Virginia Cavalry and the Jeff Davis Legion, with two light guns of the Stuart Horse Artillery, assembled on Brook Road and trotted off in the bright dawn toward Ashland. Soldiers in the camps through which they passed remarked that the Valley of Virginia lay that way and that Lee must be sending support to Jackson. Newspapers gave a similar opinion next morning. But the column, taking up a mile of the fine, wide turnpike, did not keep on

toward the valley. It passed over the Richmond, Fredericksburg and Potomac railroad, swung west of Ashland and turned
directly east down the Chickahominy.

Three days later the men who made up the column trotted
into Richmond from the opposite direction. They had ridden
over a hundred miles, completely around McClellan's army.
They had captured 166 prisoners, 260 horses and mules, and
their own loss had been one man—Captain John Latane of the
Ninth Virginia—killed while scattering an enemy force the second day of the ride. Ahead throughout, as guide, rode Mosby.
He captured a sutler's wagon at one point and, at another, executed a bit of bluff that brought amused praise from the newspapers. It came at Tunstall Station where he charged a number
of infantrymen, shouting: "Charge 'em, boys! Charge 'em!" Surprised and supposing the lone horseman was the forerunner
of heavy numbers, the Federals retreated. Then came Mosby's
turn to be surprised. He glanced over his shoulder to see riding
out of the scraggly forest the Confederate force he was trying
to give the impression he was pacing. It was a detail towered
over by the giant Prussian, Heros von Borcke, and sent ahead
by Stuart to capture the station.

The world raved over the daring ride around McClellan.
"This was service after the true Marion and Ashby fashion,"
commented the Richmond *Dispatch*. The Confederate capital
was elated. Enlivened spirit stirred in the Southern cause. But
most important of all, Lee speeded plans for the Seven Days
campaign and based them on the information supplied by the
ride.

Mosby, writing to Pauline the day after their return and
sending her some of the loot he had brought off, valued by him
at $350, told her he never had enjoyed himself so much in his
life. "I returned yesterday with General Stuart from the grand-
est scout of the war," he wrote in triumph. "I not only helped
execute it, but was the first one who conceived and demonstrated that it was practicable." He had considered changing
to Governor Floyd's command, but added now that Stuart did
not want him to go. "Told me before this affair that I should

have a commission—on returning yesterday he told me that I would have no difficulty in doing so now."

Stuart gave the scout high praise. In his official report of the ride, he stated that Mosby, among several he named, had "rendered conspicuous and gallant service during the whole expedition." To headquarters with the report went a paper pointing out that the scout was without commission. Stuart said Mosby had established a claim for position which he hoped a grateful country would not disregard, and added that his "distinguished services run back toward the beginning of the war, and present a shining record of daring and usefulness."

A few days later, the scout was mentioned in general orders for the first time. Lee named him among privates who had received special commendation.

Meantime Mosby dreamed of himself at the head of a separate command, an energetic following, one that would serve at his bid, would dash into daring feats without waiting for deliberative council of superior officers. He had discussed his ambition with others and there had been at least one attentive ear. Less than a week after the circuit of McClellan, he went to the office of Secretary of War Randolph with the following note signed by Stuart:

"Permit me to present to you John S. Mosby, who for months past has rendered time and again services of the most important and valuable nature, exposing himself regardless of danger, and, in my estimation, fairly won promotion.

"I am anxious that he should get the captaincy of a company of sharpshooters in my brigade, but the muster rolls have not yet been sent in. I commend him to your notice."

But nothing came immediately of this visit and, on June 25, Mosby trotted again with Stuart's cavalry along the Brook turnpike. He rode next day with Fitz Lee and Von Borcke, flanking Jackson, who had been brought over from the valley as planned in a surprise move and was hitting at McClellan's right wing. For four days Mosby galloped about, scouting and riding, and then, while the guns thundered around Malvern Hill, headed for the wagon camp near Richmond to get his horse shod.

He was on his way back in a pouring rain the following day and came upon several couriers gathered in front of a house a few miles from the battlefield. Through a window he could see a gray-haired officer of erect figure talking with another, of bushy beard and great figure. "That's Lee and that's Long-street," explained a courier. Presently a gaunt general with a black beard rode up, accompanied by an orderly, and went inside. Someone said it was Jackson.

Quiet followed the Seven Days campaign and gave Mosby, billeted at cavalry headquarters in Hanover County, ample time to develop his plans. Newspapers were constantly ex-tolling the virtues of the Partisan Ranger Law passed by Con-gress a few months earlier. As the scout pondered over its possibilities, something happened that stirred him to immediate action. General John Pope, taking command of the Federal forces in the valley and around Washington, announced his policy of allowing lines of retreat to take care of themselves. "Let us look before us and not behind," said Pope, and imme-diately through Mosby's mind flashed scenes which later be-came realities. He saw men falling upon the unguarded Union rear while the enemy looked to the front. He saw rich stores waiting to be snatched, wagon trains burning in the moonlight, prisoners captured by bold action. To him came a conviction stronger than that of Robin Hood, more daring than that of Marion.

Stuart listened to Mosby's argument anew. It was sound. For the first year of the war he had fought in the section around Washington where Pope's army now lay, the scout explained, and he knew the country well. This knowledge would enable him to operate more effectively, forcing cavalry to be with-drawn from the front to protect the rear. But the Confederate cavalry at the moment was preparing for an active campaign and its leader was unwilling to detach the dozen men Mosby wanted for his initial force. He suggested instead that the scout go to Jackson, who might be better able to supply his needs from infantry ranks.

Jackson had been ordered to Gordonsville a week prior to protect the Virginia Central railroad from Pope's cavalry, so, on

July 19, Mosby set out. In his haversack he carried a letter from Stuart and a newly published copy of Napoleon's "Maxims of War" the cavalry leader wanted Jackson to read. His sole companion was a man he had picked up on the streets of Richmond, a club-footed individual exempt from military service. They slept that night at the home of a farmer near Beaver Dam. Dawn found them over their morning coffee, and soon they parted, the club-foot to continue with the horses by road, Mosby to take a flying trip to visit his wife and children, whom he had not seen since winter.

At the little Beaver Dam station, the scout took off his haversack and stretched in the warm sunlight to mull over the dream that was coming true. The sun grew warmer and the scout began to nod. But suddenly he sat up. The thunder of galloping horses had come to his ears. They were coming at a rapid pace. ... He leaped to his feet. ... Before he could flee out of sight of the station, Federals seemed to be everywhere, shouting and prying and breaking. They almost rode him down.

Mosby attracted considerable attention among his captors—the Harris Light Cavalry sent from Fredericksburg to cut the Virginia Central railroad. In his haversack they found a letter, read it and threw it away. They could have saved the Union army much trouble and worry in later months had they more clearly digested the plan unfolded on its pages.

The scout's stay in Old Capitol Prison at Washington was brief and not altogether unpleasant. Ten days after he entered, he and a number of other prisoners were loaded on a ship and floated down the Potomac to Fort Monroe. There, in a flurry of craft of all kinds, they waited four days while arrangements were made for the trip up the James to the point of exchange. During this delay, Mosby's natural instincts as a scout did not fail him. He saw several transports loaded with troops and managed to learn that they had been part of Burnside's army in North Carolina. His mind developed the problem at once. Were these soldiers on their way to support McClellan at Harrison's Landing? Or were they to reinforce Pope in his advance to the Confederate capital from the direction of Fredericksburg? He ferreted the answer out of the captain of the ship on

which he waited. And on the fourth day, he stood and personally watched the vessels weigh anchor and move up the bay.

At the Rip Raps, twelve miles below Richmond, the commis-
sioners of exchange paid no attention to the spare young man
among the first prisoners to step ashore the morning of August 5. As soon as he had been identified and his name checked
from the list, he hurried up the road toward the capital, walking in the heat and dust of midsummer and carrying a satchel
filled with lemons.

It was late afternoon when guards in front of General Lee's
headquarters in Richmond stopped an unkempt figure of
stooped shoulders who said he had important news for the commander-in-chief. He protested loudly when they denied him
entrance, so loudly that a staff officer came out, heard his plea
and admitted him. General Lee's quiet manner quickly reas-
sured the scout and drove away his temporary embarrassment.
He plunged at once into his story.

"General Burnside's troops are on their way to Aquia Creek
to reinforce Pope. I have just come from Hampton Roads where
I saw them."

General Lee looked at the young soldier and then at a large
map spread on the table before him. Mosby's tone changed to
that of the lawyer arguing in Abingdon courts.

"You will know better what weight to attach to my information when I tell you that I am one of the men mentioned in
your general order in connection with General Stuart's ride
around McClellan."

Lee's eyes twinkled. "Oh, yes, I remember," he replied, and
gave an order for a courier to be ready to ride to Jackson's
headquarters immediately.[4]

Now the scene of warfare swerved back up toward Manassas
where it had been little more than a year earlier. Jackson, on
August 9, advanced toward Culpeper to prevent the concentration of Pope's scattered forces, defeated Banks at Cedar
Mountain, and then fell back when Banks was reinforced. On
the evening of the 13th, Longstreet's brigade moved by rail
to Gordonsville and behind it followed all of the remainder of

the army except two divisions which were left to watch McClellan.

On the 16th, Lee assembled his generals in counsel and outlined his plan of action. Jackson, screened by Robertson's cavalry, and Longstreet, behind Fitz Lee's brigade, would cross the Rapidan below Pope's army, turn his left flank and get in between him and Washington. The movement was set for the 18th and was agreed on as an ideal method by which to bottle up the invaders in the great "V" formed by the Rapidan and Rappahannock Rivers.

Stuart immediately sent a courier to order Fitz Lee, moving up from Hanover by way of Beaver Dam, to meet him at Raccoon Ford. But in the message he failed to make clear the time element and the vital importance that the brigade arrive before the opening of maneuvers two mornings hence.

On the 17th, Stuart rode to the signal station on Clark's Mountain. He looked down for a time on the peaceful camps of Pope off to the west and then followed the Orange Plank Road to the scheduled rendezvous with Fitz Lee. With him went Von Borcke, Major Norman Fitzhugh, Lieutenant Chiswell Dabney, Lieutenant Gibson and the disappointed Mosby. The scout still was sorely resentful over Federal interference with his plans, but was more determined than ever to set up a separate command as soon as the excitement of the present campaign died down.

About dark, they reached Verdiersville, a little hamlet deep in the woods a few miles from Orange Court House. Stuart was worried to find no signs of the approaching brigade. When residents told him no Confederate cavalry had passed and that no Yankees had been that way for a month, he sent his adjutant, Major Fitzhugh, carrying in his pocket General Lee's orders outlining in detail the plan of attack, to meet Fitz Lee and hurry him along. Then night settled over the village and, in the warm quiet, Stuart and his followers stretched on the wide porch of an old house a little back from the road and slept. Their horses, saddled, but free to graze, milled in a yard to the rear.

Dawn had just begun to break when Gibson stirred. His ears

had caught the sound of approaching cavalry. Stuart awakened to his touch, sat up quickly, staring through the early morning mist. The noise was growing louder. There was the thunder of many hoofs. Stuart stepped down from the porch, listened intently for a few breathless seconds, and ordered Mosby and Gibson to investigate. They rode off rapidly, down the road and out of sight around a curve just below the house, thinking Fitz Lee at last had arrived. The men on the porch, following them with their ears, heard the horses stop. A spatter of shots rang out. Shouts followed. The clatter of galloping horses sounded sharp on the morning air and back came the two Confederates, shouting and riding hard, hotly pursued by a detail of Federals.

There was a mad scramble at the house. Von Borcke managed to squirm his horse through the gate and took to the road. But Stuart and Dabney were forced to jump their steeds over the yard fence. The Union force, close behind, scattered through the neighborhood, searching houses and brush.

In a few minutes, Mosby came up with Von Borcke, and they circled and doubled back to see what had happened to their companions. They found Stuart, bareheaded, staring after the disappearing column of First Michigan and Fifth New York Cavalry, carrying off in triumph his plumed hat, his adjutant and his order from General Lee, for Major Fitzhugh had been captured during the night a few miles from Verdiersville.

Fitzhugh Lee's brigade arrived that night, too tired for action, and the attack was delayed until August 20. But by that time the opportunity had fled. The captured letter had given the warning, and Pope had lost no time in removing his army from the dangerous position into which he had allowed it to advance. Mosby rode again to Clark's Mountain with Stuart and watched the Federals marching rapidly back toward the safety of the Rappahannock.

On the 20th, there was cavalry action at Brandy Station, four of Stuart's regiments, mounted, driving back five of the enemy's, partly on foot. This was the first considerable cavalry engagement in Virginia, and Grumble Jones, who had been

Mosby and His Men

Mosby is depicted, in pose characteristic of the period, surrounded by a number of his hearty young fighters.

Front row, left to right: Walter W. Gosden (father of Freeman Gosden, who impersonates "Amos" on the radio team of Amos and Andy), Harry T. Sinnott, O. L. Butler, I. A. Gentry.

Middle row: Robert B. Parrott, Thomas Throop, John W. Munson, Mosby, —— Newell, —— Quarles.

Top row: Lee Howison, W. Ben Palmer, John W. Puryear, Thomas Booker, A. G. Babcock, Norman V. Randolph, Frank H. Rahm.

From a daguerreotype

Mosby as a College Student

placed in command of the Seventh Virginia after the queer election of April, came in for a lion's share of the honors. The next few days were a strain on the Confederates. They followed on the heels of the Federals, surprised them with a flank movement by Jackson's "foot cavalry" at Second Manassas, defeated them and drove them again behind the defenses at Washington.

Lee was not satisfied. He wanted this second battle to be less barren of results than the first. So, with reinforcements from Richmond, he turned northward toward the Potomac and began the first Maryland campaign, an invasion that ended with hard fighting at Sharpsburg.

Mosby galloped with Stuart's staff through it all, through this and through the dashing Chambersburg raid into Pennsylvania in October, finding himself oftener on detached duty than with the main body. His horse was wounded slightly at Manassas, and he wrote Pauline from Chantilly a few days after the battle that a bullet had passed through the top of his hat, grazing his head. At one time, he and a companion captured seven Federal cavalrymen and two infantrymen. Out of this venture he got a good Yankee horse, two fine saddles and two pistols. At Antietam, he rode behind Stuart and got his first view of the heroic Stonewall Jackson in battle. After the last attack on the lines in the woods near Dunkard Church had been repulsed, he guided his horse carefully through the windrows of dead and wounded, and once got down to place a canteen of water in the hands of a blood-stained officer.[5]

During the next few weeks, as the two armies parried with each other in Northern Virginia, the weather grew chilly and windy and sometimes served up a skim of ice on pond and hoof track. Trees shed the last of their foliage. The first snow flurries came.

Mosby had frequent opportunity to do scout duty now. He stood in the bushes near Rectortown and watched McClellan bid farewell to his staff and fellow officers. A few days later he spied on the enemy, under command of Burnside, as it gradually moved toward Fredericksburg. He reported what he had seen and was sent with nine men to ascertain the position of Sigel's corps. At Groveton, he encountered a ten-man picket, scattered his own force to make it look like a detachment of considerable size, and charged with great furor of noise and shouting. Believing Stuart's cavalry was advancing, the picket ran back on the main body, which accepted the alarm without investigating and withdrew toward Centerville.[6]

Christmas drew near and Von Borcke and others of Stuart's cavalry, stationed just south of Fredericksburg, began plans for a big headquarters dinner, with eggnog. They rounded up turkeys, hams, eggs, a quantity of apple brandy, and then, on the eve of the mammoth event, Stuart assembled 1,800 troopers, along with Pelham's guns, and set off up the river toward Dumfries. Duty called, he explained in answer to his men's protests, and besides, this was a soldier's life.

They spent Christmas Day in the saddle, riding in the bitter cold. Near Brentsville on the 28th, they had several skirmishes, none of consequence. Then they rode toward Burke's Station on the Orange and Alexandria railroad. They surprised the telegraph operator at his key at that point, and Stuart put his own operator to work, learning the disposition of the enemy and sending Quartermaster-General Meigs of the U.S. Army a complaint against the quality of mules lately furnished.

Fairfax Court House was their next destination, but they found the enemy force there too strong to attack. So they rode on into Loudoun County and stopped on the 30th, Stuart occupying a room at the home of Colonel Rogers. That night Mosby lay between blankets and pondered. He had done valuable service in his detached duty lately: the most outstanding of his feats—retreat of the large force he had caused with nine men at Groveton—still was a topic of conversation. But that was so much water over the dam. Lee's army had settled down for the winter, and Stuart at the moment lay in the exact section where the Federal rear appeared vulnerable.

Mosby was admitted to Stuart's room early next morning. He remained behind closed doors only a few minutes. When he emerged, he had permission to stay behind for a few days with nine men.

CHAPTER

7

~~~

Raiding by Customs of War

THE STRANGE LITTLE BAND that struck across Fairfax County in early January, '63, was destiny's evidence the devil had thrown loaded dice against part of the Yankee army. Silence lay over the Federal lines on the Virginia side of Washington. Except for the brief period of the first invasion of Maryland the preceding fall, this territory had not been in Rebel hands since Joe Johnston had withdrawn toward Richmond the spring prior. Behind the Rappahannock rested the Army of Northern Virginia, Longstreet's First Corps drawn up above Fredericksburg, Jackson's Second Corps below the town, toward Port Conway, while brigades of the Cavalry Division stretched on either flank. It waited as a tired champion: three invasions had been repulsed during the past year—McClellan on the Peninsula in June, Pope at Second Manassas in August, Burnside at Fredericksburg in December.

Like watchdogs ready to bark at the first movement, Union outposts centered on Fairfax Court House. The nucleus of this peaceful little village had been converted into a confusion of blue-clad infantry, cavalry and artillery, constantly shifting in vain effort to get an upper hand on the violent cold and mud. A long chain of pickets, posted within half a mile of each other, extended from Dranesville, northwest of Washington, in a giant arc by way of Centerville to the banks of the Potomac south of the city.

On the afternoon of January 10, the strange band slipped into the outskirts of Herndon Station, forested settlement on the

Alexandria, Loudoun and Hampshire railroad.[1] Directed by a wiry little leader who seldom spoke, they tethered their horses at a farm house and scattered toward the growing gloom. They had come from the direction of Middleburg, riding hard but cautiously. Their route had been over little-used paths; they had picked their way without pause. The air was crisp, clear and cold.

That night seven pickets near Herndon freshened their fire behind a windbreak of logs and settled down for the usual game of euchre. They were near the upper tip of the arc, farthermost from the Southern army. Occasionally one of them got up and walked off to listen for noises in the distance. This was a precaution taken at irregular intervals only as a matter of routine and usually in conjunction with an act of personal comfort. For months there had been no sound of hostile gunfire.

But as the hours grew late a shot suddenly broke the quiet and out of the dark leaped a circle of dusky gray figures. One Federal, reaching backward for his gun, grabbed his arm as a second blast echoed through the woods. Then there was quiet while the mysterious attackers went about their business. Prisoners were herded together and relieved of arms. Seven horses were bridled and saddled in a tiny corral of fallen trees and led off through the pines. Guns and clothing, and the cards, too, were gathered up and carried away. In less than five minutes flickering flames were the sole evidence that the post had been occupied.

Traveling silently, the band now made a circle through the trees with their captives. Two miles were covered before they halted and forced the Federals to lie down in the corner of a rail fence. Then all the Confederates except one left as a guard moved off toward another fire gleaming faintly through the trees a quarter mile away. Soon they were back, bringing five prisoners and five horses.

"Vermonters this time," announced the leader to the man left behind. "Missed a couple vedettes."

Two nights later, the ten-man Federal patrol at Frying Pan Church a few miles away tightened its guard and added a sentinel outside the small house in which the pickets slept. Word had come that a small number of the enemy were in the vicinity.

Night waned and two sentries walked back and forth in monotonous routine. They listened intently for the snap of a twig or some token of approaching danger. But there was no snap—only a dull thud as one man fell under the butt of a revolver, only a muffled grunt as the other was grabbed from behind. Men gathered from black undergrowth. They formed line in the dark and marched, with orderly tread, toward the house and the sentinel and the sleeping comrades of the sentries. At the sentinel's command to halt, delayed because of his original impression that a relief patrol had arrived, they spread in a circle around the house and blazed away at its thin weather-boarding.

On January 15 a muddy group of men drew rein at Confederate cavalry headquarters near Fredericksburg. In a matter of a few days they had terrorized Federal outposts, captured twenty-two horses with equipments, and captured and paroled twenty-two prisoners. Stuart showed great delight at their account of adventures with the enemy's pickets. Such detail excited his admiration, stirred the spirit that had led him to fall in with the plan for the ride around McClellan, and he slapped his side and roared with glee at the tale of the orderly march on the little weatherboarded house.

"I could do more with more men and more time," said Mosby.

"Very well," replied Stuart. "You shall have them."

On January 18, three days after he returned to headquarters, Mosby trotted off toward Upper Fauquier with fifteen men from Fitzhugh Lee's First Virginia Cavalry. Some had come up from Abingdon with Grumble Jones' Rifles in '61 and had been singled out by the Partisan leader; others had volunteered after word spread of the nature of the expedition.

They were hardy, virile fighters. In the group were Fount Beattie, Mosby's messmate of penitentiary-made uniform fame; Charles Buchanan, Christopher Gaul, William L. Hunter, Edward S. Hurst, Jasper and William Jones, William Keys, Benjamin Morgan, George Seibert, George M. Slater, Daniel L. Thomas, William Thomas Turner, Charles Wheatley and John Wild. Only eight were to remain Partisans.[2]

Crossing the Rappahannock at Fox' Mill, the little band headed northward. That day meant Mosby's actual farewell to the regular service, his entry into the life of the hunted. For three years, weeks past the surrender and the end of the war, he would not be able to stretch his spare figure without danger of enemy forces pouncing into his hiding place.

Hangers-on at the Warren-Green Hotel in Warrenton, the aged, the young and the disabled, pulled their chairs closer to the logs smouldering on the huge hearth and tried to think of interesting topics.

A clatter of hoofs broke the quiet. Outside, sixteen men swung from mud-coated mounts and waded through the red mire toward the porch. Except for the leader, a small man with a plume in his hat, it was just another band of transient soldiers.

An hour later the newcomers, refreshed and carrying replenished packs, remounted and disappeared in the direction of the enemy. "A foolish thing to do," commented the hotel fraternity. "They'll be prisoners by tomorrow, and the South needs those men."

The strip of country spreading toward the Blue Ridge from the Potomac at Washington, the area from Dranesville and Leesburg to Warrenton, was ideal ground for cavalry fighting. It was made up of beautiful vistas, bare rolling hills, little clumps of trees. Stone and rail fences girdled occasional wheat fields and orchards, sprinkled about expansive pasture lands. Villages were small, far apart. In the western part of this stretch is a valley, small compared to the Valley of Virginia. It is bordered on the east by the Bull Run and Catoctin mountains and on the west by the Blue Ridge, the mountain wall passing across the state from the Potomac to the southwest. This range rises to above 2,000 feet and is broken at intervals by gaps through which roads lead to the main valley. There is Snicker's Gap, opening the way to Winchester; Ashby's Gap; Manassas Gap, where the Manassas Gap railroad from Manassas Junction to Strasburg and other valley points tops the wall; still farther south, Chester Gap, around which the hills drop to afford passage to Front Royal, and finally, Thornton's Gap, making way for the road from Culpeper west. Through this country Mosby had determined to operate. It was rich and pastoral and would afford his command a not too difficult subsistence. But more important, the towering Blue Ridge and the lower-lying Bull Run range, within easy gallop of each other, would enable him to find quick cover when hard pushed by the enemy.

Before the horsemen were many miles out of Warrenton, a cold rain began to fall. It increased until the plume on the leader's hat drooped and became a waterspout. But the band rode on, heads down to keep the icy drops from their eyes. The course swung north by northeast, nearer the Bull Run Mountains, and Mosby, knowing that each turn brought them nearer enemy territory, peered more intently ahead.

Darkness blotted out the bottoms gradually, and the mellow glimmer of lamps came from the houses near the road. The leader forged ahead until his horse barely was visible to his comrades in the dusk. Some of them knew he rode in advance to take the burden of an ambush. But no ambush occurred. They moved safely along, and at last, in the very shadow of the mountains, were brought to a halt.

"You men scatter to friendly homes in this neighborhood," Mosby ordered. "Go in pairs if you must, but no more. Stay out of sight, don't get into trouble, and hide your identity. On the 28th—that's ten days from now—you will rendezvous at Mount Zion Church, on the Little River turnpike, a mile and a half east of Aldie. That's all until then." He turned and rode into the dark.

Before sunrise on the morning of January 28, horsemen trotted into the clearing at Mount Zion Church, crossroads landmark. A snow storm had set in the day before, accompanied by a northwest wind. Much of the snow melted as it fell, but eight inches were left on the ground and the condition of the roads was indescribable. Mosby rode up by a path through the woods, cheerful but not talkative. Since the 20th he had kept constantly in the saddle in an effort to acquaint

himself with the topography and military layout of the land in
which he was to operate. He had learned that the enemy kept
cavalry, infantry and artillery stationed at Fairfax Court House,
from which the outposts emanated. He also knew that the
cavalry consisted of a brigade of Fifth New York, First Vermont, Eighteenth Pennsylvania and First Virginia soldiers. The
officer in charge was Colonel Percy Wyndham, British soldier
of fortune who had fought with Garibaldi in Italy.

This week or so of observation had given the Partisan ambitious ideas and he was impatient to execute them. After the
last of his men had appeared at the woodland church, he rode
east along the Little River turnpike and settled down to a
steady jog designed to cover considerable distance in a few
hours without extreme exertion upon the horses. Soon they
turned off along a little-used byway northeastward toward
Frying Pan Church, where a little more than two weeks earlier
the ten-man picket in the weatherboarded house had been
gobbled up. But this time they found only two Federals on
duty, took them without firing a shot and then set out for Old
Chantilly Church.

Along the way Mosby added to his band a short, stout countryman named John Underwood.[3] He was thirty years old and
his body was thick and strong and muscular. He had a shock
of white hair that stood up straight from his forehead. He was
quiet, dependable, happiest when deep in the forests. To him
they were an open book. Neighbors said he knew every rabbit
path in Northern Virginia.

This man was the nucleus around which Mosby built his
efficient staff of scouts, a group from which were drawn the
battalion's guides, from which came intelligence on the enemy's
movements, each man responsible in his own light according
to the section of country around Mosby's Confederacy with
which he was most familiar. They worked tirelessly, thoroughly,
always striving to outsmart the enemy, going sometimes to such
extremes as to back their horses across sandy highways to give
an erroneous impression of their direction. At all hours they
operated, constantly in danger, and each knew this to be his
lot: "The trump of fame will never sound for him. If he fails,

it will be in the depths of some forest, where his bones will molder away undiscovered; if he survives, he will return to obscurity as a rain drop sinks into the ocean and is seen no more." [4]

Mosby had been informed a picket of nine men from the Eighteenth Pennsylvania Cavalry was on guard at Old Chantilly Church. He determined to vary from his previous nightly raids and to attack at once, reasoning that a daytime surprise might give added advantage. Extending to within a few yards of the church was a wide sweep of low pines, a dense growth with branches dropping almost to the ground. Through this covering the Partisans crawled. Above them needled tree points whispered in the cold wind of late afternoon, and birds flushed at sight of the creeping figures. Once a rabbit, frightened from his chilly couch, startled the men and caused fingers to tighten suddenly on drawn weapons.

Near the church, where they could hear distinctly the slow tread of two sentries walking post along a path beaten in the snow, Mosby crawled ahead. He returned in a few moments, as silently as he had gone, the last detail of approach worked out in his mind.

"Fount, we'll take the guards. The rest of you have your guns ready and rush in on the reserve. Crawl close to the edge of the pines before you charge. Then go together, fire your guns in the air and make all the noise you can. But be sure you're on your feet and ready to move before you begin firing."

The fight was brief. Mosby and Beattie had the drop on their men before the tumult opened at the rear of the church, and there was only one instance of bloodshed—a Federal wounded by Mosby when he attempted to escape around the building toward the sentries. John Underwood got his pick of the horses and weapons. The others were divided by lot, but the time would come when Mosby awarded spoils on a basis of merit. The harder a man fought in the hand-to-hand tussles with the enemy, the greater the reward he led away or tucked behind his saddle. Always the loot went to the men: their leader scorned it as if it were tainted.

Now the Union outpost line in Loudoun and Fairfax stirred like an angry serpent and reached out its fangs in the form of a 200-man body of cavalry that moved toward Middleburg, reputed headquarters of the elusive band playing havoc with Federal pickets. At its head rode Wyndham, madder than when he had fought under Garibaldi.

On the outskirts of Middleburg after dark on the 29th, the force halted and went into camp. Noise it created caused two men to depart hurriedly from the near-by Lorman Chancellor home. Mosby and Fount Beattie had been chatting peacefully until a servant sent to learn the cause of the disturbance brought an answer. Then they grabbed their heavy coats and galloped into the dark on an all-night ride to round up their comrades.

Daylight found Wyndham's detachment ready to move. As it turned its back on Middleburg, Mosby and seven Partisans attacked the rear, capturing one man and three horses. With this accomplished, they fell back along the street through the village and halted at the far edge. Sound of firing by the rear guard reached Wyndham up near the head of the column and he rode back in great haste. Under his direction the pursuit was organized and pushed so vigorously three of Mosby's men were captured when their horses fell, among them Beattie.

For a handful of men to charge so rashly upon the rear of an overwhelmingly larger force infuriated Wyndham. He was accustomed to hard, open fighting, face to face with the enemy, not the guerrilla tactics that made a soldier wary of every bush. Before leaving Middleburg, he rounded up some of its citizens and made a harsh threat: this band of Rebels was to disperse or he would burn the town. In mocking answer as his column resumed its march, two horsemen looked down on it from the top of a hill, silent silhouettes as still as stone statues except for a plume waving in a gray felt hat.

Snow fell anew that night in a furious storm, blanketing the countryside with white cover a foot deep. Toward morning the wind veered and a cold rain set in, sleeting over in a thick, hard crust. Wyndham was delighted with the weather change. During the night he had stationed squadrons of reserve cavalrymen at regular intervals along the line of outposts, with instructions to dash to the aid of pickets under attack at the first sound of firing. The snow would hamper the Rebels in their flight and make trailing easier.

Mosby's men, ignoring the cold and rain, gathered that day at Middleburg and set out for Fairfax, stopping for supper at a friendly house. There they left the turnpike and went toward Frying Pan, halting at the home of Ben Hatton, farmer who traded mostly with the Yankees and whose tongue loosened as the pile of Federal coins grew in his palm. Mosby had heard of him, had been told this man was one reason the cavalry under Wyndham had visited Middleburg. They found the farmer in, found the wagon tracks to his barn made late that afternoon on his return from his latest trip to the Union camp. The cold, sharp words of Mosby made him cringe: "You take us to the Federal picket post near here or we take you to Castle Thunder." [5]

The picket, composed of ten men, was stationed beside a narrow roadway. Between this post and another half a mile distant, two vedettes passed every hour. Concealing his men along the route, Mosby captured the vedettes and sent them under guard to the point where the horses had been tied. Then he ordered his command to creep forward, guided by the light of the camp fire, and to charge at the crack of his gun. Not a sound came as the Partisans moved along, following Indian file the broken path of the vedettes. Rain still splattered through the trees, and up ahead could be heard the voices of the pickets. In the very glare of the blazing fires, Mosby gave the signal. The Partisans rushed into the camp and over the surprised Federals. It was a fight that ended as quickly as it began. Men on foot surrendered without resistance. Two vedettes, who had ridden up from the post on the far side, attempted to escape. Hurst and Keys, leaping astride captured horses, gave chase, killing one man and capturing the other.

With captives herded together in an amazed huddle, the command hurried back to the point where the horses were tied. To the ears of the men as they worked over their bridles and prepared for flight came the thunder of cavalry, traveling hard

over the crusted snow. Mosby waited until the body had
passed, a few yards to the east, then rode off in the opposite
direction along the broken path it had made. Wyndham's reinforcements, hearing the gunfire, had come to do their duty, but
the Partisans had escaped from the trap and taken the bait
with them.

Mosby was delighted with his initial operations. In the short
time he had been away from Stuart, he had captured nearly
twice as many men as were in his command and more than
double as many horses. But now occurred unexpected opposition to his activities. Citizens of Middleburg, receiving a second
threat from Wyndham to burn the town if the devastating attacks were not stopped, sent the Partisan leader a petition asking him to cease. Mosby replied immediately:

"I have just received your petition requesting me to discon-
tinue my warfare on the Yankees because they have threatened
to burn your town and destroy your property in retaliation for
my acts. Not being yet prepared for any such degrading com-
promises with the Yankees, I unhesitatingly refuse to comply.

"My attacks on scouts, patrols and pickets, which have pro-
voked this threat, are sanctioned both by the customs of war
and the practice of the enemy; and you are at liberty to inform
them that no such clamor shall deter me from employing whatever legitimate weapon I can most efficiently use for their
annoyance. I will say this to you, however, that it was through
a misunderstanding of my orders that the prisoners were
brought through your town to be paroled. I was myself several
miles behind the guard that had them. As my men have never
occupied your town, I cannot see what possible complicity
there can be between my acts and you."

In this reply Mosby disposed of the last general opposition
to his plan of action from residents of the country in which it
was to be carried out. From then on, admiration for him increased. As time passed and the threat to burn Middleburg
was not executed, citizens gave him their wholehearted support. Seldom the day passed that his activities were not discussed over the dinner table or around the fireplace of their
homes.

With public complaint quieted, the raider settled down on February 4 to report officially to Stuart on his Partisan activities.[6] His account was postmarked "Fauquier County" and concluded with a gentle hint of an opening for Confederate cavalry to clean out completely the Federal force on guard at Fairfax.

"I arrived in this neighborhood about one week ago," he wrote above the signature Jno. S. Mosby. "Since then I have been, despite the bad weather, quite actively engaged with the enemy. The result, up to this time, has been the capture of 28 Yankee cavalry, together with all their horses, arms, etc. The evidence of parole I forward with this. I have also paroled a number of deserters. Col. Percy Wyndham, with over 200 cavalry, came up to Middleburg last week to punish me, as he said, for my raids on his picket line. I had a slight skirmish with him in which my loss was three men captured by the falling of their horses; the enemy's loss, one man and three horses captured.

"He set a very nice trap a few days ago to capture me in. I went into it, but contrary to the colonel's expectations, brought the trap off with me, killing one, capturing twelve, the balance running. The extent of the annoyance I have been to the Yankees may be judged by the fact that, baffled in their attempts to capture me, they threaten to retaliate on citizens for my acts.

"I forward to you some correspondence I have had on the subject. The most of the infantry have left Fairfax and gone towards Fredericksburg. In Fairfax, there are five or six regiments of cavalry; there are about 300 at Dranesville. They are so isolated from the rest of the command that nothing would be easier than their capture. I have harassed them so much that they do not keep their pickets over half a mile from the camp. There is no artillery there. I start on another trip day after tomorrow."

That same day Mosby informed his wife by letter that he was having "a gay time with the Yankees."

When his report reached Stuart a day or two later, the cavalry leader wrote the Partisan chieftain a personal letter and addressed it "captain," even though Mosby held no commission at that time. "I have heard with great gratification of your success and shall take pleasure in forwarding with my warm commendation your report of your later operations received this morning," Stuart stated. "I heartily wish you great and increasing success in the glorious career on which you have entered."

As promised, the report went forward to headquarters, and with this postscript: "Respectfully forwarded as additional proof of the prowess, daring and efficiency of Mosby (without commission) and his band of a dozen chosen spirits." And as still further recognition for the Partisan, General Lee added his indorsement when the report came to his attention: "Respectfully forwarded to the adjutant and inspector-general as evidence of the merit of Captain Mosby."

During the week following the snow, Mosby took things easy. The weather was not too bad for fighting, but the roads had turned into quagmires, and it was nothing short of cruelty to ride horses over crust which barked their forelegs and transformed them into nervous prancers. The period of inaction gave him time to attend to his correspondence and to make some necessary repairs to harness and clothing. It also afforded opportunity to plan more attacks on the enemy who, by now, was thoroughly aware of his presence and his intentions, and daily was becoming more exasperated over failure to capture his tiny band in toto.

Near the last of the week he sent out a courier with orders for an assembly February 7 at Ball's Mill on Goose Creek, not far from the Loudoun-Fairfax county line. Bright and early on the appointed date the leader was there, but only half of his raiders appeared. The others had been surprised at a dance at the Washington Vandeventer home near Wheatland the night before. A young lady and two Partisans had been wounded and four had been captured unhurt. The few who showed up at Ball's Mill talked long afterward of Mosby's fury at news of the misadventure. It was his first violent display of the strong personal force by which he was to rule desperate men, men whom even outlaw chiefs would have been afraid to trust. Those who witnessed it never forgot the fire in his eyes, the turbulence of his voice as he paced the frozen ground near his horse. They recognized justification in his wrath: he had told them to stay under cover, and disobedience in military circles merits no tolerance.

This was no ordinary Federal force that rushed in and carried off his raiders. It was an independent command of disaffected Virginians known officially as the Loudoun Rangers and recruited mostly from the German settlement northwest of Leesburg. At the moment, it was much more experienced than Mosby's band. It had been mustered into Federal service at Lovettsville June 20, 1862, under a special order of Secretary of War Stanton. But in time it was to find its paragon in men of the Forty-third Battalion and to set as its goal their extermination. Never was it the equal of the Confederate outfit, though it remained until the latter part of the war one of its major annoyances. Its leaders were Samuel C. Means, prosperous miller of Waterford, and Captain Daniel M. Keyes of Lovettsville.

Mosby had intended to renew his attacks on the picket lines in Fairfax, but, with such a diminished force to support him, this idea had to be abandoned. He decided instead to follow a foraging party that had swept into the neighborhood and was bringing loud wails from residents. These plunderers were robbers rather than soldiers. They carried off horses, stripped dwellings of such valuables as silverware, jewelry, clothing, and even deprived one Doctor Drake of his saddlebags of medicine, a scarce item. Mosby's men overtook seven members of the party a few miles from Dranesville. They looked down upon their quarry from a distance. Then they made a circuit and intercepted them, capturing the entire group, as well as the saddlebags.

With eight men the next day, Mosby set out for Fairfax, intending despite his small numbers to strike a picket post near Frying Pan Church, site of his earliest operations and far enough advanced for him not to become too entangled inside the Federal lines. Within a mile or two of their destination, a woman hailed them from a house beside the road. John Underwood whispered to Mosby that she was Laura Ratcliffe, a Southern sympathizer. Miss Ratcliffe was highly excited. She had made a round of several homes that morning, hoping to get word to Mosby, she explained. A Federal soldier had come to her home shortly before daybreak for milk. He was lonesome, wanted to talk, and he had told her in the course of their conversation that a force lay concealed in the pines farther down the road, waiting to ambush the Partisans if they came that way.

Not having enough men to justify an attack, Mosby turned aside in the direction of Herndon Station. As night fell, he allowed his men to gather around the wares of a blockade runner fresh from Washington. Purchases were made in the light of a candle on the floor of an old barn with Federal currency taken from prisoners. While the raiders were busy with their buying, a citizen approached Mosby. He knew of an enemy picket near Dranesville. Underwood was summoned to his side and from his meager directions recognized the location. An hour later the scout led the raiders directly to the spot. The vedette on duty escaped, but the fifteen men of the reserve, together with their horses, arms and equipments, were captured without trouble.

On Mosby's return to Middleburg in the small hours of the morning, he learned that an arch foe had been on his trail. Alexander F. Davis, Union sympathizer living near Aldie, dubbed "Yankee" Davis by the Southern families around him, had come into the neighborhood in broad daylight with six wagons. These wagons were guarded to all appearances by only eighteen cavalrymen, but under the canvas looped over each vehicle lay concealed six Pennsylvania infantrymen, armed to the teeth. The ruse has its counterpart in history. Abraham Lincoln's "Greeks" of '63 found "Troy," and their wooden "horses" on wheels were permitted to enter the gates of the city unmolested. But the "Trojans" were off buying goods from a blockade runner and divesting a picket post of all its war embellishments.

8

The General Leaves His Couch

～～～

FOR WEEKS WASHINGTON'S NEWSPAPERS had devoted stories to activities of Colonel Wyndham. They told early in February that he had surprised the Confederates at Warrenton, captured eighty stands of arms and sent strong patrols to the Rappahannock. They reported next that he had returned from an extensive scouting expedition to the front and had skirmished with an enemy company on the way back. No other Rebels in arms were encountered, the papers stated, signifying that the situation was well in hand. But on the afternoon of February 26 the *Evening Star* flared up with these headlines: "Who Was in Command? Forty Union Cavalry Captured!" It was reported that the picked cavalry guard out from Centerville on the Chantilly road, with the exception of one member, had been carried off the night before by a Rebel force of about 100 men. "An example," said the newspaper, "will, of course, be made of the officer commanding this picket, by dismissing him from the service summarily, for permitting this surprise to succeed!"

The lone Federal who escaped grossly overestimated the numbers of the enemy. Union soldiers whisked away from the post actually had been captives of only twenty-seven Confederates, the size of Mosby's following to date. He had called a rendezvous for the 25th at Rector's Cross Roads,[1] four miles west of Middleburg. There had been new storms in the meanwhile, one that lasted three days, and the ground was covered with nearly a foot of snow.

Among recruits who appeared that day were Walter E.

Frankland, private from the Seventeenth Virginia Infantry, George H. Whitescarver, Joseph H. Nelson and James F. Ames, a Yankee sergeant who had deserted from the Fifth New York Cavalry. This fellow Ames came on foot, unarmed, in full uniform, a large, muscular man with piercing black eyes. His legs were slightly bowed and he walked with the swing of a seaman, his reward for a few years spent before the mast. Some of the men muttered to themselves when he gave his reason for deserting. He said it was because Abraham Lincoln's Emancipation Proclamation, issued the month before, showed "the war had become a war for the Negro instead of a war to save the Union." The mutterers warned that the big cavalryman might be another Yankee trap, waiting to kill their leader or to betray the entire command. But Mosby brushed them aside. He liked this recruit. Beneath a friendly approach the Partisan recognized a reserve which indicated the newcomer could be an extremely dangerous fighter. So in the face of considerable opposition, Ames was taken in as a member. He was enrolled on the spot, but active duty would not begin for him until later. At the moment, he and Frankland were given permission to saunter forth in an effort to mount themselves from the bulging stables of the Fifth New York.

While these two men went on foot in one direction, raiders ready for action rode in another. A cold wind bit cruelly at their faces. Clouds were heavy overhead and skeletons of trees stood out black and chilled against the white countryside. John Underwood, leading the way, paid no mind to the elements and turned off at dusk to follow a winding route through the forest. Only he knew where it would lead.

Eventually a tiny speck of light blinked through the trees and slowly grew larger. They rode on, more cautiously now, close together, silent. Even the horses seemed to sense the excitement which had come over the group. In time the trees thinned and at last in the distance a sentry could be seen walking back and forth before a small fire. A quarter mile from the camp they halted and tied their horses. It was 4 A.M.

Mosby singled out Williams and Nelson, new members of the band, to capture the guard. With the others, he prepared to circle the picket post and to gain the advantage of a surprise attack from the rear. His orders were given in whispers, so soft the wind whistling in the trees almost drowned out his voice. But they were thoroughly understood. The two men slunk away to the left. Mosby led to the right, aiming to come in behind several small, unchinked log houses he could see in the reflection from the fire. They reached a parallel with the line of houses, stopped briefly to survey the situation, and then suddenly the sentry fired his gun and ran back toward the buildings, screaming loudly.

Mosby was prepared for this turn of affairs. Into the circle of light he leaped, calling for his men to charge. In they came for the finish. Some of the Federals tried to escape to a thicket a few yards away. Others attempted to resist and were shot down. When the flurry of shooting was over, four men in blue, including a lieutenant, lay dead and several were wounded.

News of the attack, Mosby's greatest stroke to date, traveled rapidly. It went up and down the line of Federal outposts. Jeb Stuart heard about it officially the next day in a report from the Partisan leader who praised his men and offered to mount some of the dismounted members of the First Cavalry if they were sent to him.[2]

At the time Mosby was preparing his report, General Robert E. Lee was busy on general orders of great import to the Partisan. Lee called attention in the message to the "series of successes" of the cavalry of Northern Virginia during the winter months, "in spite of the obstacles of almost impassable roads, limited forage, swollen streams and inclement weather." In concluding, he observed that "Lieutenant Mosby, with his detachment, has done much to harass the enemy, attacking them boldly on several occasions, and capturing many prisoners."[3] The title of lieutenant was authentic: Mosby's commission finally had come through.

The Germantown raid also was felt at Federal headquarters. Wyndham was furious. For two months these irregular attacks by a handful of men had occurred when least expected—from behind or from the front, by dark or by daylight, at severe cost to the attacked, at virtually no cost to the attackers. They came as an insolent wound to his British pride and were made all the more exasperating by the comment of Washington newspapers. He ranted, and in his vexation could think of no worse epithet to call Mosby than a horse thief. This denunciation, passed on through citizens of the neighborhood, brought a reply from the denounced. He said all the horses he had stolen had had riders and all the riders had had sabers and pistols.

On March 1 Wyndham ordered Major Joseph Gilmer of the Eighteenth Pennsylvania Cavalry to move late that night with 200 men toward Middleburg. There was some degree of self-preservation behind Wyndham's action in sending out this expedition. Information had been received that the Rebels were busy rounding up grain for threshing in that vicinity. And a rumor was afloat in the capital that Wyndham himself had been captured, along with 800 cavalry. Some busybody had gone so far as to inquire into the report and had received a telegram of denial from the indignant Britisher.

Gilmer's orders were to proceed carefully and to send back couriers at intervals throughout the night with reports on whether the enemy had been sighted. He was not to cross Cub Run until daylight, and then was to send out flankers and small detached parties to gain information. He had these instructions well in mind as he set out, but the night was cold and somewhere along the line of horsemen a bottle was started. Another appeared, and another, and another.

At Cub Run, in the wee hours, Gilmer's orders still read for him to wait until daybreak to cross, but the fiery spirits he had been drinking told him to go ahead. A few miles farther on slept Middleburg and Mosby and his men and all the troubles which awaited Federal outposts. Now was the time to strike—before they awakened. He rode on. Somewhere in his thoughts had been lost that little item about sending back couriers.

It was a noisy, drunken mob of soldiers who took over Middleburg before daylight. A cordon of pickets was thrown around the place; extra patrols were stationed to assist them, and the main body continued on to the hotel to drag Mosby out of bed and parade him before the townspeople. But the hotel was empty of raiders, and its larder was shorn of meat and biscuit.

A stubborn streak arose in Gilmer. He sent soldiers to arrest every man they could find. Soon the net was drawn in, bringing a miserable huddle of old men. "Let's make them march!" someone cried. And back and forth along the street in the growing light the old fellows stumbled, prey of a drunken major.

That morning Mosby met his men at Rector's Cross Roads. Some of them brought word that Middleburg was occupied by Federals. Mosby waited until he had seventeen followers and then set out for the village, hoping to cut off straggling parties pillaging the neighborhood. But they learned before they reached the outskirts that the enemy had gone, drunks and all. The Confederates dashed in at full gallop to find themselves in the midst of a throng of angry women, crying children and barking dogs. The Federals, according to the predominantly female population, had ridden in the direction of Aldie at daylight, with the old men perched behind them.

Mosby learned afterwards that things had not gone well with the abductors. A few miles beyond Aldie, their advance saw guns glisten in the distance, saw tiny figures spread out to skirmish, and fell back without delay. Major Gilmer's befuddled brain was unequal to the test: it gave him pictures of his entire command gobbled up by this ferocious enemy he had been positive he could find in Middleburg and who now most certainly was between him and home base. Without detailing a party to reconnoiter, he turned off in the direction of Groveton, racing horses at full speed to gain Centerville. Forgotten in the rush and dropped beside the road were the old men.

Some of the soberer members of the command failed to be drawn into the panic and proceeded cautiously along the Little River turnpike in the direction of the unidentified skirmishers. They soon recognized Companies H and M of the First Vermont Cavalry, under Captains Hutton and Woodward, also sent toward Middleburg on reconnaissance. Together they rode into Aldie.

From Middleburg to Aldie is a ride of five miles over rolling hills, clear for a few yards back from the roadway and crowned on top by little clusters of trees. It is beautiful country to live in, but tricky for fighting. Mosby and his men covered the distance that morning in short order. Their first halt came as they topped one of the hills on the edge of Aldie. There they ran horse to horse into two surprised Federal vedettes and captured them.

From this point the road sloped gently through Aldie, past the water-fed mill that gave the village its importance, across Little River to the Bull Run Mountains, almost within stone's throw to the east. Near the bottom of the long slope on the other side of the stream Mosby made out several mounted men. He took them to be part of the rear guard of Gilmer's column and ordered a charge. He was riding that day a high-spirited bay captured from the enemy and unaccustomed to spurs. As he sank his heels into its flanks, the animal raised up, took the bit in its teeth and dashed madly toward the Federals. "I had no more control over him than Mezeppa had over the Ukraine steed to which he was bound," Mosby recorded in classical strain.[4] Down the hill the bay sped, its heels throwing mud high in the air. Past the mill where dismounted soldiers in blue fed their horses. Past the few scattered houses of the village. On toward the bridge in a thunder of heavy hoofs.

The small body of cavalry waiting on the far side of the stream was amazed at the sight of a plumed figure dashing toward them on a crazy horse. They waited in fascination and fear. They saw the rider rise in the saddle, swing out into the air and land, feet first, in a sea of mud. Then, as if they took this foolhardy Rebel to be the forerunner of a powerful enemy, they turned and raced away in a body. Behind them trailed the frightened bay, still at full gallop.

It was the foghorn voice of Dick Moran, one of the new stalwarts of the command, that announced to Middleburg the extent of their captures at Aldie—nineteen men, including two captains, and twenty-three horses with accoutrements. Waiting to hear the tidings were Frankland and Ames, Frankland with a story that brought loud laughter. Ames, he related, had made his way into the Federal camp around midnight, had boldly saddled two horses and had ridden off in plain view of the guard.

Washington newspapers were highly agitated over what had happened at Aldie. For the first time they turned on Wyndham. "Another bungle has taken place on our front," one of them wrote. "It is ascertained certainly that there is no enemy in or about Middleburg. What is imperatively necessary here is some cavalry commander who can enforce such discipline among his men as to keep them always in the state of caution as will prevent his pickets from being gobbled up through the careless and gross negligence of the officers he sends out in command of detachments." [5]

In his report of the Aldie fight, Lieutenant-Colonel Robert Johnstone, commanding the Cavalry Division, gave Gilmer no quarter except in his estimate of Mosby's seventeen men, which Johnstone placed at seventy. He immediately put Gilmer under arrest and filed charges of cowardice and drunkenness.[6] "The horses returned exhausted from being run at full speed for miles," he complained to headquarters.

Against the Partisans Johnstone made a charge that was to be repeated freely, and often unjustly: "Major Gilmer lost but one man, belonging to the Fifth New York Cavalry, who was mortally wounded by the enemy and afterwards robbed. He was away from the command and on this side of Aldie, his horse having given out. The enemy seemed to have been concealed along the line of march and murdered this man, when returning, without provocation." A squirrel rifle in the hands of some patriotic agrarian, voluntarily and stealthily doing his bit for the South, often deserved blame for pot-shots fired at the invading enemy from the cover of tree or copse. But in most instances these incidents were chalked up to Mosby's men.

For weeks Mosby had been running through his head a bold plan, a scheme that had taken on new life with the arrival of Ames. It was bolder even than Stuart's ride around McClellan. In its calculation, success was based on the theory that to all appearances it was an impossibility. At Fairfax Court House, well within the Federal lines, was the headquarters of the British adventurer who had called Mosby a horse thief. Great would be the revenge and great the surprise if the Partisans sneaked through the outposts and plucked the officer from the midst of the thousands of soldiers protecting the roads west of Washington. It was in line with the suggestion to Stuart, now obviously ignored, that the cavalry at Fairfax was isolated and that "nothing would be easier than their capture." [7]

Mosby worked carefully. Prisoners were questioned at length. Investigations went on relentlessly, but quietly. Frequently Ames, already popular with the men and endowed with the friendly moniker of "Big Yankee," was called into conference.[8] The enemy's strength, Mosby learned, was overwhelmingly against the venture. On Little River turnpike a mile or two from Fairfax Court House were three regiments of cavalry. Within a few hundred yards of the town were two infantry regiments. Another lay at Fairfax Station, between two and three miles to the south, and at Centerville was stationed an infantry brigade, supported by cavalry and artillery. To all appearances the way was blocked. If he went by the turnpike, Wyndham's horsemen would meet him face to face. On the other hand, if he chose the route by Centerville, the road along which Gilmer's frightened horse had galloped back into camp, troopers of all arms would stand in his way. The only two highway approaches were out. But folks said John Underwood knew paths not even rabbits had found.

Mosby ordered an assembly at Dover on the afternoon of Sunday, March 8. The Federals had shown no offensive since their disastrous experience at Aldie the Monday previous, allowing the raiders ample opportunity to recuperate and to condition their horses.

Twenty-nine men appeared at Dover. The leader watched them come in and was satisfied. He was pleased particularly with weather conditions. A melting snow lay over the ground, and, toward night, a drizzling rain began to fall. Darkness closed in rapidly, dense and impenetrable, a curtain to all that stood or moved.

Of the followers on hand, only Underwood and Ames knew the direction they were to take. The command moved westward through Aldie Gap, and three miles from Chantilly turned off to the right along an obscure path that placed responsibility squarely in the hands of the guide. It was steady riding now. The continual creak of saddle leather, the muffled crunch of leaden feet and the silky purr of horses breathing were the only sounds that rose from the silent column. Never increasing or abating, the rain seemed to tuck them protectively into their oilcloth coats, bringing stable odors strongly to their nostrils.

Mosby's idea was to cut through the triangle formed by the Little River turnpike, the highway from Warrenton through Centerville to Fairfax, and the Frying Pan road, in this manner avoiding the pickets on each of the two main highways and passing through the Federal outpost line in the woods north of Centerville. If details worked as planned, they would reach their destination shortly after midnight, do their deviltry and be outside the enemy bailiwick before daybreak. This schedule must be maintained if they were to proceed with any degree of safety. In the darkness, they would be mistaken for a friendly scouting party; by light of day, they would be identified and the entire command shot down or captured.

Delay came early: en route single file through a dense growth of pines, half the men got separated and stopped, helpless without a guide. Some wanted to return to Fauquier, some to wait until Mosby sent back for them, some to keep on in the hope they would stumble on the trail of the others. They were unaware of the assignment ahead of them, and this made their situation all the more complicated. But they were unanimous in their desire to share in the excitement, and finally the idea of continuing prevailed. They moved slowly forward, the men in front literally feeling their way and leading their horses. This kept up for what seemed an interminable period and some of the raiders began to talk of the futility of proceeding farther. But a short distance ahead a light glimmered faintly through the trees and hopes soared. They worked their way cautiously toward it. Presently they made out a tiny hut and heard voices, some of which they recognized as those of their companions.

More than an hour had been lost, and now Mosby urged them along at faster pace, stopping at intervals to be sure none had fallen behind. Soon after they left the hut, they crept through the outpost line. Each man was dismounted and ready to stifle the slightest snort or neigh from his horse. A vedette hailed them at one point and allowed them to approach after they assured him they were from the Fifth New York Cavalry. Underwood took him prisoner.

Once inside the lines they traveled at a fast trot, knowing anyone they met would accept them as Federals, particularly since their raincoats hid the gray of their uniforms. Pretty soon their path emerged on the Warrenton road, midway between Fairfax and Centerville, and the men halted to cut telegraph wires so no alarm could be given from headquarters. Continuing, they flanked to the right some distance farther to avoid infantry camps and then went on in a southeastwardly direction until they struck the road from Fairfax Station to the courthouse.

It was 2 A.M. when they drew up on the outskirts of their destination. The entire village seemed asleep. Streets were deserted. No noise came from the houses. Scarcely a light was visible. Here was what Mosby had hoped for: headquarters so confident of safety far behind the lines that it went to bed at night without the precaution of heavy sentry detail. Riding to the front, he halted and turned sidewise on his horse, facing his men. "Our work must be fast," he said after unfolding his plans. "Take every man you can find, particularly officers, and let's get away from here. We must be out of the lines before dawn."

Gum coats swished and revolver cylinders clicked formidably in the dark.

They rode along the street almost to the point where it intersected with the Little River turnpike in front of the village hotel, converted into a hospital. There they halted while "Big Yankee" and Frankland dismounted and approached a sentry, barely visible as he walked post before a light shining faintly from a window of the building.

What happened during the next hour was pieced together

partly in the report of Provost-Marshal D. L. O'Connor, who set the strength of the invaders at 300:

"Captain Mosby, with his command, entered the village by an easterly direction, then advanced upon my outer vedette, when he challenged (no countersign out). The Rebel picket or scout advanced, presenting at the same time two revolvers to his head and threatening to blow his brains out if he said a word, demanding his arms, etc., when the force came up and captured every man on patrol, with horses, equipments, etc., until reaching the provost marshal's stables, when they halted and entered the stables, taking every horse available with them. Then they proceeded to . . . Stoughton's stables, captured his guard, took his horses and those of his aides. Then they proceeded to Colonel Wyndham's headquarters and took all the horses and movable property with them. In the meantime, others (of Mosby's command) were dispatched to all quarters where officers were lodged, taking them out of their beds, together with the telegraph operator, assistant, etc. They searched the provost-marshal's office and, finding him absent, went to the post hospital and there made diligent search for him, offering a reward for him. The provost-marshal had just left the street, say ten minutes before they entered, and went across some vacant lots to ascertain from one of his vedettes if he had caught any horses or horse thieves."

On reaching the heart of the village, Mosby had proceeded much along the lines O'Connor described. Several detachments were sent to the stables with instructions to round up all available horses and to herd them in the street in front of the hotel. Mosby proceeded with part of the command to the Murray home, at which he had been informed Wyndham had his headquarters. But he soon discovered his mistake. The Murrays said the officer was at the Judge Thomas residence in the other end of town.

Mosby returned to the courthouse to find a number of horses already in the street, herded together, fully equipped, champing their bits and nickering. Others could be heard approaching. Joe Nelson found a tent in the courtyard and dragged from it a sleepy-eyed telegraph operator. He also captured a soldier who told him he was one of the guard at the headquarters of Brigadier-General Edwin H. Stoughton, a Vermonter. Mention of Stoughton gave Mosby a new idea. Directing Ames to go with a detachment to Wyndham's quarters, he himself set out to find the brigadier-general. With him went five men— Joe Nelson, William Hunter, George Whitescarver, Welt Hatcher and Frank Williams, all destined to bring the command much praise through their deeds.

At the brick home of Dr. Gunnell, sitting back a hundred yards or so from the main road past the courthouse, they stopped. Mosby gave a loud knock, and in a few seconds an upper window was raised and someone called down sleepily, "Who's there?"

"Fifth New York Cavalry with a dispatch for General Stoughton," replied Mosby.

The window was closed, a light flickered and footsteps could be heard coming down the stairs. The door was thrown back by Lieutenant Prentiss of Stoughton's staff, dressed in shirt and long drawers, looking more like a farmer roused from his couch by chicken thieves than an officer in the United States Army facing a group of desperate Partisan raiders.

Mosby grabbed him by the shirt and poked a gun in his ribs. "Lead me to the general's room," he said coldly.

Nelson, Hunter and Williams followed, revolvers in hand. Up the stairs they trailed and in a large room the lieutenant pointed to the general.

Stoughton lay in a sound sleep, heavy covers accenting his figure in a sloping mound. Near at hand stood several empty champagne bottles, mute evidence of revelry the night before. Mosby walked to the bed and pulled down the quilts. Stoughton was on his side, snoring. Lack of covering caused him only to double his knees more closely against his stomach. But he kicked and raised on one elbow in sputtering confusion when the Partisan lifted his nightshirt and spanked him on the behind.

"General, did you ever hear of Mosby?" the figure bending over him asked.

"Yes, have you caught him?"

"He has caught you."

"What is this!" roared the general, sitting up in bed. "Lieutenant, what is the meaning of this?"

Mosby answered before Prentiss could speak.

"It means, General, that Stuart's cavalry have taken over Fairfax and General Jackson is at Centerville."

Stoughton groaned. "Is Fitz Lee here?"

"Yes," lied Mosby.

"Then take me to him. We were classmates at West Point."

The Partisans helped the general and the lieutenant into clothes. At the front door, Williams gave Stoughton his watch, overlooked by him in the excitement.

Whitescarver and Hatcher had not been idle while the others were upstairs. They had captured seven headquarters couriers from tents in the yard, as well as several horses which had been standing by bridled and saddled. These were all waiting at the gate, ready to move.

Mosby was determined Stoughton should not escape, so he directed Hunter to hold his reins and to ride by his side. This worked successfully with the brigadier, but somewhere in the dark Prentiss slipped away. Back at the courthouse square more than 100 prisoners and horses were waiting. Ames was there with bad news. Wyndham, acting brigadier, had gone to Washington the afternoon before, but the deserter had succeeded in raiding his quarters and capturing the assistant adjutant-general, Captain A. Barker.[9]

For more than an hour the Partisans remained in the village and not a shot was fired. They worked in close harmony, each performing his duty as instructed, and so active were they that the prisoners were unanimous in believing that the entire Confederate cavalry had broken through the Federal lines. There was no resistance. But Mosby knew the command would not be safe until it passed Centerville and that that must be done before daylight. Riding among the milling horses and men in the darkness, he finally got the column in motion, directing Underwood to lead it along the same route they had come.

As they passed through the street on their way out, an upstairs window of one home was raised and a man, bellowing

with authority, asked the identity of the cavalry. A chorus of
laughter from the riders was the answer. Realizing this must
be an officer of rank, Mosby sent Nelson and Hatcher to make
the capture. They crashed through the front door and there
were met by a fighting tigress, a woman who fought and
scratched to delay them until her husband could escape. For
ten minutes the two Partisans combed the building and its
surroundings, but nowhere could they find the inquisitive Federal. By his clothing, which they brought off, they learned that
he was Colonel Robert Johnstone, commanding the cavalry
division, and the same individual who had filed charges against
the drunken Major Gilmer. It was days later they heard the
object of their search had fled, barefooted and in nightshirt, to
take refuge beneath a privy at the back of the garden, there to
shiver in misery until his wife signaled him to return.

The column proceeded toward Fairfax Station, swung to the
right around the infantry camps, and continued to the southwest. It was beginning to turn faintly gray along the eastern
sky to the rear as they circled the fortifications at Centerville.
A mile or so farther on they reached Cub Run, a swift little
stream between high banks, now swollen into a churning torrent by melting snow. Mosby urged his horse through the mist
along the bank and into the icy water, spurring the steed gently
until it was well out in the current. On the bank its quick
snorts could be heard above the gentle, encouraging voice of
its rider and the noise of the torrent. Then it got its stroke and
moved rapidly across, emerging at a point some distance down-
stream. Other riders followed, some so surrounded with horses
as to resemble flotillas of sea elephants. Not a man or a horse
was lost.

It was an unparalleled exploit this cavalcade was bringing to
a conclusion: twenty-nine men behind a bold leader had
wormed their way through strong picket lines to the very point
where enemy officers slept, yanked them out of bed, laughed at
the guards on their way past, and disappeared ahead of the
rising sun. When they hurried into Warrenton later in the day,
their column still included Stoughton, two captains and thirty

privates, as well as fifty-eight horses, most of them fine, well-bred animals from officers' stables.

Early next morning Mosby turned his captives over to Fitz Lee at Culpeper. On his arrival he was given further cause to dislike the man who had succeeded Grumble Jones. Lee cordially greeted Stoughton and invited him into his headquarters. But Mosby was left on the outside, a lieutenant, without praise or commendation from his superior.[10]

A few hours later Jeb Stuart detrained at Culpeper with the gallant John Pelham, only a few days separated from his death at Kelly's Ford. Stuart's golden laughter echoed around the little railway station as Mosby unfolded his account of the adventure in Fairfax. Before they parted, Stuart handed the lieutenant a commission as captain in the Virginia troops. The Partisan stared at it dubiously: there were no such troops now that the Confederate government had taken over all armed forces in the South. But Stuart said he was confident the War Department would recognize it.

On the 12th the Fairfax raid was praised by Stuart in general orders. The same day came six precious words from General Robert E. Lee, passed on to the Partisan by Stuart: "Mosby has covered himself with honors." [11]

Stoughton's capture awakened Washington suddenly to the fact that a Partisan leader whom newspapers persisted in calling "Moseby" and "Moseley" had been the root of the recent troubles along the Federal capital's outposts. "There is a screw loose somewhere, and we need a larger force in front," reasoned the *Star*. And later: "It is about time that our brigadier-generals at exposed points brightened up their spectacles a bit."

First reports, based on the capture by John Underwood of the vedette on the outskirts of Fairfax, said Mosby had been able to get into the town by seizing an orderly who was carrying the countersign in his pocket for deliverance to officers at the posts. In the excitement a number of citizens were arrested and sent to the Old Capitol Prison in Washington. Among these were a former sheriff and several merchants and farmers.

As the Federals continued their investigation, the finger of suspicion came to rest on a young lady of the town, Miss Antonia Ford. Her father, E. R. Ford, merchant, had been one of the first persons arrested. A letter written from Fairfax by a soldier four days before Stoughton's capture was the strongest bit of evidence against her. It read:

"General Stoughton, who commands the Second Vermont Brigade, has his headquarters in the village, although his brigade is five or six miles away. What he could or would do in case of an attack, I don't know, but it seems to me that a general should be with his men. If he is so fancy that he can't put up with them, the government had better put him out.

"There is a woman living in the town by the name of Ford, not married, who has been of great service to General Stuart in giving information, et cetera—so much so that Stuart has conferred on her the rank of major in the Rebel army. She belongs to his staff. Why our people do not send her beyond the lines is another question. I understand that she and Stoughton are very intimate. If he gets picked up some night, he may thank her for it. Her father lives here, and is known to harbor and give all the aid he can to the Rebs, and this in the little hole of Fairfax, under the nose of the provost-marshal, who is always full of bad whiskey. So things go, and it is all right. No wonder we don't get along faster." [12]

Newspapers reported that Colonel L. C. Baker, provost-marshal, had positive information that Mosby slept at the Ford home, that the girl had gone around with him to point out the homes occupied by the principal Federal officers, and that she had helped him in planning and executing the raid.

On Friday, March 13, Antonia Ford was arrested. At her home were found letters which indicated she had been corresponding with Confederate authorities at Richmond. One document, later reproduced in Washington newspapers, was of particular interest to the Federals. It was the original commission as "honorary aide-de-camp" Jeb Stuart playfully had given her while the Confederate lines lay around Washington in the fall of '61.

Antonia was interned at Old Capitol Prison on Sunday, there to think over her patriotic misdeeds while people came to her defense. Among these was Moses Sweetser, Union merchant and sutler whose principal warehouses were located at Fair-fax. He wrote that Miss Ford was "a young lady of refinement, education and great modesty ... as pure and chaste as the morning sunbeam." But for the moment the Federal high command was in no mood to dismiss the matter on personal assurances, or to take stock in the comparison involving anything so ethereal as the forenoon sun.

9

Chantilly and Miskel Farm

—————〰〰〰—————

THE FAIRFAX RAID WAS FOLLOWED by a break in the early March cold. A deafening thunder storm, with severe lightning, swept over on the night of the 15th and was slow in spending its violent fury. Little damage was done. But telegraph operators at Washington and along the capital's outposts were much alarmed when communication suddenly was cut off between Fairfax Court House, Fairfax Station, Union Mills and other points. They spread the warning as far as their messages would carry: Rebels were cutting telegraph lines in Fairfax County, certain evidence of impending attack. Panicky hours were spent before dawn arrived and the truth was ascertained.

This scare brought necessary repairs to the communications system and it also strengthened the alarm which had existed since Stoughton's capture. Within twenty-four hours the *Star* was on the streets proclaiming: "We believe it has been determined to remove from the immediate vicinity of our lines, in Fairfax, all residents not known to be reliably loyal. Events of the last month have amply demonstrated the pressing necessity for putting in force this expedient."

Encouraged by the change of weather, President Lincoln and his general-in-chief, the West Point-trained Halleck, clamored for fighting. In answer, General Joe Hooker, moving cautiously in view of Burnside's rough treatment at the hands of the Rebels, sent Averell with 3,000 sabers and some guns by way of Kelly's Ford to break up Fitz Lee's brigade at Culpeper.

Averell, too, was careful. As he advanced he detached 900 men to watch his flanks and rear. Small parties had been so active north of the Rappahannock during the late winter that it was suspected a large Rebel force was maintained somewhere above Warrenton.

But these small parties were Mosby's, and Mosby at the moment was not interested in Averell. On the morning of March 16 he wrote two letters, enclosing in the first, addressed to his wife, fifty dollars. "Come on immediately," he urged. ". . . The place I have selected for you to stay is Mr. Hathaway's, a very nice place about four miles from White Plains . . ." [1] It was the second time he had encouraged her to join him. On March 3 he had informed her that General Wager had offered to meet her at Culpeper Court House any day she chose and to escort her to Fauquier County.

The home Mosby had selected was a fine Virginia mansion built in 1850 by James H. Hathaway, Southern patriot. A two-story brick structure, it sat on a mound deep in the forest, far off the beaten path of Federal troops. As true a part of the Confederacy as its owner, it was constantly a haven for the Partisan legion. Many times over Rebels stopped there for food and rest, and more than one visitor was sent from its hospitable roof to independent service. If Mosby had a home he could call headquarters, this was it. The Federals knew of the traitorous designs which went on beneath its roof, and frequently they searched it, but for all the tangible evidence they could lay their hands on, it was just another center of domestic felicity.

The other letter Mosby wrote that day was to Stuart. [2] It informed the cavalry commander that there had been no activity since the two had parted at Culpeper. "I start with my command today to go down in the neighborhood of Dranesville," Mosby announced. "I expect to flush some game before returning. I have received several more recruits. Public sentiment seems now entirely changed, and I think it is the universal desire for me to remain . . ."

Forty men met him that afternoon at Rector's Cross Roads, a meeting place preferred because of its access from all directions, giving more opportunity for escape in case of surprise. Several new faces were present, vouched for by someone who had been on previous raids, and the entire group, old and new, cheered lustily when Stuart's general order lauding the command for the capture of Stoughton was read.

Along Little River turnpike they jogged after climbing into their saddles. Then they turned northward and followed John Underwood into the foothills of Catoctin Mountain, to bivouac in the neighborhood of Goose Creek and Ball's Mill. Next morning they were up early. Mosby rode in from the home of Nat Skinner, citizen whose tricky eye, dedicated to the cause of the Confederacy, was the best scouting service the Partisans had in that part of the country. Underwood took a route that made his followers suspect his main purpose was to deceive them instead of the enemy. Along highways, across open fields, through unbroken bypaths, into dense tangles of forest and scrub they moved. Toward noon they crossed the Alexandria, Loudoun and Hampshire railroad about three miles northwest of Herndon Station and plunged into a sweeping stretch of pines along the tracks toward Alexandria. Another hour's ride and the guide halted in a small clearing.

Mosby slipped nimbly from his horse and disappeared through the trees. His men waited, sitting their mounts as still as statues. Not even the champ of a bit, the stamp of a hoof broke in on the stiff March breeze soughing among the pine tops. Occasionally from along a gully-like declivity to the left sounded the drone of distant voices, and now and then a burst of raucous laughter.

Mosby came back as stealthily as he had gone. He motioned to two men. They slid from their horses and stepped to the edge of the glade. He whispered instructions and then swung back into the saddle as they disappeared among the trees. Around him sat the other Partisans, still-faced, serious, listening.

In less than ten minutes the two men returned, bringing a captive, a surprised Federal picket who still clung to the newspaper he had been reading before the two men hurtled upon him, one from the trees in front, the other from the side. A gun held close to his ribs as he entered the glade reminded him to keep quiet and tread lightly.

Now the entire command dismounted and Mosby led the way down a narrow path beside the declivity. For nearly a hundred yards he moved, almost on tiptoe, then halted and pointed ahead. Plainly through the trees a few yards farther on could be seen a number of the pickets, lounging about an old sawmill, some playing cards on clean piles of yellow sawdust, others lying about sleeping or reading.

The Partisans closed up. Each drew his revolvers and gave them a final checking over. From the camp came a loud burst of laughter. Mosby waved his arm, scythe-like. His men stole forward, a few more yards. Then they rushed in upon their prey with screams that drowned out the soughing wind. "The surprise was so complete that the men made but little or no resistance," reported Major Charles F. Taggart, commanding the Federals in that area. "The enemy . . . entered on foot by a bridle path in rear of the post, capturing the vedette stationed on the road before he was able to give the alarm."

In a brief report of the raid in which he announced his loss was "nothing," Mosby passed on the information that the enemy cavalry had been moved from Germantown to beyond Fairfax Court House, on the Alexandria pike.[3] This contraction of Federal outposts was one of the objects he had promised Stuart his operations as an independent would accomplish. Mosby's report was forwarded by Fitz Lee with the terse indorsement that "such performances need no comment." General Robert E. Lee, however, postscripted that it was forwarded "as an evidence of the merit and continued success" of Mosby, attaching to it this note to President Jefferson Davis:

"You will, I know, be gratified to learn by the enclosed dispatch that the appointment you conferred a few days since on Captain J. S. Mosby was not unworthily bestowed. The point where he struck at the enemy is north of Fairfax Court House, near the Potomac, and far within the lines of the enemy. I wish I could receive his appointment, or some official notification of it, that I might announce it to him."

The official notice Lee requested appeared in Special Order No. 82: "His excellency, the President, has been pleased to show his appreciation of the good services and many daring exploits of the daring J. S. Mosby, by promoting the latter to a captaincy in the Provincial Army of the Confederacy. The general commanding is confident that this manifestation of the approbation of his superiors will but serve to incite Captain Mosby to still greater efforts to advance the good of the cause in which we are engaged. He will at once proceed to organize his command, as indicated in letter of instructions this day forwarded to him from these headquarters."

Fifty-five men answered a call on the 23rd. Mosby surveyed the growing group carefully. It was his finest gathering to date. Adventurous spirits in increasing numbers were coming into the country where rumor placed his headquarters.[4] Many of these, for love of fighting, signed up for the duration of the war; others enlisted for duty only until they could ride back to the regular army on contraband horses. Some were on leave of absence from the famous Black Horse Cavalry, recruited originally from Fauquier County; some were farmers from the immediate neighborhood, attracted by the appeal of independent warfare and the reputation service with Mosby would give them; others were floaters, youths under conscript age, young men from Maryland, nomads drawn by the opportunity to ride, fight and plunder. Still another element, a major factor at the beginning of operations, had dropped out completely. These were the convalescents, a group of wounded men left in a hospital at Middleburg by Lee's army on its return from the Maryland campaign. Crutches and bandages were common among them. But only the bedridden failed to sneak out at night when word came that Mosby's men were on the rampage. They fought by dark; they convalesced by day. It was a dual existence that continued with great success until one of them got killed in a raid and was identified.

Deserters hurried to the scene of Mosby's operations and were promptly turned away. Whatever fault his superiors found with the foxy Partisan leader, they never justly could say he was unfriendly to the conscript officer. He knew his band never would survive if it became a refuge for the men who fled their posts in the regular ranks, even though they continued to bend their efforts toward a Southern victory.

The men Mosby admitted to his command were called "spoiled darlings," "feather-bed soldiers" and "carpet knights" by members of the regular service, but these names were far from descriptive of the life they lived. There were no camps. Men who boarded at private homes did so at the risk of their liberty and even their necks. Many preferred the open, even in winter. On one occasion a Ranger rubbed his eyes in the morning sun beside a stone fence to find that a column of the enemy had marched along the other side during the night. It was chiefly because the Federals might stumble upon him that Jim Sinclair chose a graveyard as his bunk whenever possible. The ground of these hallowed plots was softer, the grass longer, and usually there was a barrier of stone or rail to keep his horse within bounds during his nap. Once while he nodded in a setting of tombstones he made out faintly in the moonlight a small object on the cap rock of the enclosure some yards away. It sat there for a moment and then disappeared. Presently it was back, stationary, and again it dropped to the ground. This kept up until Jim, puzzled and curious, pulled one of his revolvers from its holster and fired. The object came back no more, and the raider fell asleep. Next morning he walked over to take a look at the perch of the nocturnal ghost. Prone on the ground beyond the stone fence lay his charger, its blazed face pierced by a bullet. A gap in the wall told the story: through the opening the horse had wandered to graze in deeper clover and stare over the fence while it munched.[5]

Looking over the company that day at Rector's Cross Roads and ignoring its unsoldierly appearance, Mosby spied several new faces that gave him courage and inspired him to greater deeds. There was James William Foster of The Plains, veteran of Ashby's cavalry, and Captain George S. Kennon, hardy survivor of Wheat's celebrated Louisiana Tigers, a profane but highly-educated, well-bred gentleman who had fought with Walker in the Nicaraguan expedition. Already he had started a flow of talk that was to win him the distinguishing reputa-

tion of the biggest liar in the command. Another promising face
was that of Bradford Smith Hoskins, an Englishman. He was
small of frame, muscular, firmly knit and looked out of place
with his neat British uniform and saber against some of the
brawnier members clad in anything from overalls to homespun. He had come in with a letter of introduction from Stuart
that told he had been a captain in the English army and had
won the Crimean medal while fighting with the Forty-fourth
Royal Infantry, that he had joined Garibaldi in his Sicilian
expedition, that he was devoted to the profession of arms and
that he came to the Partisans at his own request.

Farther along the line, Mosby's eye rested on a grizzled,
hardened little man well past his fiftieth birthday. He had
given his name as William Hibbs, Loudoun County blacksmith.
Some of the Partisans said he had two sons off fighting with
the regular army. His hat, a faded felt riddled by sparks from
the forge, rested sidewise on his head, above a matting of gray
hair that hung low over his forehead like a fetlock trusted with
the care of a pair of small black eyes. The only part of his
raiment that represented the army was an old gray military
coat, held together by a strange array of buttons, only two of
which bore the initials of the Confederacy. Some of the friskier
members dubbed him "Major" on the spot.

There was no roll call that day—nor had there ever been.
Mosby knew his command by name and face, and the new
recruits got there only by personal indorsement from the seasoned members.

As they got to horse, they followed again their favorite lane
to the battlefront—the Little River turnpike—a path along
which each variation of its course, each boulder at its side, each
tree shading its ruts, was beginning to have some pet memory.
Six miles from Chantilly they turned to the right, continued
eastward through the woods, parallel with the road. John Underwood was leading.

It was Mosby's object to circle to the rear of the outposts
and to advance from a direction opposite that in which he
would be expected. But in this he was disappointed. As his
band emerged late in the afternoon from a body of woods about

a mile from Chantilly, they came upon two vedettes who flushed like a covey of birds and galloped back toward the main body of pickets. Realizing his plans for a surprise had miscarried, Mosby turned back. Soon riders in the rear reported Federals were in pursuit. More than a hundred, some estimates said.

Mosby galloped to spread the warning among the men in advance. Ahead was a half-mile stretch of woods through which he had passed while scouting with Underwood a few days before. He and his riders trotted toward it. They moved at the same unhurried pace they had set before the enemy was sighted, neared it, and disappeared. Colonel Johnstone informed Federal Brigade headquarters of what followed:

"Between Saunders' toll gate and Cub Run there is a strip of woods about half a mile wide through which the road runs. Within the woods, and about a quarter of a mile apart, are two barricades of fallen trees; our troops pursued the enemy between these barricades. Behind the latter some of the enemy were concealed. The head of the column was here stopped by a fire of carbines and pistols, and also by a fire upon the flank from the woods. The column broke and was pursued by the enemy one and a half miles." [6]

It had been a strange drama. One moment gray horsemen rode into the forest, pursued by a more numerous enemy in blue; the next, shouts and gunfire sounded deep in the wood and out of it came the men in blue, chased by the less numerous troops in gray.

Coming up with a reserve from Frying Pan, the Federals attempted to rally, but their efforts developed into no more than a momentary stand. Their horses were exhausted and they were afraid the enemy had them far outnumbered. As his men withdrew, Mosby called a halt on the far side of the woods and checked results. Five of the enemy had been killed, a number wounded, and one lieutenant and thirty-five men, as well as a large number of horses, captured. Not a Partisan had been scratched.

On his return that night Mosby wired Stuart of the success. Back came an answer:

"Your telegram, announcing your brilliant achievement near Chantilly, was duly received and forwarded to General Lee. He exclaimed upon reading it, 'Hurrah for Mosby! I wish I had a hundred like him!' "

Federals would have been much interested in the carriage that rolled along the wooded road toward the Hathaway place one windy March day. A woman and two little children sat behind the uniformed soldier in the driver's seat, and an escort of soldiers trotted along as a bodyguard fore and aft. The horses were army horses, big, powerful animals from Stuart's cavalry. Pauline Mosby was on the last leg of the journey to join her husband.

Other cheerful developments came at this time. One was the order from Lee for Mosby to organize his company, with the understanding that it was to be placed on a footing with all troops of the line and that it was to be mustered unconditionally into the Confederate service for the remainder of the war.[7]

"Though you are to be its captain," instructions stated, "the men will have the privilege of electing the lieutenants as soon as its members reach the legal standard. You will report your progress from time to time, and when the requisite number of men are enrolled, an officer will be designated to muster the company into service."

Mosby read the order carefully. The part about the election of lieutenants did not meet with his approval.

Stuart also sent advice:

"I enclose your evidence of appointment by the President in the Provisional Army of the Confederate States. You will perceive by General Lee's accompanying instructions that you will be continued in your present sphere of conduct and enterprise and already a captain, you will proceed to organize a band of permanent followers for the war, but by all means ignore the term 'Partisan Ranger.' It is in bad repute. Call your command 'Mosby's Regulars,' and it will give it a tone of meaning and solid worth which all the world will soon recognize, and you will inscribe that name of a fearless band of heroes on the pages of our country's history, and enshrine it in the hearts of a grateful people. Let 'Mosby's Regulars' be a name of pride with friends and respectful trepidation with enemies." [8]

This advice Mosby, if he gave it any heed at all, promptly forgot. It was his aim to be irregular. He had been that way in varying degree as a boy, as a college student, as a lawyer and as a soldier, and he had no intention to change now. His operations were built around his ability to be different, to baffle his enemies through his refusal to follow the routine prescribed by the military academies.

Stuart warned also against incorporating deserters from other branches of the service. "As there is no time within which you are required to raise this command," he reminded, "you ought to be very fastidious in choosing your men, and make them always stand the test of battle and temptation to neglect duty before acceptance." Swinging from this more serious business, Stuart next thanked Mosby for sending him Stoughton's saddle, a gift the Partisan had forwarded soon after they had met at Culpeper, and asked for whatever evidence the raider could furnish of the innocence of Miss Antonia Ford.[9] He wanted it, he explained, so that he could insist on her release from prison. "We must have that unprincipled scoundrel, Wyndham," Stuart added. "Can you catch him?" And then, fearing the rashness of the young independent in carrying out this suggestion, he cautioned: "Do not get caught. Be vigilant about your own safety and do not have any established head-quarters anywhere but 'in the saddle.'" [10]

"I hope Mrs. Mosby reached you in safety," Stuart concluded. "My regards to her if still with you. Your praise is on every lip, and the compliment the President has paid you is as marked as it is deserved."

On the 30th of March the Federals heard that Stuart had arrived at Aldie and that Mosby with another force was on his left.[11] This was not entirely true. It was the next day before the Partisans assembled, and then they came together neither in support of the Confederate cavalry nor in opposition to the enemy at that particular point. Mosby had his eye on something else.

Sixty-nine men were present, a number of them new, several from the Black Horse. Without delay they set out for Dranesville, in the direction of those isolated outposts Mosby had written Stuart about at the same time he had mentioned the situation around Fairfax. But at Herndon Station, where two weeks earlier the command had surprised the First Vermont Cavalry at the sawmill, it was learned late in the afternoon that the pickets had been moved behind Difficult Run, a stream properly named because of its few fordable points. Darkness came on rapidly and Mosby inquired about forage. Residents shook their heads. Forage was a rare item in those parts and hard to find for friend or foe, they said.

At 10 o'clock that night Mosby found feed for the horses at the Miskel farm, north of Leesburg, a rich tract tucked down in the northern tip of Loudoun County where Goose Creek runs into the Potomac. Leaving the horses after they had been fed in the confines of a high board fence around the barnyard, the raiders dropped to sleep like children, exhausted after forty miles of riding. A majority of them took to the hay in the huge barn, snuggling deep for warmth. Mosby and a few others stretched on the floor in front of an open fireplace at the house.

The route they had taken that afternoon had not gone unnoticed. A woman resident had watched them ride by, had checked on their numbers, and had dispatched her brother to carry the news to Major Taggart, commanding the post beyond Difficult Run. Taggart recognized the opportunity at once. Mosby's entire command of sixty-nine men could be caught in the angle between two impassable streams, and there easily bottled up. Taggart selected Captain Flint and 150 seasoned fighters for the task.

Early next morning one of the Partisans from the barn aroused Mosby. Signals had been noticed at a cantonment of Northern troops, plainly visible on the highlands of the Maryland side of the Potomac.

Mosby walked out into the morning air. The smell of spring was strong, though a few banks of snow left by the violent winter still hid in sheltered places. He raised his glasses and stared in the direction of the enemy camp. He could see no cause for alarm.

But suddenly he heard faint shots at his back. Turning, he saw a figure emerge from the woods on the far side of the clearing next to the road. He trained his glasses. It was Dick Moran, riding madly across field and screaming at the top of his powerful voice. The evening before Moran had dropped off to spend the night at the near-by home of a friend.

The shouts were a tocsin. Men ran out of the house, out of the barn, some still half asleep. They crowded around Mosby, and his hand raised for silence. Moran's yell could be heard distinctly: "The Yanks are coming!"

Mosby glanced toward the gateway in an angle of the fence on the far side of the clearing. Blue figures already were riding out of the forest.

Miskel's barnyard turned into a hive of noisy action. Men ran about yelling and cursing in their haste to prepare for fight. Not a horse was saddled or bridled; most of them were running loose and had to be caught.

Meanwhile one squadron of Federals had ridden through the gate and toward the house, spreading out fanwise to hem in the Partisans. Another squadron halted at the barrier to block it with fence rails, an added precaution against the escape of these infernal raiders they at last had bottled up. Down to the gate from the boarded barnyard, parallel with the fence at one edge of the clearing, ran the only road leading out of Miskel farm.

On foot, Mosby, revolver in hand, kicked open the gate at the barn and ran out, shouting for his men to charge. John Farrar grabbed the barrier and held it ajar.

The enemy had come close. They fired scattered shots, and the lead pellets spattered against the boards of the fence and the barn.

Horsemen began to pour out of the yard, some with saddles, some without. All were shouting, revolvers ready. Moran was in front, his foghorn voice booming like thunder. So was "Big Yankee" Ames, towering above them all. Harry Hatcher of

Middleburg, on furlough from the Seventh Virginia Cavalry, rode through, leaped nimbly from his horse and handed the reins tc Mosby. The agile chieftain grabbed them and swung into the saddle.

A screaming confusion broke loose a few yards from the barnyard. Men cursed and shouted. Horses plunged and reared. Guns roared at close range. Sabers in blue-sleeved hands hacked and clashed and rattled in the gray dawn.

More men came out of the barnyard. Hoskins was there with his British sword, fighting back at the Yankees in their own fashion, the only one he knew. The confusion thickened and more Federals rode up from the second squadron at the gate.

Mosby's men were in their glory. Blacksmith Hibbs seemed a superman, grinning through his gray whiskers in happy diversion. A new recruit, William H. Chapman, lieutenant fresh from the Dixie Artillery, and his brother Sam, a divinity student, were terrors. Harry Hatcher had found another horse and was back, striving to get into the thick of the fight. Hunter, Wellington, Tom Turner of Kinloch, Wild, Sowers, Seibert—all were battling, back to back, some with their reins in their mouths and their guns roaring.

The scrambled mass thinned out momentarily and it could be seen men were down, some in blue, some in gray. The enemy ganged on the savage Sam Chapman, and Hunter broke away and came to his rescue. These Chapmans were fighters. It was their battery in Longstreet's Corps that shattered Fitz-John Porter's lines in the assault on Jackson at Groveton Heights in '62.

Davis of Kentucky fell with a mortal wound. Hart, Hurst, Keys had been slashed deeply and were on the ground, trying to dodge the hoofs of the crazed horses.

Mosby saw them. He was in the midst of the turmoil, shooting, dodging, parrying. He rose in his stirrups and his voice came in a high-pitched shout above the din, sharp, piercing. His men heard. They closed back in, ready for the final push, the furious stroke that brought them victory against heavy odds.

The Federals gave way against this new ferocity. The shouting swelled louder. Officers tried to reform their men. But it was too late.

Union horsemen turned and galloped at full speed toward the blocked gateway. Members of the second squadron, waiting there, caught the excitement, got panicky and tried in desperation to throw aside the rails fixed in the barrier. These rails had been placed with no thought of the turn the fight had taken. Horses could not be stopped. They forced into the angle of the fence, rearing, champing, neighing shrilly, frightened so that their cries sounded like those of human beings.

Captain Flint rode into the tumult. He shouted and waved his saber, striving frantically to start a rally. His face was red, the veins bulged to finger size on his neck. The charging Rebels spied him. They shot him down, riddling his body. They shot his horse. They shot Lieutenant Charles A. Woodbury, killing him on the spot. Nothing could stop these Partisans in their fury. They shot before sabers could strike.

The angle had become a bloody trap. Men were down, trampled by the horses. The jam became worse. Federals pushed to get through, spurred from behind by the lunging Confederates.

At last the rails gave way, and the horsemen spurted out of the gate like water from a spillway. Men on foot strove to catch riderless horses in the melee. The pressure was too great. Some were struck down, others dropped their weapons and ran to the woods.

"We drove them in confusion seven or eight miles down the pike," Mosby reported to Stuart. "We left on the field nine of them killed—among them a captain and a lieutenant—and about fifteen too badly wounded for removal; in this lot two lieutenants. We brought off eighty-two prisoners, many of these also wounded. . . . The enemy sent up a flag of truce for their dead and wounded, but many of them being severely wounded, they established a hospital on the ground. The surgeon who attended them informs me that a great number of those who escaped were wounded." Among the Federals in the temporary hospital was Lieutenant Josiah Grout, Jr., one day to be Governor of Vermont.

"Mosby was completely surprised and wholly unprepared for an attack from our forces," recorded Major-General Julius Stahel, cavalry officer who had replaced Wyndham after the embarrassment of Stoughton's capture. "...I regret to be obliged to inform the commanding general that the forces sent out by Major Taggart missed so good an opportunity of capturing this Rebel guerrilla. It is only to be ascribed to the bad management on the part of the officers and the cowardice of the men. I have ordered Colonel Price to make a thorough investigation of this matter, and shall recommend those officers who are guilty be stricken from the rolls." [12]

Stuart forwarded Mosby's report "as in perfect keeping with his other brilliant achievements," and at the bottom of this record James A. Seddon, Confederate Secretary of War, added: "Nominated for promotion, if it has not been previously done."

It had been done. In a letter to the President in which he told of the Miskel farm fight and that the enemy had evacuated Dranesville, General Lee announced: "I had the pleasure to send by return courier to Major Mosby his commission as major of Partisan Rangers, for which I am obliged to your excellency." [13] This came two weeks after Mosby had been made a captain.

10

Raiders Along the Railroad

APRIL PASSED RAPIDLY FOR MOSBY, keeping him extremely busy. While he maintained constant watch for new conquests, the Yankees staged such a campaign of activity against him he was convinced they had renewed their vows to effect his capture. Three times during the month they sent expeditions into Loudoun and Fauquier. This had been done mainly at the insistence of Abraham Lincoln. Four days after Stoughton's capture, Stahel was summoned by the President and entrusted with Wyndham's post. He was cautioned that the lines in front of Washington were insecure, that raids upon them must stop. There was fear Mosby and his band might come charging into the capital. Certainly men who were bold enough to take a general from the midst of his army would not stop at the White House gates.

The *Star* hailed Stahel's appointment. It said that the cavalry attached to the Department of Washington had been handicapped so far by its need for an "experienced and efficient" commander, one who would watch "every movement of the small bands of guerrillas and other irregular troops that have alone perpetrated the mischief that has taken place in the course of the last four weeks." [1]

Cheers along Warrenton streets the Saturday afternoon of May 2 carried the same rebellious spirit for the South that tempered the firing barely audible from Confederate guns toward Chancellorsville. Mosby's command had ridden in unannounced, and the townspeople had swarmed out to greet them. Not since March, when they appeared early in the morning with the unhappy Stoughton, had these hardy fighters been seen in this part of the country.

But there was little time for chitchat that day. Everybody was excited. Up and down the line of riders could be seen familiar faces, milling in the praise and excitement. The handsome Chapmans. The grizzled blacksmith, "Major" Hibbs, corn pressing specialist. The colorful Captain Hoskins and the equally colorful Captain Kennon. The faithful Beattie, paler than the others because of his months in prison. Loud-mouthed Dick Moran, easily singled out. Joe Nelson, the holy terror. Tom Richards, student from Washington. The silent John Underwood, white lock bulging from the band of his cap. Near by, his brother, Sam, newly arrived. Tom Turner, Prince Georges County Marylander. George Whitescarver . . . Frank Williams . . . Mighty names and mighty people.

"Big Yankee" Ames would have been there, too, but for one of those three Federal expeditions the previous month. During the first of these, he had met five Federals in the road near Middleburg and had attempted to rout them with the aid of two brothers, Harry and Dan Hatcher, both from the Seventh Virginia Cavalry and riding temporarily with Mosby. The enemy was scattered, Ames battling toward the end with a bullet wound through the shoulder.

It was by luck that still another person was on hand that day. Mosby himself had had a narrow escape. The last of the expeditions had been led by Stahel in person, supported by 2,500 men and four pieces of artillery. So harried was the Union leader by small bands of Mosby's men staring down from hills along the way that he shelled a small body of woods near Middleburg before he went into camp there. Mosby brushed him close the next day, but no shots were fired. And on the following day, he brushed Mosby close. The raider, who had spent the night with Fount Beattie at the George McArty home on the outskirts of Middleburg, had to run the gauntlet through the entire 2,500 men. Stahel, unaware of who slept near by, had come up in the wee hours and bivouacked in the surrounding fields.

The crowd was thickest that day at Warrenton around the Partisan leader. He sat astride his spirited bay near the center of town, smiling, not saying much. It was whispered about that he planned to tear up the Orange and Alexandria railroad somewhere near Warrenton Junction,[2] weakly guarded since Stoneman's withdrawal. Another rumor said the destination would be Hooker's lines of communications at Falmouth.

But the firing toward Chancellorsville ...

On the morning of April 29, hours before Mosby and Beattie had made their dash from the McArty home to escape Stahel's unsuspecting troopers, Hooker had pushed across the Rappahannock in the fog. This meant the beginning of action on a large scale at the very point where the armies had left off in '62. It was a general offensive, the making of a pair of gigantic pincers designed to squeeze the fight out of the Army of Northern Virginia. Lee had spread his diminishing forces to the maximum. Stonewall Jackson moved off at 4 A.M. May 2 to circle the right wing, to press in on the flank and rear of the enemy. Soon afterward it was that he rode into a hail of death bullets from his own men in the pines at Chancellorsville.

Now was the time when Mosby could help the regular army. Hooker was worried enough as it was. What would be his dilemma if someone broke his line of communications, his heart string with Washington?

Mosby bivouacked the night of the 2nd a mile or two from Warrenton, in the open, where his command could scamper as emergency demanded. He was up early next morning, urging his men to hurry. The firing toward Chancellorsville was louder.

Daylight was opening rapidly in the east when they finally got to horse and hurried away. In the air was the smell of spring, the fresh feeling of new things, and there was indication the day would be warm. They had covered most of the eight or nine miles to Warrenton Junction when a bugle bleated ahead. Mosby signaled for a halt. He nodded to one Partisan, and the fellow slid from his horse and crept away. Pretty soon he was back, bringing the surprised bugler. The Federal was badly frightened, but he managed to talk. He said there was an infantry brigade directly in their path, that cavalry was on the railroad at the junction. Cavalry could ride to the aid of infantry, but infantry could not ride to the aid of cavalry, Mosby reasoned.

It was shortly after 9 o'clock in the morning when the command neared the edge of the woods surrounding the little settlement of railroad buildings at the junction. The sun was shining bright, and not 300 yards away they could see the Federals lounging about in a field in the forks of the tracks where the line branched off to Warrenton. Their horses were unbridled and grazing.

Now came the usual preparations for a Partisan dash. All the way back along the column men loosened their revolvers and examined the cylinders. There must be six bullets in each. A few dropped down and tightened the girths of their saddles. Some extended the reins to their mouths, testing to be sure they could have both hands free if necessary. Their leader, peeping out of the woods, estimated the odds would be three to one against him.

All was ready. Mosby rode into the open. Others pressed close behind him. There was no shouting. They were playing for time. Each step before they were recognized would be of great advantage when the charge came.

The Federals stared at the approaching horsemen without concern. For days they had been scouring the country in search of Mosby. They had been to Upperville, Salem, The Plains, Rectortown, Aldie and Middleburg in a vain hunt, and the other half of their command still were off searching on the opposite side of the railroad. Or perhaps it was returning now.

For the first few seconds no one stirred among the Federals. Then someone recognized the gray plumed hat. He shouted "Mosby! Mosby!" frantically and ran toward the protection of the houses. The Partisans let loose ... they blazed away with their revolvers ... they raced their horses down on the scampering enemy ... they screamed with blood-curdling effect.

Confusion grew. The Federals scrambled to near-by buildings, running, stumbling, cursing hoarsely. Their horses, useless without bridles, stampeded in all directions. One blue-clad soldier was dropped by a Rebel bullet as he darted into a house. He sprawled across the doorstep. His companions pulled him in, closed the portal and fired from a window.

Smoke became thick, but it got thicker as the Partisans threw the reins over their horses' heads and crawled behind trees for steady firing at the buildings. The bark of the revolvers was a staccato tattoo against the heavier volume of the Federal carbines. The Confederates centered their attack on two out-houses. For five, ten minutes it kept up before a white hand-kerchief was waved from one of the buildings. Those in the other small house saw it and a second white flag appeared.

Now attention was turned to the main building into which more than a hundred of the enemy had jammed. They were firing from the window and their bullets nipped close to the Rebels behind the trees. One tore dangerously near Mosby's shoulder and it made him furious. He leaped up from the ground, gun in hand, a devil with eyes his own men feared. He raced toward the structure. The Yankees on that side saw him coming. They saw his smoking weapons and they shot wild. ... They lost sight of him.... They wondered if he were down. ... They thought he was and were ready to rejoice.... Then they heard him firing again, at close range, from the safety of a chimney.

Several of his men had taken to horse. They dashed in circles around the building, firing at the openings as they passed. Mosby's men were hard to hit in the saddle. They clung to the off side, down low, giving scarcely a boot heel for a target.

This circus riding kept up. Young Robert S. Walker, hardy recruit, rolled over the grass as his horse fell, shot through the head. He got up, grabbed another with enemy accoutrements and reentered the fray. Meantime horrible scenes had crept in. Off to one side lay Templeton, one of Stonewall Jackson's best scouts, fresh from Washington. His mouth was open and his eyes stared blindly up at the trees. He had got his death wound on his first ride with Mosby.

The firing went back and forth. It was evident many on the inside had been hit. Several Partisans lay in the open, wounded or dead, too much exposed to be dragged to safety. Guns blazed from a background of peeping faces, grimly black from powder smoke. Mosby yelled for the finish. He directed Alfred Glasscock to bring straw and brushwood so that a fire could be started around the building. The first armfuls were dumped at the base of the structure. A match, heavy with sulphur, blazed, and a spark of fire took hold, swelled into an angry tongue, lapped at the inflammable pile.

But before the flames could climb high along the bullet-speckled weatherboarding there was loud cheering. Sam Chapman, the fighting divinity student, had burst in the door, followed by Harry Sweeting, John DeButts, Robert Walker and others. Standing at the bottom of the stairs, Chapman called above for a surrender. Twenty men filed down, hands raised. But there were more, including officers, who refused to give up. The men in the lower room on the left marched out. The door to the chamber opposite was barricaded. DeButts fired through, and a man with his shoulder against the portal on the other side dropped. Sweeting and the others poured in, firing through the dense smoke until the Federals yelled for mercy.

Chapman shouted again for surrender from above. There was an uncertain period of waiting, and then the remainder of the force filed down. In less than half an hour after the Partisans rode out of the woods, Mosby was in undisputed possession of Warrenton Junction.

The salvage now began, all hands taking part, flushed with victory. Pistols and sabers were gathered up, dumped in sacks and thrown across saddles. A fine ambulance was rolled out. Saddles, camp equipage and other valuable accoutrements were tossed into it. One detail began digging with shovels to bury the dead. Others scattered in all directions to round up the stampeded horses. The burning building was enveloped in flames.

Suddenly came an unexpected alarm.

"I was sitting on my horse near the house, giving directions for getting ready to leave with the prisoners and spoil," Mosby recorded, "when one of my men named Wild, who had chased a horse some distance down the railroad, came at full speed and reported a heavy column of cavalry coming up. I turned to one of my men, Alfred Glasscock, and said to him, 'Now we will whip them.' I had hardly spoken the words when I saw a large body of Union cavalry, not over 200 or 300 yards off, rapidly advancing." ⸰

Mosby rode into the field toward the enemy, trying to form his men for the usual concerted thrust. But there was no chance. The command was disorganized, widely scattered. They took to their heels, closely pursued, leaving the prisoners and most of the loot. Mosby and a few others dashed into the nearest cover of pines. The firing at their backs was heavy. William Jones, one of the first fifteen to fight with Mosby, fell from his horse, badly wounded. His brother, Jasper, another original, was infuriated. He whirled and turned on the horde of advancing Federals, but they were too numerous and he, too, reeled and fell from his horse.

The onslaught became overwhelming. For the first time in their four months of operations, the Partisans were routed. They scampered to the winds in confusion, every man for himself.

What had happened that bright Sunday morning in May had been the very thing Mosby had guarded against during his thrusts at the enemy outposts in Fairfax: while his men cheered and blazed away at the barricaded First Virginia, the Fifth New York, camped unknown to him within hearing distance, had realized something was wrong and had come to investigate. It was what Stuart had in mind when he warned Mosby to stay far enough away from brigade camps to enable him to carry off his plunder and prisoners.

For the first time since he had been operating, Mosby had to admit defeat in a report. How much better would it have been had he ignored the cavalry at the junction, slipped through the lines, and gone on toward Falmouth and Hooker's communications. Maybe the South would have rejoiced over his deeds at that point and maybe general orders from the mouth of the beloved Lee would have heaped still greater praise on his command. But the occurrences of May 3, '63, were another part of the uncertainties of war. Mosby knew in his own mind that he had made a mistake and he subsequently confessed it:

"I committed a great error in allowing myself to be diverted from the purpose of my expedition. The cavalry at Warrenton Junction was perfectly harmless where it was and could not help Hooker in the great battle then raging. I should, at least, have endeavored to avoid a fight by marching around them. If I had succeeded in destroying them all, it would hardly have been equivalent to the damage I might have done to Hooker by appearing at United States Ford during the agony of the fight."[4]

From Warrenton Junction on the 23rd came word that Mosby was at Catlett's at 6 A.M., that several pickets had been fired on during the night. A little later it was added that the Rebel had established his own pickets in that area and that the infantry at Catlett's reported continual sound as of wagons or artillery moving toward Bristow. A spy informed Stahel that Mosby's men were scouting the country in small parties, that the leader sent nine men to Dranesville and five down the Little River turnpike on the 26th, that on the 27th he was collecting a party of men with the intention of making a raid "in some direction not ascertained." At the same time a report from the provost-marshal general's office said Mosby was above Warrenton with 200 men and, in far more important and mysterious language, that "the Confederate army is under marching orders, and an order from General Lee was very lately read to the troops, announcing a campaign of long marches and hard fighting, in a part of the country where they would have no railroad transportation."

On the 28th, Colonel W. D. Mann, commanding near Bristow Station, reported the return of five different searching parties, all from fruitless expeditions. They had touched such points as The Plains, Warrenton, Salem, Waterloo, Hopewell Gap, Middleburg, New Baltimore, Georgetown and Thoroughfare Gap. Back with them they brought news that sounded more like idle gossip. A wild-eyed citizen had told them the

Partisans had brought in a piece of artillery by way of Waterloo and now had it somewhere in or about Aldie.

This was not idle talk. Back in April Stuart had reminded Mosby that "there is now a splendid opportunity to strike the enemy in the rear of Warrenton Junction." The cavalry leader suggested capture of a train, as well as interruption of the operation of the railroad. But he warned the raider to keep far enough from brigade camps to escape with plunder and prisoners.[5] Mosby came back with a request for a howitzer.[6] His plea was based on much greater logic than it would seem at first sight. If Stuart wanted Federal trains smashed or captured, such was not work for a gun which hung from the hip.

The gun was delivered promptly. It had been captured from the Yankees at Ball's Bluff in '61 and had been used by the Rebel cavalry on numerous occasions. Practice in handling it was started immediately. Sam Chapman, old hand from the Dixie Battery, rounded up men out of the command who had had previous artillery experience and put them to practicing. Other Partisans looked on in mild anticipation.

Mosby was impatient to try his luck with the howitzer. The time seemed opportune. Preliminary movements leading to the Gettysburg campaign had been started by Lee along the south bank of the Rappahannock and Hooker was following him on the other side. Mosby's scouts informed him both cavalry and infantry patrols were thick along the Orange and Alexandria railroad between the Rappahannock and Washington. Camps lay within a mile or two of each other, and detachments constantly passed back and forth. Trains, steaming down with valuable stores of food for the Union army, were guarded heavily by infantry.

Forty-eight men answered his summons on the 29th of May. The day was warm and bright, inviting, too beautiful to be wasted in idleness. For an hour Sam Chapman ran his artillery crew through their routine and then reported that the formidable little twelve-pounder was ready for action. Mosby swung south to outflank the Bull Run Mountains and struck across country toward the railroad. Supper was eaten at Greenwich, not far from Catlett's, and they bivouacked for the night a few miles farther on, deep in the pines. No fires were lit. Men slept without blankets on the needled flooring in a circle around the howitzer.

Notes of reveille in the near-by Union camps awoke them next morning. It was another clear day, giving early signs of rising temperature, and the Partisans went quickly to work. Along a narrow path they moved to within a hundred yards of the railroad. There Sam Chapman swung the artillery piece about and prepared to put it into position. In a few seconds the muzzle pointed wickedly down toward the narrow bands of steel lying northward toward Washington, southward toward Hooker's army. On that long stretch of rail you could see an engine's smoke two miles away. The gun was loaded, aimed and primed. It was well concealed and there was nothing to signal in either direction the trouble awaiting Federal transportation up in that hillside growth of pines.

In the meantime other Partisans had clipped the telegraph wires and loosened a rail on the side next to the howitzer. It had been exciting work. Shoulder to shoulder, a bit frantically, they struggled in the bright sunlight, casting nervous glances up and down for signs of approaching train or patrol. Perspiration flowed freely.

At last all was ready. The gun in the pines was no longer the point of interest. Under cover in the fringe of trees along the railroad lay the main body, most of those nearest the rails armed with carbines. A lone watchman was posted out on the track. This was different warfare from the slash-bang cavalry attack of Mosby's early operations.

Minutes dragged into an eternity. The man out on the track wiped his brow. His companions back in the undergrowth watched him closely. They spat tobacco juice with unerring aim, competed with each other for accuracy, and fingered their weapons impatiently. But they kept their positions. There was no smoking, no talking. One of the horses neighed, yards behind, and they turned in alarm. There must be no slip.

Their bodies suddenly tensed. The watchman had raised his hand as a signal that he had heard or seen something. He dropped and placed his ear to the rail. Then he stood up, shaded his eyes with his hat and stared beyond the point where the track disappeared in the distance. Motionless, for one minute, two minutes, three minutes, he stood before he ducked and ran to cover.

Mosby sneaked to the edge of the pines for a glance. Northward toward Manassas Junction a growing trail of smoke could be seen rising above the horizon, dark and menacing. The leader moved about quickly, spreading the alarm. Men tightened the wires attached to the loose rail. Higher up behind them, Sam Chapman gave the artillery piece a final inspection. He found everything ready and patted the weapon tenderly.

The train rapidly rolled nearer. Minutes went by. Each chug of the locomotive could be heard distinctly. The rumble deepened and the earth began to tremble. A screeching blast from the whistle spread over the countryside, and Confederate pulses quickened. On thundered the monster. It paralleled the stretch of pines. Then there was a great clatter, a din of heavy metal hitting together, and the chugging stopped abruptly. The engine had dashed into the gap where only a second before had been a rail. Loud voices and gun firing rose above the echo. Then, suddenly, like a clap from heaven, came the roar of the howitzer. It belched forth a volume of smoke and sent a shell flying into the boiler of the locomotive. The hiss of escaping steam added to the tumult.

The engine and several of the string of twelve cars had been derailed. Infantry on board were answering the fire from the carbineers along the fringe of pines nearest the track. It was a hot exchange. A second blast came from the tiny cannon and a second shell struck the train, this time near the middle. The guard, convinced the attackers were a force from Stuart's cavalry, fled to the woods on the opposite side.

Out from cover dashed a majority of Mosby's forty-eight men. They ransacked the abandoned cars. They ate and pillaged simultaneously. There were choice items—oranges, lemons, candy. Somebody threw out bundles of shoe leather, and in one car they found a store of fresh shad. It had been some time since the fortunes of war had been so generous.

There was no delay. Along the entire line of cars men were at work, tossing out things to be salvaged. They shouted and made merry over their good luck, but they did not waste time. After a few minutes, they brought forth bundles of hay, cut the bales and scattered the contents under the entire train. Soon smoke carried the signal to enemy camps.

Mosby was aware of their danger and kept urging the men to greater action. Chapman packed the little howitzer, ready to travel. The men rounded up their horses and tied their loot, including shad, on the back of their saddles. Then the entire force streaked off toward Greenwich.

But they did not get far before Federal horsemen from the Fifth New York Cavalry appeared on a hill in front of them. Only a few of the enemy could be seen, but from the dust at their rear it was evident that they had come in force. Sam Chapman rushed up with the little gun, and he and his crew unlimbered it and fired a shell. This landed beyond the hill, killing the horse of an officer, and the enemy retreated to a neighboring elevation. Mosby sent William Foster and several men in their direction as an indication of confidence and fearlessness, but these members soon were recalled. The leader was afraid to separate his command for fear of an attack from behind.

Again the Rebels pushed on, this time with Foster and several others riding farther back as a rear guard. Drums and bugles sounded in the distance. They were evidence that the enemy now was thoroughly alarmed. Mosby was not worried. He had destroyed a train, and his men, as they had done on other occasions, could take care of themselves if the pressure became too great. One thing was in his favor: the Federals knew that he did not fight with artillery and they would be slow to pursue an unidentified column of unknown strength.

Several times the rear guard checked the Union troops coming up on their trail. Once the howitzer was swung about and fired. But the pursuers were growing in numbers and Mosby realized he could not keep up such a fight. He instructed Chapman to push on with the gun and to find a suitable position from which to put it into action. "We'll make them pay for it before they take it!" he yelled encouragingly to the trusty divinity student.

As the howitzer disappeared, Mosby galloped back, through a scattering of shad and other loot along the roadside. The pursuit must be delayed until the gun was placed. It would involve a difficult task: numbers were greatly against them. A swarm of Federals were close behind, and once there was a hot little clash. Mosby and four others dashed into the face of the Blue column. There was a mad scramble, a salvo of firing. Two Yankees dropped, but others took their places. The Partisans fell back, rapidly now, leaving behind the gallant Captain Hoskins, prone beside his sword. He was mortally wounded.

Mosby and the three men left with him overtook Sam Chapman two miles southwest of Greenwich. Sam had posted the howitzer on a hill overlooking the road. In such position he could command the enemy's only route of attack—a narrow lane flanked on each side by a high rail fence. Mosby and the rear guard galloped back behind the gun and waited, concealed in the underbrush. An orange-tinted dust covered the countryside, blotting out the green along the roadway. Larger and denser clouds of it could be seen rising above the trees through which the enemy was approaching.

Chapman, face grimy and streaked with sweat, gave the gun another going-over, the way he did when the train chugged up toward it. He was satisfied with what he saw. He stood back to wait.

In a few seconds the Yankees rode into view. They were the Fifth New York, the troops who shied at that first shell in the road. They were ashamed of themselves. They had discovered that it was only a handful of men and one little gun they were chasing. The howitzer pointed at them through the dust and they cheered at sight of it.

With the remainder of their support up, they prepared to charge. It was an orderly affair, parade-like in its uniformity, neatly executed. They rode up the lane in column of fours. Dust was caked on the damp nostrils of their horses, on their sweaty flanks, on the riders' faces, wherever there was perspiration. It was so thick on their unforms it gave them a coppery effect. More of it swelled from the earth with each step of their mounts.

Only the noise of the advancing column could be heard. All was silence on the hill, but there hostile figures waited, ready to lunge. Bridle reins were taut; guns cocked, in hand, pointing for the blow.

To within fifty yards of the crest the Federals rode before the little gun kicked back on its heels and vomited a death load of grape. Ten men in the front ranks dropped, three as dead as the shot that had riddled their bodies. The column faltered, closed up, uncertain. Then from the trees on the hill burst a demoniacal, bloodthirsty band of Rebels, terrible in their ferocity. The column broke before it and scurried in wild flight, all thought of order gone. For half a mile it fled before it met reinforcements from the First Vermont Cavalry and halted for a stand. Mosby, aware of the hopeless numbers against him, drew off his men and returned to the howitzer.

Twice more the Federals charged and twice more they were driven back after they had been checked by a load of grape and canister. There was a lot of noise, a lot of riding, a lot of dust. A few were wounded; some were dead. Bill Elzey halted, hot on the Yankees' heels, and spat out a bullet and a handful of teeth. Mosby, beside him, laughed and cheered him on.

They returned from the third pursuit. Sam Chapman yelled to Mosby: "This is our last round!" The leader nodded and shouted: "Make it a good one!"

Again the Federals charged; again the little twelve-pounder kicked back on its heels and stopped them. There was a lull, and then down the hill dashed Mosby on his spirited horse. Behind him came Charley McDonough and a string of others. Mosby overtook the retreating column. He rode among them. A big cavalryman turned and struck him across the shoulder with his saber, almost knocking the Partisan from his saddle. One of his revolvers roared and the cavalryman dropped. There was more hand-to-hand fighting before the Confederates retreated, this time with Blue soldiers close after them. The Federals pushed on up the narrow lane, past the point where their men had fallen, up to the crest of the hill. The little gun had been silenced by an empty limber chest, but a hot affair was in progress around it. Sam Chapman, Montjoy and Beattie, battling on foot, were defending it to the last. George Turberville, its driver, rode off with its caisson, deep into the forest, leaving it where it would not be found for days.

It was desperate fighting. Sam Chapman, threshing at the Federals with the rammer of the gun, was shot through the thigh and fell, helpless. Montjoy was overpowered and captured. Beattie, remembering his days in prison, leaped on a free horse and dashed away. Off at one side a few Partisans still carried on. A limb slapped Mosby in the face, knocking off his hat. At the same time, more of the enemy came up, and the Partisan took to the woods, accompanied by a hail of Yankee bullets.

As the thunder of Rebel horses died in the distance, the bruised Federals turned away from the fateful howitzer that had come back into their hands after a stormy career. They looked to their wounds, happy at heart, and they went along the road gathering up shad and sole leather.

CHAPTER

11

Advancing on Gettysburg

CHEERED BY WORD FROM STUART that another gun might be
sold for the same price as that at Catlett's Station,[1] Mosby
sent out a grapevine broadcast in early June calling his command together for its most important rendezvous to date. The
message went straight; Washington suspected nothing. It said
the meeting would be held at Rector's Cross Roads on the 10th.
Rumors had been circulating rapidly in Federal circles during
the last few days. Many of them had grown out of the report
current in the North that Lee was preparing for an invasion.
The Southern army was said to be in several different places—
Kelly's Ford, Thoroughfare Gap, Harper's Ferry. It was prophe-
sied that there would be a third battle on the bloody ground of
Manassas. The only one of the bits of hearsay that took reliable
shape was Mosby's raid on the Orange and Alexandria at
Catlett's. First information reported two pieces of artillery had
been captured, but the number later was reduced to one.

Excitement grew as the day neared for the rendezvous of
the 10th. Word was given on good authority that Mosby
planned to organize his command formally and to muster it
into the army. Some folks scoffed at the idea. They said no
matter how much Mosby's men were organized they never
would stand for the formality of military routine.

Mosby had his own ideas about an organization that too
closely resembled the regular service. A place on the Confederate roster would give his men prestige and recognition,
and would bring them much credit for their daring deeds.

From a painting by Beancé

Mosby Planning an Attack

From Munsey's Magazine

Fighting at Dranesville

Moreover, he could see no reason why it should dampen their ardor or limit their freedom. They still would be independent, operating solely by his direction, and there should be no encumbrance to their surprise attacks on Federal outposts. He made sure, too, that they still would be able to divide spoils on a basis of gallantry, the system he had devised to create healthy rivalry among his men and to remove all inducement to leave the fight for plunder. But two phases of his instructions from headquarters he recognized as dangerous to his original plan of action: Lee had ordered that his lieutenants should be elected by the men who would serve under them; Stuart had suggested that he ignore the term Partisan Ranger and select in its stead Mosby's Regulars.

One detail had been thrashed out after a flurry of correspondence. Mosby laid the matter before Stuart: "I have received from the War Office a notice of my appointment as captain of Partisan Rangers. The letter of Captain Taylor says that they are to be organized with the understanding that they are to be on the same footing with other cavalry. The men who have joined me have done so under the impression that they are to be entitled to the privileges allowed in the Partisan Ranger Act. If they are to be denied them, I cannot accept the appointment. Please let me know." Stuart sent Mosby's letter to Lee, who returned it with the following notation: "No authority has been given Major Mosby to raise Partisan troops, nor has it been so intended. He was commissioned as such to give him rank, pay and command until he could organize companies that could be mustered regularly into the service. He was so informed when his commission was sent him, to prevent mistake. His commission was limited to himself, and did not extend to his troops." [2]

It seemed that Mosby's ambitious plans had been squashed with that single notation. But the raider still would not give up. He saw as the question at issue the interpretation which should be placed on the commission, so he appealed to Secretary of War Seddon. In due time he was informed by the secretary that his commission entitled him to recruit a command for

the Partisan service. There the matter ended and not again was
it broached.

Before daylight June 10th, horses clattered along the four
routes leading to Rector's Cross Roads. They came from the
north, out of Leesburg and Hamilton; from the east along
Little River turnpike, in the direction of Middleburg and Aldie
and Fairfax; from the south, toward Piedmont and Salem and
Warrenton, and from the west, along the silent slopes of the
Blue Ridge. In small groups riders gathered out of sight in the
trees around the meeting point, waiting, watching. And when
Mosby rode up from the Hathaway place after sunrise, they
emerged from the underbrush like quail from the scrub. Close
to a hundred were there, including thirty from the independent
cavalry unit commanded by Captain William G. Brawner of
Prince William County.

Mosby sat his horse calmly in the blazing sunshine and stared
at the circle of faces. His uniform was neat, his boots shined.
The hat knocked from his head at Catlett's Station had been replaced by another plumed gray felt, cleaner and a bit cockier
than its predecessor.

Against the green background his men formed a colorful
band more turned to the gonfalons of tribal chiefs than to the
scientific fighting of a major war. A few persons Mosby wanted
particularly to include in the command were missing. Among
these were "Big Yankee" Ames, Dick Moran, Sam Underwood,
Tom Richards, Sam Chapman, "Major" Hibbs and Montjoy,
absent because of capture or injury. These were a part of the
foundation on which his operations had got a start.

Satisfied with the assemblage except for these absences,
Mosby turned quickly to the order of business. Vedettes were
placed along each of the four routes, far enough away for a
pistol shot to give the main body ample time to escape. Then
the task of preparing a roster began, directed by a representative from the War Department at Richmond. This took considerable time, each man coming forward to give his name and to
aid with the correct spelling. When it was completed, the
enrollees formed line along the crest of a hill. Mosby rode to
their center and swung his horse around to face them. He spoke

in a voice that carried distinctly along the surrounding slopes:

"You will be known as the Forty-third Battalion of Partisan Rangers. It is my desire now to organize you who have gathered here as Company A of this unit. These are the men you are to ballot on for your officers."

He read out the ticket slowly and clearly: James William Foster, captain; William Thomas Turner, first lieutenant; William L. Hunter, second lieutenant; George H. Whitescarver, third lieutenant. There was no nepotism in this slate—and no alternates. It was picked by Mosby solely on a basis of his judgment of the men and their ability. His closest friend and war companion, Fount Beattie, was not included. The man he chose to head the company had entered the regular service in May, '62, as a private in Turner Ashby's cavalry. He had had a horse shot from under him at Kernstown, had been promoted to a sergeancy for his gallantry and had joined Mosby while recruiting horses in Fauquier. He had caught the Partisan chieftain's eye in the Chantilly fight, his first with the command, and had strengthened this estimate at Catlett's Station.

"What is your will, men?" Mosby called.

As the leader anticipated, not a dissenting voice was heard among the chorus of ayes. He had used an effective counter to a bad situation, letting it be known in advance that he would send to the regular army the man who did not vote the straight ticket. The formality of an election, apparently useless in the face of such dictatorship, was necessary in view of Lee's instructions, but the control Mosby maintained over the outcome was the battalion's protection against one of the greatest weaknesses of the Southern army. He had seen the election system at work in '62. He had watched it take the command from capable officers in many instances and place it in the hands of men pitifully lacking in military proficiency.

With the organization routine over, Mosby waved his arm with a sweeping motion and spurred his horse down the hill to the road leading east toward Middleburg. A shot brought in the sentries, who caught up separately with the column strung out along the highway, each member wondering what was in the leader's mind. Experience long ago had taught that

Mosby kept his plans to himself, for his own welfare as well as theirs. He rode now at the front of the column, head erect, not once looking back to see that all were following. It was whispered among some that he was figuring out details of the raid on which they were starting. They had seen him do this before— ride twenty miles without uttering a word and then suddenly, with his movements mentally outlined, join in on the conversation.

A quarter mile or so east of Rector's Cross Roads he turned left, northward toward Leesburg, along a narrow, winding route. This swing away from the turnpike raised questions and brought comment, none of it loud enough to carry to the head of the column. Point of Rocks and the Potomac and the Chesapeake and Ohio canal were up that way, men recalled, and some of them grew eager in anticipation of what awaited them on their first foray as the Forty-third Battalion. It was the opening page of a book that already had had an active and exciting prelude.

At dawn next morning, they plunged across the Potomac at a ford a mile below Seneca, burned a boat on the canal and struck a more numerous enemy force drawn up at Seneca Mills. There was heavy fighting before the Federals fled in a running battle, leaving their flag behind. Along that day for the excitement was Frank Stringfellow of Stuart's scouts, said to have sworn he never would be captured alive.[3] He was riding beside Mosby during the pursuit. They came upon a figure in gray uniform lying face down in the road. They got down and turned the body over. A well-aimed bullet had snuffed out the life of Lieutenant George Whitescarver. Death struck again farther along. Captain Brawner, the Prince William County independent, was mortally wounded in the waning dust of the chase.

After directing destruction of the camp, found to have been occupied by troops from the Sixth Michigan Cavalry, Mosby headed back across the river. At Middleburg he halted to report to Stuart and to send him the captured flag.

Mosby's appearance north of the Potomac had the desired effect. Troops were rushed in force up the left bank of the river from Washington. DeForest's cavalry was ordered from the camp on Difficult Run to upper Fauquier. Stahel dashed madly across country from Fairfax, bent anew on capturing the foe he had been chasing since spring. Mosby had gone when Stahel got to Middleburg, but somewhere in the village the Federals found the unsuspecting Captain Foster and a prize white horse, awarded him for his bravery at Seneca.

Federal Brigadier-General Alfred Pleasanton, Cavalry Corps, commanding, wrote Chief Quartermaster Ingalls on June 12: "Ask the General how much of a bribe he can stand to get Mosby's services. There is a chance for him, and just now he could do valuable service in the way of information, as well as humbugging the enemy." Rufus Ingalls answered: "If you think your scheme will succeed in regard to Mosby, do not hesitate as to the matter of money. Use your own judgment and do precisely what you think best for the public interest." [4]

But Mosby had no thought of humbugging anyone except the Federals themselves. There was work for him to do. Up from Fredericksburg on a tangent to the northwest was swinging the bulk of the Southern army, facing its greatest venture to date. Ewell was marching toward Winchester. Twenty-five miles behind moved Longstreet; still farther back, A. P. Hill. Off on the flank nearest the Bull Run Mountains galloped Stuart's cavalry, suddenly apprised at Fleetwood on the 9th that the Union cavalry had learned to ride and fight at the same time. Somewhere back along the line, General Lee studied maps and pondered over the possibility that Hooker had guessed his strategy. It was evident the Federals knew something. As the Gray troops fell away from Fredericksburg, three of Hooker's corps dropped behind to keep the base at Aquia Creek, and the other half of his army moved toward the Centerville area. This worried Lee. He desired to cross the Potomac, using the Blue Ridge as a shield, and collect his troops in Pennsylvania before the enemy perceived his intentions.

By the 15th, all roads leading from Fredericksburg to Culpeper and northwestward along the slopes of the Blue Ridge, on both sides, were marked by low-hanging clouds of dust.

They were kicked up by the heels of the South's hungry soldiers, marching toward the better-filled barns and larders of the Cumberland Valley in enemy territory. Ewell had cleared Berryville and was preparing to drive Milroy out of Winchester. He had been instructed not to delay for a siege there, and Lee supposed he already was en route to Hagerstown. Behind him in stride the next day followed two other links in the Confederate movement. Longstreet marched from Culpeper, and two of Hill's divisions were on the road from Fredericksburg, with the third ready to move at a moment's notice.

On the 16th Stuart drew up at the home of Miss Kitty Shacklett, near Piedmont in Fauquier, and pitched his headquarters tent in the front yard, near the road. Next morning, early, a dusty horseman, followed by a small entourage of roughly-dressed men, rode up and dismounted. It was Mosby, ready to join forces with his superior, whom he had not seen since the day General Stoughton was paraded at Culpeper. Trotting behind him was a gift for Jeb—a fine, spirited sorrel, former property of a Michigan lieutenant.

The day before, the scout had been lower down along the Bull Run range, in the vicinity of Thoroughfare Gap, and had learned from Hooker's campfires that the Federals, while retiring on Washington, had the head of their column up toward the Potomac. It was news Lee had asked for, news Stuart had been instructed to obtain while watching Longstreet's flank, and the bearded cavalryman all but clasped the slender Partisan to his breast.[5] They talked briefly and parted with the understanding that they would meet again later that day at Middleburg.

Mosby was on time, riding in with thirty or forty of his command, at that later rendezvous. Stuart, who had arrived earlier and was standing in the street, dismounted, had never seen so many of the Rangers together at one time and he made jocular, but complimentary, remarks about their appearance, primarily for the benefit of the young ladies of the town who had gathered near by. Mosby ignored the quips: Jeb Stuart was his hero, the man who had given him his chance to rise above the ranks.

They held a second brief conference. Some of Fitz Lee's regiments were a few miles ahead, watching the gap in the Bull Run Mountains at Aldie. Pleasanton, Stuart explained, was out there looking west and trying to determine what the Confederates were up to: Rebel horse must impair his focus. Mosby had a plan intended to create diversion and to gather information. He would ride with his command to Seneca, where he had been just a week prior, stir up a commotion in that area and observe Hooker's movements at the same time. The Federals would be unable to explain an enemy force so far inside their lines; certainly they would not expect him to cross the Potomac again so soon. Stuart nodded.

"You'll soon hear from me!" Mosby shouted as he galloped away, the plume of his hat, a miniature of that worn by Stuart, waving with the stride of his horse.

The Ranger command had ridden ahead, and Mosby, silent about his plans, overtook it a mile from town. They pushed on in the boiling heat of afternoon and, three miles from Aldie, turned off and struck north toward Seneca. Some time later, while they quaffed buttermilk in the shade on a farmhouse lawn, the sound of artillery firing came to them from the direction of Aldie Gap. In an instant the command was in the saddle, riding toward the mountains. Prisoners picked up along the way confirmed the belief that the Union cavalry was crowding in from the east. At the top of the range, Mosby stared toward Aldie, where Kilpatrick of Gregg's division was driving in Munford's pickets; toward Fairfax and toward the Potomac, where long, stringy clouds of dust marked the path of the Union army. To reach Seneca, his men would have to make their way through compact columns of Blue infantry.

The Partisan leader sent his prisoners and a dispatch back to Stuart at Middleburg, giving him all the information at hand. Then he concealed his men in the woods to wait until dark. He had forsaken the Seneca trip: the line of communication extending from Pleasanton's cavalry back to Hooker's headquarters near Fairfax Court House looked like greener pastures for the moment.

When nightfall formed a curtain, the Rangers came out of

hiding and picked their way behind John Underwood toward
the Little River turnpike east of Aldie. It was still early
evening. Near the road, they halted to listen to a steady stream
of Federal troops filing past. Everything was in a stir. Guns
rumbled through the blackness, kicking up unseen clouds of
dust, dust that coated everything and stuffed the lungs of men.
There was song, sporadic, and the sound of horses and marching feet. Campfires blazed in all directions.

Mosby posted the command in the forest again and rode off
with Joe Nelson, Charlie Hall and Norment Smith. The gray of
their uniforms was unnoticed in the dark. They made good
time, wending in and out among infantry brigades, and drew
up between 10 and 11 o'clock at the roadside home of a Union
sympathizer named Almond Birch, native of Saratoga County,
New York. Three horses waited at the front gate in care of an
orderly.

"Whose horses are these?" demanded Mosby.

"Major Stirling's and Captain Fisher's—jist from General
Hooker's headquarters," announced the orderly in Irish brogue.

Mosby told him to come closer, then grasped him by the
collar and whispered in his ear, "You're my prisoner—this is
Mosby."

The orderly misunderstood.

"You're a dom liar," he fired. "I'm as goot a Union man as
iver there were."

Mosby pressed his revolver against the Irishman's cheek.
"Be still," he said, and in a still lower tone he directed Nelson
and Hall to serve as a reception committee for the officers.

It was hard to convince the two men of their captors' identity when they emerged from the house a few minutes later.
Only a few feet away sounded the steady tramp of Union feet,
a surplus of support for the helpless prisoners, but the little
drama at the gate went unnoticed.

At a friendly farmhouse a short distance away, Mosby
studied a dispatch found on the officers. It was from Hooker
to Pleasanton, and gave a fairly clear picture of what was
running through the Federal commander's mind.[6] He was looking with solicitude to Aldie, occupied by Pleasanton with cav-

alry and infantry, and he planned a cavalry reconnaissance in
force toward Warrenton and Culpeper. Also included was intelligence valuable to Lee: "The advance of the infantry is suspended until further information of the enemy's movements."
And also: "If Lee's army is in rear of his cavalry, we shall move
up by forced marches with the infantry." The same dispatch
further revealed that pontoons were being assembled at the
mouth of the Monocacy, which empties into the Potomac
directly east of the Catoctin range.

Mosby hurried the captured message off to Stuart by Norment Smith. The courier reached Middleburg by daybreak to
find that there had been excitement the evening before. Colonel
A. N. Duffie, impetuous Frenchman with the First Rhode
Island, had come up through Thoroughfare Gap and closed on
the town around 4 P.M. Pickets were driven in so suddenly
Stuart and company, including the gallant von Borcke, gay
plumage and all, were forced to run the gauntlet. But Robertson and Chambliss were near, and Stuart used them to turn
on the Federal Duffie and stem the tide. There was spirited
fighting, brief and hot in the late afternoon sun, before the
Union regiment was shattered. Then the Rebels piled back
into town to celebrate around the fiddle.

Stuart's reaction was still gay when the captured dispatch
from Mosby was handed him next morning. He studied it carefully; then sent a courier off to meet Wade Hampton, coming
by way of Warrenton from Beverley Ford, and to instruct him
to check the cavalry advance in that direction, a thing the
South Carolinian did without difficulty. As for the remainder
of Hooker's message, Stuart paid little heed to any part except
that giving the number of enemy divisions beyond the Bull Run
Mountains. By this he was persuaded in no event to attack
Pleasanton and Aldie with cavalry alone.

Meanwhile the Federals were shouting blue murder. There
was no excuse for such an important message to be lost so far
within their own lines and in the midst of vast hordes of armed
men. In Union minds blame lay at the proper door—guerrillas.
The morning Norment Smith rode up to Stuart, Major-General
David Butterfield, chief of staff of the Army of the Poto-

mac, gave orders to "catch and kill any guerrillas, then try them. . . ." [7] But this was much more easily ordered than done. The little independent bands of Rebels moving back and forth between the two armies were brazen and hard to find. Mosby, for instance, only a few hours before had snuggled down for a brief nap within half a mile of Meade's corps at Gum Spring in Loudoun. And up toward Point of Rocks on the Potomac, another force like Mosby's, under Colonel E. V. White, often mistaken for the Rangers, lurked in the bushes after one of its biggest successes. It had stopped a train en route from Sandy Hook to Baltimore and had destroyed the engine and twenty-two cars.

Pleasanton, on the 18th, reported that from all the information he could gather Mosby was raiding in Pennsylvania. But in this he soon learned he was mistaken. Mosby spent most of the day along the flanks of the marching Blue columns on Little River turnpike, gathering up prisoners and horses and listening to what was said. As night drew on, he turned west toward the mountains, taking an unguarded bridle path over the Bull Run range that the enemy apparently had not discovered. In the shortest time he was at headquarters unfolding his information and adventures to Stuart.

On the 19th heavy fighting along the turnpike from Middleburg toward Upperville caused Stuart to withdraw his brigades to the west for more concentrated battle. Gregg pounced on him a mile west of Middleburg, but Beckham's guns and the spirited Rebel cavalry stopped the Federal rush and, by nightfall, only a half mile of territory had been lost and the roads to the Blue Ridge still were blocked. The 20th was comparatively quiet, darkened by a slow, continuous rain.

Meanwhile, back at the Army of the Potomac's cavalry headquarters at Aldie, the mysterious disappearance of Hooker's message to Pleasanton had been explained, and it dawned suddenly on the Union command that Mosby's activities might be a very serious blow to the army's success. Promptly, Gregg, up front pushing Stuart, was cautioned to search all houses along the line of march for concealed soldiers. The warning was made still more potent: "The general commanding has information which he considers reliable that all of the citizens of Middleburg belong to or are implicated with Mosby, and therefore directs that you have all the men arrested and sent down to him and that you give direction that the women be not allowed to leave their premises during our occupation." [8] Again the people of Middleburg, who had petitioned Mosby before swinging to his support, were to suffer for their loyalty.

Early on the 21st the Federal advance stiffened, driving Stuart back on Ashby's Gap, where his line held. In the heat of the action, Mosby and his doughty Rangers slipped away through the steady rain to make another raid on Pleasanton's rear.

All afternoon they watched the Federal horse from an elevation a mile off the turnpike. As night drew on, they moved east toward the Bull Run range and the unguarded bridle path along which they had traveled just three days prior. Somewhere in the dark on the mountainside hours later, a Ranger dropped his hat. Men behind halted to help him search; the others, unaware of the delay that had befallen their companions, rode on, led by Mosby. The break in the column went unnoticed until those in advance bivouacked in a hollow near the crest.

Next morning Major-General George G. Meade, soon to succeed Hooker as commander-in-chief of the Federal army, sent a message back from Ashby's Gap with a report that the Confederate army was in the Shenandoah Valley, that Lee and Longstreet were at Winchester, that A. P. Hill was coming up to join them. That was the substance of the news given by Pleasanton, but Meade had other news he relayed in rueful tone: "I came near catching our friend Mosby this morning. I had reliable intelligence of his expected passing a place about four miles from here at sunrise. I sent forty mounted men, all I have, and 100 infantry, who succeeded in posting themselves in ambush at the designated spot. Sure enough, Mr. Mosby, together with thirty of his followers, made their appearance before sunrise, but I regret to say, their exit also, from what I can learn, through the fault of both foot and horse. It appears Mosby saw the cavalry and immediately charged them. They ran (that is, my horses) toward the infantry, posted behind a fence. The infantry, instead of rising and deliberately delivering their fire, fired lying on the ground; did not hit a Rebel, who immediately scattered and dispersed, and thus the prettiest chance in the world to dispose of Mr. Mosby was lost." [9]

Meade's report was an honest admission of failure in another lunge at the charmed Partisan chieftain. The flying heels of the Rebel horses, kicking up a shower of muck from the night's rain, had been a Confederate raspberry in the face of the pursuing Yankees.

The affair, though a failure, was carefully planned. A Negro brought word the Rangers were on their way. At 1 o'clock that morning, safely concealed by the rain and darkness, Captain Harvey Brown, with 100 men and three officers from the Seventeenth Pennsylvania Volunteers, rode out from a camp near Aldie and took the Thoroughfare Gap road. His object was to reach Ewell's Chapel, a country church in the eastern foothills of the Bull Run Mountains, and to post his men there before daylight, near the point where Mosby's men would emerge from the bridle path.

But the detachment was stopped several times by its own picket lines, causing unexpected delay, and added to this were the difficulties of the heavy roads. Consequently, it was broad daylight when the force drew up at its destination. There, because of the open country, Captain Brown found little choice in stationing his men. He placed half the cavalry and part of the infantry in rear of the little chapel and at the head of a lane leading up to the home of Dr. Ewell, landowner from whom the church had got its name. It was supposed the Partisans would pass that point. To further fortify the trap, the others were stretched on the left of the lane, facing the house. Up front, as bait, was sent a small body of cavalry.

Scarcely had the infantry flattened themselves in the wet undergrowth when the watch, posted in a tree top, gave warning the enemy approached. Men on the ground looked again to their rifles; cavalrymen raised in their stirrups and stared in the direction of the low-lying mist toward the mountains. It was rolling terrain and gave them little chance for a clear sweep of the lane nearest the house; moreover, clouds had dropped down and were growing darker in promise of a new downpour.

In a minute or two the thirty men who had gone ahead with Mosby in the blackness of the mountainside the night before came in sight. They were riding at a rapid clip. When they saw the Blue horsemen in their path, they halted and waited until their leader, who had fallen behind, caught up. There seemed to be a brief consultation before they surged forward in a charge. It was the usual hot spur of the Partisans, seasoned by clattering hoofs and yelling men.

Federal riders, feeling jubilant, held their ground. When the quarry came within pistol range, they exchanged a few shots and fell back toward the chapel, feigning nervousness. Plans were working out nicely. But suddenly the Rebel leader warned his men in a shrill cry, keenly penetrating above the thunder of the charge, and the entire band whirled, low on their horses' necks, and fled back toward the mountains. The surprised Federals were caught flat-footed. The infantry fired at the raiders' backs and the cavalry gave chase for more than a mile, but the entire Ranger force made cover easily. Back at the chapel lay the sole fatality of the brief encounter, a sergeant of the Seventeenth Pennsylvania.

On the way Mosby kept an eye open for horses and mules. Stuart's quartermaster had complained of a shortage and, in response, the raider captain had cheered him in the presence of other officers at headquarters with a reminder that the enemy had plenty. Before they had ridden far, four wagons, each drawn by six mules, rolled in view. The Rangers made quick work of them, looked over the cargo and sent the pickings on a circuit toward the Confederate lines. Later, within a mile of General Birney's camp, they met twenty wagons, heavily loaded and guarded by a cavalry escort that had galloped in advance confident that it was foolish to expect the enemy so far within Union territory. It was a cinch for the raiders, despite their small numbers. With scarcely one man to a wagon, they slipped in on the drivers and made quick work of the entire train. But before they could get away with their

prizes, the guard, somehow sensing trouble, charged back, captured three of the Rebels and regained some of the animals.

The efforts of Mosby and his small band this time caused an
important change. Stahel, in obedience to Hooker's orders, had
set out that day from Fairfax with three cavalry brigades and
a battery of artillery on a second reconnaissance to the Rappahannock. Hampton had driven him back from an expedition
he had attempted two days earlier. On the 23rd, while the
first brigade was crossing the river, a second order arrived,
countermanding the first and calling Stahel back at once.
Hooker had heard of the attack on the first train and had sent
the later order by way of General Hancock at Thoroughfare
Gap. Butterfield followed this up with a telegram to Hancock
shortly afterward: "The general thinks you had better not send
in any train until General Stahel's command comes in, and then
move with them. A party of about 100 men of the enemy are
inside our lines and have today attacked a train en route for
Aldie."

This alteration of plans saved the Confederate army possible
serious trouble. On the other side of the Rappahannock, Lee's
line of communications was uncovered. Stahel's return was
futile, for the captured horses and mules had been delivered
to Stuart's quartermaster long before Hooker's second message
reached its destination. When Stahel learned that "the party
inside our lines" was Mosby's midnight marauders, already a
thorn in the side of the Hungarian soldier Lincoln had entrusted with their capture, he wrote in plaintive tone to the
Secretary of War about Hooker's order calling him back: "It
was with feelings of bitter regret and disappointment I received this order, inasmuch as I was just crossing the Rappahannock with three brigades of cavalry and a battery of horse
artillery, who were fresh from camp.... All of Lee's supplies
had to pass between the Rappahannock and the Blue Ridge
Mountains across the Shenandoah Valley, and my force was
sufficient to have destroyed his entire trains and cut off General
Lee completely from his supplies.... I was compelled by this
order to abandon my movement and restrained from dealing
so fatal a blow to the enemy, and return with my whole divi-

sion to disperse about 100 guerrillas, who had escaped back of
our lines before I ever received the order to return."

At Stuart's headquarters, Mosby learned there had been fine
doings on the other side of the Bull Run Mountains while he
was escaping from General Meade's trap at Ewell Chapel and
rounding up wagon trains along the turnpike. Pleasanton,
blocked by the stout resistance facing him in Ashby's Gap, had
withdrawn to Aldie and Stuart had followed him, stopping
with his cavalry spread out around Rector's Cross Roads.

The Rebel raider found Stuart in a quandary. That day, the
22nd, had come a message from Lee giving the cavalry orders
to move into Maryland and to overtake Ewell. But there was
doubt concerning the best route to follow. Confederate infantry and trains were fording upstream at Williamsport and
Shepherdstown, west of the Blue Ridge, and it would take him
forty miles out of the way, besides delaying him, to fall in behind these slow-moving columns. Federal troops still held
Harper's Ferry, and there was doubt that he would be able to
force a crossing east of the mountains.

Mosby had a plan that bordered on the daringness of the
ride he had induced Stuart to make around McClellan. He had
rubbed shoulders with the Federal army, had lost his fear of
contact with it, and he knew its exact disposition at present.
Hooker's corps were widely separated. The ideal move, he said,
would be to swing through unguarded Glasscock Gap in the
Bull Run Mountains, a few miles south of Hancock at Thoroughfare, and to proceed by way of Haymarket, through Hooker's army, to the ford at Seneca. This would be feasible, he
argued, and there would be no force to block the crossing at
the Potomac. There was much to be gained by so daring a
move. It would head along the most direct line to Maryland
and would conceal to a degree the plans of the gray-clad infantry west of the Blue Ridge. Hooker's transportation could
be cut along the way and communications between Washington and the North could be broken up. On the other side of the
Potomac, the canal and railway from the capital to Edward's
Ferry, where Federal pontoons had been laid, could be de-

stroyed. As still another possible advantage of the plan, Union cavalry no doubt would be withdrawn from the front and dis‹ patched after Stuart, the very thing Lee wanted.

Stuart gave an attentive ear. Richmond newspapers were scoring him for his showing at Fleetwood, and this might be the feat that would restore his reputation. While they talked, Generals Hampton and Fitz Lee walked into the room and there was still more serious consideration. Soon afterward a courier was sent off to convey the plan to the commanding general in the valley.

But Stuart had still other troubles. In his message that day, General Lee had expressed fear that Hooker would steal a march on them and get across the Potomac before they were aware of it. "If you find that he is moving northward, and that two brigades can guard the Blue Ridge and take care of your rear," he wrote, "you can move with the other three into Maryland...." That was an important "if," considered from any angle. Was Hooker moving? Mosby volunteered to find out, even though his sleep for the last three days consisted only of the brief nap in the rain on the mountain top the night before.

The rainy spell of the last few days continued as Mosby rode into the night. This trip was to be for reconnaissance, not for fighting, so he allowed only two men to accompany him.

Dawn found the trio riding through the Federal camps. Twice during the morning prisoners were captured. Mosby sent them back by his companions, along with dispatches to Stuart, and rode on alone toward the east to make certain Hooker was not moving. Near Frying Pan, he stopped to see Laura Ratcliffe, the Southern sympathizer who had warned him of the ambush early in February.

The Ratcliffe family had not seen Mosby often enough to keep him well in mind, and not until he threw back his rubber cape and displayed a Rebel uniform set off by the insignia of a major did they recognize him. While he perused the latest newspapers at hand, they hid his horse for fear the enemy would surprise him. But no Federals appeared—not until that evening, hours after he had gone. Then two privates dropped

House at Fairfax, Virginia, where Mosby captured
General Stoughton in March, 1863.

From a photograph taken during the war

William H. Chapman

by with an exciting tale. They had ridden for miles that day with the guerrilla Mosby, had returned his cheerful "good evening" when they parted and had not learned until later of the praise which would have been theirs had they turned their guns on this pleasant companion. With license for her trickery, Laura pooh-poohed the idea and declared it was very improbable the stranger was Mosby.

Late in the afternoon Mosby worked his way back toward the unguarded bridle path. At one point he stopped at a farmhouse to inquire the shortest way to Little River turnpike. The farmer was Southern in sympathy, but was reluctant to talk. He had been tricked by the Federals before and had too much at stake to let his tongue lead him into trouble again. While Mosby tried futilely to convince the man of his identity, two Union soldiers trotted up the lane toward the house and stopped at a tree a few yards away to pick cherries. The Partisan drew his gun beneath his cape and rode slowly up to them. He learned they were from Reynolds' corps, camped near by at Guilford, and then took them prisoners. It was done without getting his gun wet. In six months the name of Mosby had become one of dread.

With his captives, the raider set out in the general direction of the turnpike. His judgment of directions proved sufficient, for eventually he found his bearings. But as he came in view of the road, his hopes fell. Moving slowly along, flanked on each side by a strong cavalry guard, was a long wagon train. He called a halt to study the situation. As far as he could see were the heavy army vehicles, steadily, doggedly rolling onward, separated from each other by only a few feet of space. Somehow he must pass through this apparently endless caravan to the mountains beyond, and it must be done soon. Only by reaching the bridle path before dark would he be able to find the route back through the wilderness to headquarters.

Pulling his unrevealing cape tighter about him, he drew his twin revolvers beneath it and spoke in a cold voice: "We're going through that train. If you make any sign or utter a word to have me captured, I will blow your brains out and trust to the speed of my horse to escape."

They rode toward the line of wagons, the prisoners on each side a step in advance of the nervy, sandy-haired Partisan. A gap in front admitted them to the pike. Mosby had noticed as they approached that there was no opening on the opposite side and that the fence was too high for their horses to jump it.

After reaching the road, he nodded his head to direct the prisoners between two wagons. They were in the cavalry guard now, riding close, surrounded. The noise of the train—suck of horses' feet in the mud, creak of wagon bodies heavily laden, lumber of giant axles, crack of whips and the bellowing voices of the drivers, mostly Negroes—seemed to drag Mosby in and carry him along. For 200 yards they rode before a narrow lane appeared ahead. He spurred his horse around in order to put both captives between him and the outside. At one point his elbow brushed a guardsman who had come up unseen. Beneath the cape, his grip tightened on his revolvers, but outwardly he gave no notice of the contact, keeping his head straight to the front, not daring to glance at the cavalryman out of the corner of his eye.

Opposite the lane the pressure of his horse edging toward the outside gently forced his prisoners into the side road, giving the appearance that all three had had the same thought. For more than a hundred yards they continued in the clear before a thin covering of trees gave Mosby a chance to relax. Then he sheathed his revolvers and looked hopefully toward the mountains.

At headquarters next morning he learned that Stuart had received another letter of "ifs" from General Lee during his absence: "If General Hooker's army remains inactive, you can leave two brigades to watch and withdraw with the three others, but should he not appear to be moving northward, I think you had better withdraw this side of the mountain tomorrow night, cross at Shepherdstown next day and move over to Fredericktown. You will, however, be able to judge whether you can pass around their army without hindrance, doing them all the damage you can, and cross the river east of the mountains. In either case, after crossing the river, you must move on and feel the right of Ewell's troops, collecting information, provisions, etc." Near the end, Lee gave Stuart still further incentive for his later action: "... I think the sooner you cross into Maryland, after tomorrow, the better."

Mosby reported that Hooker definitely was not on the move that he had been through Loudoun and Fairfax Counties where the heart of the Federal army was located, and had found the troops at ease in their camps, apparently waiting for Lee to indicate his intentions. Stuart promptly wrote Lee his final message before setting out on the circuitous route that was to throw him late at Gettysburg. In it, guided partly by the advice of the scout at his side, he gave a description of the exact path he would follow, the identical line of march suggested by Mosby two days prior.

That afternoon, with a part of his command gathered around him, Mosby started again for the unguarded bridle path over the Bull Run Mountains—on his fifth journey inside the Federal army in nine days. Stuart had instructed him to scout toward Dranesville to be sure the way was open, to meet him next day at Gum Spring, and there to take charge of his advance detail.

A few hours later, with three days' rations prepared, Hampton, Fitz Lee and W. H. F. Lee's brigades set out under cover of darkness for a secret rendezvous at Salem, leaving Jones and Robertson's brigades to watch the front at Middleburg. An hour after midnight they started southward toward Glasscock's Gap, moving as rapidly as possible over the rain-soaked roads. Stuart wanted to avoid the eyes which would be peering at them at daybreak from the ridge of the Bull Run range.

Daylight found Mosby and his companions at a spring on the slope of the mountains making a quick breakfast of captured sutlers' stores. Two raiders stood guard at the approaches. As the men at the spring ate, a fusillade of shots sounded suddenly from the direction of the vedettes. Food was forgotten. Partisans leaped into their saddles on the run, fleeing from the second ambuscade in four days.

As the men urged their horses through the woods extending down the mountain from the spring, they heard the roar of guns from the direction of Haymarket. Stuart explained the firing in his report: "As we neared Haymarket, we found that Hancock's corps was en route through Haymarket for Gum Spring, his infantry well distributed through his trains. I chose a good position and opened with artillery on his passing column with effect, scattering men, wagons and horses in a wild confusion; disabled one of the enemy's caissons, which he abandoned, and compelled him to advance in order of battle to compel us to desist." [10]

The ominous sound of the guns burst into full meaning when Mosby reached the turnpike and found blue-clad forces marching in a steady stream. During the night had happened the very thing that would knock the bottom out of the plan he had unfolded to Stuart. The entire Federal army had begun to move northward, the development he had watched for so carefully on his last trip over the mountains. The troops that had come in and taken the right-of-way from Stuart, cutting off his contact with Mosby and his most direct route to Maryland, were those of Hancock, stationed at Thoroughfare on the left of Hooker's line. Ewell, cutting up in Pennsylvania, and the marching Gray hordes on the west of the Blue Ridge, as seen finally by Union signal stations, had given the alarm. The grand march was on.

It was on the 27th, two days behind schedule, that Stuart, forced to make a wider circuit by way of Brentsville, crossed the Potomac at Seneca. Too many elements enter into the battle of Gettysburg to fix definitely the blame for the South's bloody defeat there. Had Stuart been able to get through to Maryland as planned and had he not delayed further to capture a supply train, even after Hancock had blocked him, there is no telling what the result might have been. In defense of Mosby's plan to ride through the Federal army, it was approved by Lee, Longstreet and Stuart, three of the Confederacy's mightiest generals, and doubtless would have brought great praise from the press and public alike had it succeeded. That it did not apparently was one of the gambles of war no amount of preparatory scouting could have saved. It was daring from start to finish, and it threw great fright into the heads of government at Washington. Mosby's greatest praise for his work in the campaign came in the report of Stuart: ". . . the fearless and indefatigable Major Mosby was particularly active and efficient. His information was always accurate and reliable." [11]

CHAPTER

12

The Spur of a Cavalier

M OSBY SPENT THE REMAINDER of his first year of operations in a concerted campaign on enemy wagon trains. After missing Stuart at Gum Spring, he had dashed through Maryland and had set himself up for a few hours as provost-marshal of Hagerstown. Then he went on into Pennsylvania, as far as Mercersburg, whirling about there at news that Lee's army was on its way back to Virginia.

His war on wagon trains caused him to move in a wide circuit over miles of country, striking with such repeated success as to draw strong praise out of Richmond, especially from Secretary of War Seddon. In view of the repeated attacks, Colonel Lowell at Vienna advised that it would be well to delay all wagon trains without heavy escort until definite information on Mosby's movements could be learned. He also suggested that strong infantry pickets be posted along the road to ambush the raider. The latter of these suggestions was carried out, along railroads as well as highways. For miles on the tracks in every direction out of Washington, sentinels were stationed so close together they could see the next in line on each side while they were walking post.

But none of these precautions stopped Mosby's raiders. One night a long wagon train came to a halt in the dark a few miles out of Warrenton. When officers in charge finally awakened to the fact that something was wrong, they went to investigate and found between forty and fifty deserted wagons in the center of the caravan. From the vehicles had been taken 145

152

horses and mules. In Fairfax one day another string of wagons came to a fork in the road. The lead team swung to the right, most contrary to orders. Behind at intervals of only a few yards, came the others, twenty-nine of them. Farther on, a band of raiders watched from a hiding place in the trees. As the first wagon appeared, they recognized their own Jack Barnes, humming crazy tunes and talking sassy to the subdued Yankee driver beside him. Fresh in the mind of the Federal were the twin guns of a man in a plumed hat. This man sat on Wagon No. 30, rubbing elbows with another disgusted teamster. Between wagons 1 and 30 were twenty-eight drivers, all unaware that their train had been taken by Mosby.

At the headquarters camp of the pale and pious General Howard, forty artillerymen lay one day in a field, forming a human fence around a number of mules grazing with their eyes on the green foliage of near-by mountains. To the west a handful of horsemen emerged from the woods and picked their way slowly toward the long rows of tents. On the other side of the field another band rode leisurely out of cover and headed directly for camp. To all appearances, these were tired reconnaissance parties returning from a long overnight jaunt. But suddenly, on the very edge of the camp, the two little bands came to life, spread out in a circle, flashing revolvers, and swept the field of artillerists and mules. They were gone before the Federals lying about in the tents realized what had happened.

A few nights later, John Underwood crept into a Union corral, disguising his approach with occasional jangles from a cowbell around his neck. In the stampede that followed, the Confederate horse supply was stepped up by dozens.

Sutlers, too, came in for their share of misery. Some of them told of a strange ravine to which they were taken after capture. In it were remains of wagons, trunks, boxes and clothing. Their captors, neatly dressed and heavily armed, wore uniforms of gray pantaloons with a yellow cord down the seam, dark jackets and gray felt hats, one side turned up and fastened with a rosette, the other set off by a black feather.

This concerted campaign of raiding had its effect across the Potomac. J. H. Taylor, chief of staff, sent out a notice: "No mercy need be shown to bushwhackers. These guerrillas must be destroyed." As if this notice had set off the spark of retribution, Federal cavalry turned on the raiders with terrific force at Gooden's Tavern, wounding Mosby in the side and thigh and killing Norment E. Smith, the man who had taken the captured message of General Hooker to Stuart. The press grew hot with reports on this turn of affairs. It was said one day the Ranger leader's wounds were fatal; the next, that his leg was amputated at the thigh. To aggravate these rumors, a woman brought word to Washington that she had seen Mosby's men conducting him along a road near Upperville. "As he lay in the open wagon supported on pillows and shielded from the sun by umbrellas," she said, "his face had the ghastly hue of death upon it."

By late September the Union knew Mosby was not dead. Colonel D. H. Dulaney, aide to Francis H. Pierpont, governor of the "pretended state government" formed in counties of Western Virginia in sympathy with the North and moved to Alexandria after that area was taken over by Federal troops, was spirited away from his home one night, much on the order of Stoughton. His own son, French Dulaney, member of Company A, was one of the abductors. So was Mosby.

Shortly afterward, the raider organized his second unit, Company B, with William R. Smith as captain and, a little later, Company C, captained by William Chapman. This period also marked the arrival in Ranger ranks of Mosby's brother, William H., not long past his seventeenth birthday. And on the heels of this came another family development—Mrs. Mosby gave birth to a second son, named by her John Singleton Mosby, Jr.

As the weather grew colder and the fighting in late '63 waned, the main armies shifted and settled down for the winter. Lee's line lay behind the Rappahannock, retired, but Meade spread his troops around Warrenton and along the Orange and Alexandria railroad, nervous, impatient, but reluctant to act. There the two great hordes lay, face to face, spitting at each other with occasional cavalry thrusts across the river.

Mosby's presence in the neighborhood caused Warrenton to

become a trouble center. General Gregg, sent there to determine what could be done to prevent the Partisan assaults, reported that it would be impossible to exterminate the little bands under methods then in use. He proposed that the town be completely enveloped, "so as to bring it within our lines and cut off communications between its disloyal inhabitants and the guerrillas who infest the country about."

Through the cordon thus thrown around Warrenton on Gregg's advice seeped a letter from a Confederate soldier to a pretty young maiden, Roberta Pollock. Phrased patriotically, it asked her as a friend of the South to remain constantly alert for information which might be of use to Rebel scouts and guerrillas.

Roberta's home was at a point where it was surrounded by picket lines by day, outside of them by night. On the morning of December 22, she walked into town on a routine trip. The weather was clear and cold. About her she observed a scene that brought a choking sensation to her throat. The little town's natural charm had vanished in less time than it had taken to build some of the houses which had come up within her recollection.

At the home of a friend, she spread her skirts before the fire to talk. This friend had exciting news. She had seen a strange Negro man a few minutes earlier walk through the streets under escort in the direction of the provost-marshal's office. She was positive his presence foreboded evil for the Confederates.

A few minutes later, Roberta approached the sentinel on duty in front of the provost-marshal's office and spoke pleasantly. The soldier, a young recruit, willingly ceased his monotonous pacing and presented arms. She told him coyly she was in trouble, and the demure look in her eyes bore her out. Would he, kind sir, let her pass? It was vital that she talk with her A'nt Felicia, one of the Negro servants in the basement. A family matter. A recipe for an herb root potion her ailing mother needed. Coins touched the Yankee's palm. There was an embarrassed pause. Then he clutched the money, shouldered his gun and resumed his tiresome tread.

Once inside, Roberta became a changed woman. Her coyness disappeared and in its stead came a desperate calm. She tiptoed along the corridor. Opposite a room from which sounded the chatter of Negro voices, she turned into another chamber, a damp, dark, unfloored cell that fitted her purpose admirably. Above her she could hear men talking, the sharp, quick words of the Federal officers and the more deliberate drawl of the slave escorted to headquarters. Her ears picked up their words. The Federals were harassing the Negro, badgering him for information. After lengthy questioning, much of which confused the darky, his tone changed. Roberta could hear plainly, "Sho, I kin lead you to Mosby, 'specially ifen you gimme de money you done promised." He could show them houses where Mosby's men stayed and he could show them where the raiders had stored a lot of corn. All he needed was the money and for the "Nawthun gen'muns" to protect him from the white folks if he "pinted" the way.

Roberta tiptoed out of the basement, nodded pleasantly at the sentinel and walked on through town. At a farmhouse on the outskirts she borrowed a horse, Kitty Grey. A little farther along, at another house, she took up behind her after talking briefly with his parents a small boy, more for the courage of companionship than for physical protection. It was Roberta's plan to ride until she could pass on to some Southern soldier the information she had acquired.

By this time it was late afternoon and much colder. Throughout the day the temperature had dropped steadily. A blustering wind had kicked up somewhere, and the skies were covered with moving masses of black clouds. With the lad's arms clasped tightly around her waist she rode on, for miles, through country that became stranger with each turn. The weather seemed to grow rapidly more severe, the darkness deeper, the wind higher and higher. Nightfall came and her face ached with cold. More time passed, more riding during which they huddled miserably and listened to the monotonous clatter of the horse and the creak of the saddle. The agony became steadily worse. Roberta's fingers lost their sensation, and the bridle reins fell from them and lay across the pommel. Since before dark she had kept anxious watch for a farm house at which to warm and, when at last the glow of a bonfire shone through the trees, she allowed the horse to go toward it without thought of whether it had been kindled by friend or foe. She could see no one as she approached.

Staring about her while warming, Roberta suddenly spied a large tree against the skyline and recognized it as the "view tree," an old giant to which lovers and now soldiers came to obtain a better survey of the countryside. It brought a gasp of surprise from her. She had ridden eight miles or so and had arrived at a spot only four miles from Warrenton. The fire, it occurred to her, must have been built by Southern scouts who had left or been driven away.

She turned the horse about and rode out of the circle of light. It seemed to her to be darker than before, but all at once the clouds parted and the glow of a full moon gave her a glimpse of her route. The boy's arms tightened about her suddenly. He whispered, "Look, look there!" Moving slowly forward in V formation at her right was a body of men, each with raised carbine. Roberta neither increased nor decreased the pace of her mount. Instead she patted the mittened hands of her companion to give him courage and steeled herself against the challenge she was positive would be shouted at her. But no challenge, no gunfire came, and in a few seconds the clouds slid mercifully back over the moon, blotting out the landscape. She rode on breathlessly through the sheltering darkness, wondering why there had been no call.

Half an hour later, while Kitty Grey kept up a steady trot, a single horseman blocked their path. "Halt!" he called, and Roberta, in answer, did something she later could not explain. She raised her arm and shouted in a voice made hoarse by the cold wind—"Surrender or I'll blow your brains out!" A moment's interlude, and then she heard the clatter of hoofs retreating down the road.

Nerved with the thought that she surely by now had passed the last picket, she urged the horse along faster. But her spirits sank again when she topped a hill to stare down on the lights of Warrenton less than three miles distant. Once more she had lost her direction. To continue toward the town would lead her toward the Yankees. If she turned and, by chance, became entirely lost, it would be easy to guess what might happen to the boy and to herself on such a night. But thought of the disadvantages under which Mosby's men operated gave her courage. She turned the horse and rode into the blackness.

Some time later she was startled by a voice calling for her to halt. She drew rein and waited. A Federal picket approached cautiously. "Where are you going?" he asked when he had come close.

She replied in a tremulous voice. "I was trying to go to the neighborhood of Salem to see a sick friend, but my horse has traveled so slowly that night has overtaken me and I've lost my way."

The soldier spoke with command. "It's my duty to take you to the reserve where you will be detained and taken to headquarters in the morning."

His words angered the girl. "You may shoot me on the spot, but I will not spend the night unprotected among your soldiers. You shan't perform your duty."

There was a moment of indecision on the part of the soldier, and then he spoke in a more kindly tone. "Nor am I willing to perform it. Do you see that light yonder? Go to that house. They'll let you stay."

The girl turned off and tried to follow a path. "Not that way!" called the soldier. "That leads to the reserve!"

He walked over and led her horse into the right path. "Goodbye," he said. "I shall have three hours on picket to think of a freezing lady."

Next morning Roberta was given an explanation of why no call or gunfire had come on the hillside. The answer was supplied by six Federal soldiers who arrived at the home to which she had been directed. They were in talkative mood, searching for eggs and milk. They were celebrating, they said, because they had outsmarted Mosby. "His men tried to trick us," one of them explained. "They sent a single rider in advance in our sector last night, thinking we would all fire on him and not be ready for the rest when they came up. But we were too sharp for them. We held our fire and they were afraid to attack us."

By judicious questioning, Roberta learned also that no party had been sent out with the Negro to guide them. An hour or so afterward, she slipped off by direction to a spot in the nearby mountains and imparted her warning.

Meanwhile the countryside prepared to celebrate Christmas in as lavish a manner as the privations of war would permit. The Rangers themselves made plans to participate in the festivities, and word of their intentions got around. It reached the headquarters of the Army of the Potomac and from there on Christmas Day was passed on to Colonel John P. Taylor, commanding the Second Cavalry Division. "Dispatch just received," the message read, "states that Mosby has made great preparation to have a frolic, with his principal officers, at the house of Dr. Bispham and Mrs. Murray in Salem tonight. Dr. Bispham's is the second house as you go in the village from Warrenton, and Mrs. Murray lives about the middle of the street, in a large white house. The major-general commanding directs that you send a party from the brigade which is at Warrenton, under the command of a smart and competent officer, to capture them." [1]

Salem is a little village topping a ridge of rolling terrain fifteen miles northwest of Warrenton. More and more, as the war advanced, it came to be recognized as the center around which Mosby's men could be found in varying numbers at all times. There were reasons for this. To begin with, it was near the heart of Mosby's Confederacy and it had highways leading into it from all directions, giving ready ingress and egress. Around it, protectively for independent soldiers, were small bodies of wood and the little clumps of trees characteristic of that part of Northern Virginia. Up to its edge meandered the Manassas Gap railroad and its defunct tracks, with scattered ties and bent rails. But its main attraction as a Partisan hangout was its location midway between the Bull Run and Blue Ridge Mountains. No matter from which direction the enemy approached, Rangers could flee from the village with consolation that a haven lay ahead of them. Residents professed a certain feeling of safety during the war due to the presence of Mosby's men. They said they could shout or wave a handkerchief from a window and know that one or more of the Rangers would catch the signal.

So it was natural for the Federal command to put much credence in the report of a Christmas celebration at Salem. But the raid on the large white house and the house that stood second in the village from Warrenton netted nothing. The party sent to investigate found the two homes as quiet as Sunday night. Mosby's scouts had sounded the alarm.

During Christmas week, while Roberta Pollock and several girl guests were preparing for bed, a strange tapping sounded on a window of her home. Roberta threw on a wrap. In the yard, pale in the faint glow of lamp light from the front doorway, she could see a small circle of horsemen. They raised their hats and bowed, and the leader, pointed out by a waving plume, briefly expressed his thanks for her daring ride to give them warning. But he wondered if she could direct them to the exact position of the pickets and vedettes.

"I think so," replied the girl. "At least I can give you a general idea." She hesitated uncertainly, and then went on. "There is a hill near here from which I could point out their position more exactly."

One of the horsemen urged his mount a step or two forward. "Major, may I have the honor to accompany her there?" It was Captain Smith, senior of company officers.

Roberta disappeared into the house and was back shortly, well wrapped. "We can walk there in a very short time," she said to Smith, who prepared to help her into the saddle. At this suggestion, he looped the bridle over his arm and caught stride with her. Other Rangers accompanied them as far as the barnyard, voicing in low tone their wishes for success. Then along a path Roberta had followed since childhood, across a pasture, through low pines and toward a body of larger trees the couple walked. The moon shone brightly, covered only by a veil of fleecy clouds. As they proceeded—the hardened rider and the frail, light-stepping girl—they became gay and buoyant in their conversation, forgetful for the moment of war and its terrors. Behind them the horse followed obediently, in perfect understanding of its master's mood.

But their joviality ended suddenly. As they neared the woods a picket stepped from behind a tree. In the breathless moment that followed, Roberta was given an idea of the alertness, the quick action by which Mosby's men saved their necks in an emergency. Before she had fully taken in the situation, Smith leaped on his horse, grabbed her beneath the arms and threw her across the saddle. A bullet seemed to graze their ears. The animal lunged, darted off to the side, took them swiftly through the pines. Behind sounded shouts. They heard the entire picket line take up the alarm, heard the spasmodic signal shots, and then there was silence.

"A little romance for you," whispered Smith as they drew up, safe, in a clump of trees. Later, as she undressed for bed, Roberta found in the hem of her skirt a jagged rent. She told herself it was made by the spur of a cavalier.[2]

13

Loudoun Heights

———◇◇◇◇———

A HARD-RIDING UNIT OF SEVENTY-EIGHT MEN out of the Second
Maryland Cavalry from Harper's Ferry was sent New
Year's Day to search for Mosby's Rangers. These troopers rode
like devils in a high wind. From Hillsboro to Waterford to
Purcellville they dashed in fine fashion. Nothing stopped them
and they saw nothing for which they would bother to stop. But
at Upperville the story changed. A mysterious rifle blast out of
nowhere left one of them dangling from his stirrups, dead of
a bullet wound in the head.

Captain A. N. Hunter, their leader, was a cautious man. He
directed a careful search of the neighborhood, and found nothing. Then he galloped with his command to Rectortown, and
there encountered a situation that gave him even more uneasy
concern. Sinister against the skyline around the town could
be seen figures on horseback, mysterious, strangely still, like
scavengers waiting for the carrion. Nearly every hilltop and
prominence had its coterie. These riders were widely scattered
and there was no evidence that they planned to attack, but
sight of them, in sharp, cold relief against the wintry skies,
sitting their horses and calmly looking down on what they
evidently considered fair prey, gave the Yankees a creepy sensation that was worse on morale than the sound of firearms.

Hunter was baffled. He waited at Rectortown most of the
day for something to happen and, when nothing did, ventured
out of the village in grave apprehension. He instructed each
man to keep his own lookout, pushed them close together to

prevent straggling and struck off afield toward Middleburg. But his precautions were useless. Near Five Points a band of thirty-five Rangers swept down on his detail of Marylanders and completely routed them.

On January 3 the skies blackened and there followed the worst storm of the winter. Snow fell fast, whipped about by a cold, furious wind. It reached a depth of several inches, with no sign of letup. Because of the screen afforded the Rangers by such weather, the Federal picket line around Warrenton was strengthened heavily. Soldiers were instructed to be particularly vigilant and, as further precaution, citizens were not permitted to pass in or out of town. In the customary routine of changes, Captain Gillmore of the Third Pennsylvania Cavalry was sent with a force to relieve a detachment of the First Brigade. He took up a line established on the Sulphur Springs[1] road.

Some time during the early morning hours a corporal from Gillmore's detail started with the relief scheduled to go on duty at that time. The wind had become more violent during the night and was sweeping furiously across the deep covering of snow, blowing hard, frozen flakes stingingly against the soldiers' faces. As the corporal approached No. 3 post he spied in the glow from the picket's bonfire ten or twelve men drawn up in line. He immediately returned to camp and reported what he had seen. Gillmore assigned a lieutenant to return to the post with ten men and investigate. The lieutenant scouted the entire circuit of the line, finding nothing, not even tracks in the whipping snow.

Pickets were warned to be doubly on guard, and after No. 3 post had been resupplied, things again settled to a routine watch. As the morning advanced, the wind reached blizzard proportions. Snow was swept into drifts and pasted against sides of trees. As seen from the northwest, everything was covered in white.

Between 4 and 5 A.M., the second relief left the reserve camp to go on duty. Its members took a last warming back rub at a fire blazing in front of the cook tent, pulled their heavy coats snugly about them and plunged into the storm. In the stillness

left behind at the camp, a gust of wind rolled a stick from the
fire. It sent up a shower of sparks and brightened the glow,
pointing the way for thirty-one Rangers who suddenly pounced
from behind a ridge. They surrounded the tents, covered the
openings and shouted for the Federals to surrender. Captain
Gillmore, leaping to his feet in the confusion of such a sudden
awakening, called loudly for his men to rally. But before he
could organize them, he was shot down and surrounded by a
dozen raiders. The surprise planned at a time when two reliefs
would be absent was complete.

So angered were the Federals at this assault that 100 men
from near-by camps rode in pursuit until their horses were
broken down. A full investigation was held after daylight. In
the snow a faint trail told what had happened. Due to misunderstanding among Union officers, a vedette had been removed from the line, leaving a gap between Gillmore's extreme
left post and the right of the First Pennsylvania Cavalry pickets. Through that little break in the chain the Partisans had
crawled, one at a time, and had reassembled at the rear of the
tents. "The reports furnished and examinations made," wrote
General Gregg, "convince me that the officer in command of the
reserve is responsible for the disaster, which resulted from in-
attention and gross neglect of duty. The officers and enlisted
men responsible will be brought to trial." [2]

Near the end of the severe storm that left nearly a foot of
snow on the ground, a courier rode into Mosby's Confederacy
with an important message. He said Stringfellow had spied
around Harper's Ferry and had found a vulnerable spot for the
Rangers to strike. The Maryland cavalry camp on Loudoun
Heights was in such position that it could be taken at night.
The surprise, however, must be complete and must be executed
with lightning stroke, so the invaders could flee before support
arrived from the Ferry, a mile distant. This information
sounded attractive on face value, but more appealing was the
fact that the camp was under command of Major Henry A.
Cole. This officer was extremely unpopular with residents of the
border counties.

On Saturday, January 9, Mosby waited for his men at Upperville. They rode up out of the horizon in all directions and approached slowly, alone or in small groups, cutting their own paths across the unbroken expanse. Some had been through massive drifts, as attested by the snow still clinging to the horses' sleek coats. It had been a terrific blizzard. Even now the skies were gray and foreboding, and some of the younger men predicted there would be more snow before night. But the older members shook their heads. Too cold, they said.

By noon, 106 men, made up of about an equal representation from each of the three companies, had arrived. The size of the force seemed to satisfy Mosby and he took the lead as they moved off, striking north. At dusk the cavalcade, bearing anything but a military appearance with its wide assortment of heavy coats, mufflers and boots, stopped at the home of Henry Heaton, well up in Loudoun County. This Ranger had forged ahead to notify his family of the approach of the horde of hungry fighters. When they arrived, fires blazed in every room of the spacious mansion, and downstairs in the large dining room awaited the kind of food best suited to the cold ride ahead.

One, two, three hours passed in quick succession. At last a courier appeared from Stringfellow. The scout, this messenger said, had been over the entire area again and had found everything favorable to attack. He was waiting up near Harper's Ferry with ten men.

Mosby ordered his command into the saddle. It was 9 P.M. The clouds of the morning and afternoon had disappeared, and in their stead had come a clear stillness and a bluish-black canopy dotted by shivering stars.

For hours through the bitter cold the Rangers rode. Each man bore his own troubles; there was no talking. As they trotted along, many held the reins in their teeth and slid their hands under the saddle blankets next to the warm skin of their mounts. Quite a few cut holes for their heads in the center of blankets and draped them like tents over their shoulders. Now and then some of them, to get their blood in circulation, dropped stiffly from the saddle and trotted along in the spray of fine snow kicked up by the horses' muffled hoofs.

Some time in the aching hours of early morning, Mosby halted and ordered fires built. John Underwood and others accustomed to the forest scattered through the trees, feeling for sticks and underbrush. In a few seconds, the wood was crackling and sizzling. Raiders pushed up to the flames in relays. Smith and William Chapman found themselves side by side. Smith brought out a beautiful gold watch, snapped open its case and peeped at the dial. A birthday gift from his wife, he announced proudly to Chapman.

After another ride that seemed interminable, the courier who had come in at Heaton's led them to a sheltered spot on the Potomac River, a mile and a half below Harper's Ferry, where Stringfellow and his party waited. Thus reinforced, the Partisans traveled northwestward along the bank of the stream toward the Ferry. It was nearing the dead hour of morning and the cold had reached its severest stage. Clear and white stretched the frozen river. At one point along the way, sentries could be seen passing back and forth against fires blazing on the opposite shore. Mosby had made no announcement of his plans, and some of his raiders thought this camp across the river was the object of their expedition. But shortly afterward, when a locomotive whistle came in a long, lonesome blast, they supposed it was the train they were after.

Harper's Ferry had received rough treatment during the war. It had passed back and forth, from one army to the other, and its arsenal had been destroyed. Now in the hands of the Federals, it had been fortified to a high degree and was garrisoned by both cavalry and infantry. Rising high above it on the north was Maryland Heights, a bluff covered with trees and undergrowth, and on the Virginia side, where the Shenandoah empties into the Potomac, another spur of the Blue Ridge, Loudoun Heights, jutting up equally as towering. Stringfellow steered the Rangers toward these mountain bulwarks visible against the stars. Near a bridge across a small stream where he knew pickets were stationed, he turned off to the left, then led the way into a dense pine thicket for about 200 yards to the bridge across the Shenandoah River. Stringfellow said it

was Cole's headquarters they could see on the left of the road—
a tall, bulky frame building—and that the camp was beyond it.

The party moved out of the thicket, advanced farther to the
left and halted at the base of a wooded cliff, which they must
scale to reach the camp. Men were allowed to close up and
then, one by one, leading their horses, they began to climb.
Often they floundered in the snow and clung desperately to
bushes and other objects that gave them a handhold. There
was no noise beyond the snorts of the animals and the heavy
breathing of the men.

Mosby was among the first to make the climb. At the crest
he found just enough room for his raiders to wedge in between
the first row of tents and the cliff. Leaving Smith to hurry the
remainder of the force up the hazardous route, he set off in a
half run to scout the camp, moving stealthily and silently. In a
few minutes he was back. Over the entire camp he had found
nothing but sleeping men. Except for the snores of the snugly-
wrapped Federals, the entire plateau was as quiet as a tomb.

All the raiders were up by this time, ready for action, and
Mosby was confident capture of the camp was a certainty. Up
to dark, Stringfellow had been able to determine that between
175 and 200 men were on duty there. This would be a victory
worth all the torture they had suffered to bring it about.

From back along the mountain side, the wind came in a low
moan, kicking up runners of snow and sending them scurrying
in and out like field mice along the rows of tents. A canvas flap
near the waiting men broke loose and slapped futilely in the
dying gust, then fitted back into the deathly stillness.

The wiry leader glanced once more through the camp, white
and ghostly in the darkness. He turned to his lieutenants. One
by one they moved off to execute his orders—Stringfellow and
ten men to surround the house on the point of the hill and to
capture Major Cole and his staff; Captain Smith and party to
secure the horses and mules; Montjoy, with six men, to capture
the picket they had avoided at the bridge on the way in, while
the leader attacked the camp with the remainder of the men.

The blankets with holes in their centers were lifted from the
shoulders of the men and strapped behind saddles. Mufflers and

overcoats were loosened. Tingling fingers, partly paralyzed with cold, were drawn reluctantly from gloves and fitted against the steel chill of revolvers. The torture seemed less severe to the Rangers in their excitement.

While he waited for the various parties to reach their destinations, Mosby dismounted a number of the men left with him and scattered them through the camp, ready to grab the surprised Yankees when they darted, sleepy-eyed, out of their cots. In a few minutes his entire force was stationed, revolvers ready, their eyes on the line of tents. The other parties must be almost in place.

Then, suddenly, like a clap of thunder, a shot sounded, startlingly loud, sharp and cutting. It came from the direction Stringfellow had taken.

Cause of the blast was never established definitely. In front of the stable where the officers' horses were quartered were several army wagons to which had been tied a number of mules. Perhaps the raiders who went after this prize spoke too loud. Perhaps there was someone awake at headquarters. Perhaps Stringfellow's men deserted him after they entered Cole's quarters. Perhaps a numbed finger pressed too tightly on a sensitive trigger. Perhaps someone in the tents was awake. The real answer, more likely, was snuffed out with the lives of men who fell during the furious fighting of the next few minutes.

Immediately following the shot, Mosby and the men with him waited in breathless suspense. Then over the hill from headquarters came horsemen, charging wildly. They were from Stringfellow's party, but their identity was blacked out by the darkness. The Rangers poured a deadly fire at them, wounding and killing six before the mistake was discovered.

Like a flash now the camp came to life. Gun barrels appeared out of tent flaps and fired their death loads in the dark. Along the tent rows the furore was picked up and increased. "Fire at every man on horseback!" "Men, do not take to your horses!" "Fire the tents and shoot 'em by the light!"

Frightened Federals, seeking the explanation of this sudden interruption to their sleep, dashed out into the snow and were shot at, or found their comrades and formed behind some bar-

rier to blaze away with their carbines at the unidentified attackers. Some ran into the bushes on the mountain side and
from there poured a deadly fire into the camp.

The voices of Mosby, Smith, Turner, Chapman and others
could be heard in the confusion, shouting for their men to
charge. The fire became hotter. Tents were riddled with bullets. Figures, in gray and in blue, lay about, some in pools of
blood; others tried to crawl to safety, Turner among them.
Someone found him, got help, dragged him away.

Federal fire was coming now from the headquarters buildings and the barns. Captain Vernon of Cole's battalion rallied
the Yankee cavalry at one side of the camp and set up a stiff
resistance. Mosby felt it, felt the disadvantage under which his
men were fighting, saw them firing at each other in the confusion.

The signal gun on the heights sounded. In a few minutes, reinforcements from the thousands of infantry troops at Harper's
Ferry would be on them. Mosby realized that longer resistance
was useless. In a shrill voice he called for a retreat toward
Hillsboro.

But his cry did not reach all the Rangers. Some of them could
hear only the pleas of their wounded comrades. Fount Beattie
was down, crawling on the ground, with the second wound of
his Partisan career. So were Charlie Paxson and William E.
Colston, both just back from sick leave, both fatally wounded.
So were others. John Robinson, Scotchman and ex-captain in
the English army, was dead. Near by, dying, lay Joseph W.
Owens.

Chapman rushed back into the camp. He had the idea Mosby
was in there wounded. He spied Captain Smith on horseback,
carrying away Henry Edmonds. "Come on!" shouted Chapman.
"Mosby's in there—let's get him!"

Edmonds was left with another Ranger, and the two rode
back. They recognized Lieutenant Gray and three others, including John Tyler Grayson, at one corner of the camp. Grayson joined them. The firing had shifted to the rear of the camp,
next to the mountain, where the Federals were making a stand
in the bushes, up where Captain Vernon of Cole's cavalry lay

helpless with a serious wound in the head. Charlie Paxson spied the trio. "You're not going to leave me here!" he called. Grayson turned back to get an extra horse. Just then, from a near-by tent, a shot was fired. Smith and Chapman returned it. A Yankee sergeant gripped his carbine. He dropped to his knees, raised his piece, pushed aside the tent flap and pulled the trigger without aim. Smith leaped suddenly up from his saddle and fell from the right side. Both feet were caught in the stirrups and his head dangled in the snow in a pool of blood.

Chapman sprang from his horse and called to his comrade, but there was no answer. He endeavored to lift Smith into the saddle: the wounded man was too heavy. Then he thought of the birthday watch and fumbled in the overcoat for the pocket where it was kept. His numb fingers could not loosen a single button. He knocked Smith's feet from the stirrups and led his horse out of the camp. He found Gray and asked him to help recover Smith's body and look for Mosby. Gray said Mosby had ordered a retreat and that they were the only men left. The pair galloped after the retreating Rangers.

Federals quickly formed pursuit. As dawn broke, they easily picked up the trail of Rebel horses in the snow and rode at a gallop. Up along the Shenandoah River, miles above where it empties into the Potomac at Harper's Ferry, the maze of tracks led. Union riders presumed they were getting nearer their quarry. But suddenly the hoof prints swung down the bank to the edge of the water, at a point directly across from a high cliff. There the pursuit ended. Search along each side of the stream failed to reveal the spot where the Loudoun Heights raiders had emerged.

14

A Bearded Enemy Arrives

N O SETBACK IN MOSBY'S CAREER had been or would be as
costly as that at Loudoun Heights.[1] In his report of the
affair a few days later, he revealed that he had come away with
six prisoners and between fifty and sixty horses. But he added
that his own loss was severe, "more so in the worth than the
number of slain." He listed four killed, seven wounded, of
whom four later died, and one captured. His casualties included two of his three commanding officers—Smith and
Turner. They were among his veterans, his choice of the ablest
fighters of his command. In many of his reports, particularly
of late, they had been lauded by him directly and through cita-
tion of their accomplishments.

Along with other champions of the Forty-third Battalion,
Stuart feared the effect the outcome at Loudoun Heights would
have on Mosby's operations. To offset the worst, he attached to
the report an indorsement rich with praise, concluding:

"Since I first knew him, in 1861, he has never once alluded
to his own rank or promotion; thus far it has come by the force
of his own merit. While self-consciousness of having done his
duty well is the patriot soldier's best reward, yet the evidence
of the appreciation of his country is a powerful incentive to renewed effort, which should not be undervalued by those who
have risen to the highest point of military and civic eminence.
That evidence is promotion. If Major Mosby has not won it, no
more can daring deeds essay to do it."

With the Confederacy at low ebb and war activity paralyzed

by cold and mud of winter, Southern military leaders suddenly swung from the gunfire of the battlefront to the verbal fire of criticism. Their disapproval was aimed at the myriad Rebel bands which had sprung up and were plying back and forth with reckless abandon between the two main armies. These little groups brought to the service a generally bad influence that began to outweigh their amazing accomplishments.

When the Partisan Ranger Law had been adopted by the Confederate Congress, a certain romance was in the air. Guerrilla warfare was looked on as symbolic of Southern independence and courage, a dash of the chivalry of plantation aristocracy. To hear sons of families well established in history say in '61 and '62 that they planned to set up their own commands was recognized as an outburst of the elan handed down by cavalier ancestors. It was the fine and proper thing to do. Legend running well back into the centuries, repeated over and over in story book and fairy tale, told of similar courage by men of all races and creeds. Fable had awarded them an enviable niche in the hall of fame.

But the tide changed. The war that was to have lasted only a few months stretched into years, and the Northern blockade began to choke the South. The romance of the great adventure paled in the wake of a losing cause. Men who tramped through the dust of summer and the mud of winter under strict regular army routine began to look longingly off toward the independent bands pillaging and plundering to their own personal gain. Out there was excitement and adventure they themselves had expected in the ranks. As food became scarce the situation became worse. Soldiers went home on furlough to find their families starving. Desperately aroused to a sense of self-preservation that overshadowed their patriotism, they returned to join up with some guerrilla chieftain, to place themselves in line for the contraband prizes which would help dependents left behind.

General Lee noticed this gradual desertion from the regular service. He knew his great army was dwindling, that something must be done. When he got word that some of his soldiers had been drafted into Morgan's command while they were at Richmond, he wrote President Davis that "you will see if this conduct is allowed that all discipline is destroyed and our armies will be ruined." [2]

Before this there had been criticism of irregular activities—during the preceding August especially, when newspapers had announced that Yankee plunder sold by Mosby and his men at Charlottesville had brought $30,000. War Secretary Seddon immediately launched an investigation, and Lee censured the Partisan for operating with so few men and centering his attention on the capture of sutlers' wagons rather than injury to the enemy's communications. Earlier, the commander had written Stuart that he feared Mosby exercised too little control over his men.

Still other adverse attention to the raider's activities had been brought by a newspaper correspondent who observed that "Mosby is doing much good in his present sphere, and though he eminently deserves it, it is feared his usefulness may be spoiled by too rapid promotion." [3] This had stimulated response citing the Partisan's early refusal to accept a commission and his recent acceptance of one primarily at the suggestion of Stuart.

But it was left to Brigadier-General Thomas L. Rosser, commanding the Valley District, to give the most thorough statement of the case against independent warfare as the regulars saw it. [4] He was stationed in a section through which were operating a number of these little bands, and he could see the direct effect of their alluring activity. His complaint, worded in a letter to General Lee, termed the irregular outfits a nuisance and an evil to the service. "Without discipline, order or organization," he charged, "they roam broadcast over the country, a band of thieves, stealing, pillaging, plundering and doing every manner of mischief and crime. They are a terror to the citizens and an injury to the cause. They never fight; can't be made to fight. Their leaders are generally brave, but few of the men are good soldiers and have engaged in this business for the sake of gain."

Rosser's letter passed all the way up the line to the head of the Confederate War Department and drew varying comment as it advanced. Stuart, the man who had given Mosby his start, said the Forty-third Battalion was the only efficient band of Rangers he knew of, but added criticism might be due the Partisan leader for operating with only a fourth of his nominal strength. "Such organizations, as a rule," he admitted, "are detrimental to the best interest of the army at large." General Lee struck at the matter broadside: "As far as my knowledge and experience extends, there is much truth in the statement of General Rosser. I recommend that the law authorizing these Partisan corps be abolished. The evils resulting from their organization more than counterbalance the good they accomplish."

Things looked bad for Mosby. In short order, the Confederate Congress, acting on recommendation of the best military advice, did away with the bill authorizing independent warfare. The repeal was drafted by Secretary of War Seddon.

Complying with the act, General Lee prepared a list of all recognized Partisan bands operating as a part of the Confederate service: the Fourth and Fifth North Carolina Cavalry, then in North Carolina; Mosby's battalion; Captain Kincheloe's company, in Prince William; Captain McNeill's company, Major Gilmore's battalion and Major O'Farrell's battalion, in the Valley District. Of these he recommended all be disbanded except one. "I am making," he said of this one, "an effort to have ... Mosby's battalion mustered into the regular service. If this cannot be done, I recommend that this battalion be retained as Partisans for the present. . . . Mosby has done excellent service, and from the reports of citizens and others I am inclined to believe that he is strict in discipline and a protection to the country in which he operates." Seddon agreed with Lee's recommendations in all but one respect. He preferred, and so ordered, that McNeill's command also be retained.

There was considerable foresight in Lee's recommendation. With him, it developed, rested the life of the Forty-third Battalion—and a six-month extension of the life of the Confederate cause. Lincoln and Stanton and Grant and Sheridan would have had a much simpler problem to deal with had there been no enemy force in Northern Virginia.

On February 1, the very day Congress was preparing to consider the bill that would mean the death knell of most Partisan Ranger organizations, Mosby prepared a report of his January operations. It was his last act before setting out on a brief visit to his family, staying then at Charlottesville, and to Richmond, where he had business pertaining to the move to dismember his command.

Some of the horses and mules mentioned in the report as captured had reached the Partisans in unorthodox fashion. At 1 o'clock in the morning a party of fifteen Rangers had moved to the outskirts of a camp near Vienna. Three times they slipped into the unguarded stables and brought out animals before Baron von Massow, Prussian lieutenant who recently had come to Mosby with letters of recommendation from Stuart, broke up the night's fun with the remark: "Ah, this is not fighting; it's horse stealing."

On February 11, Jeb Stuart, ever the gallant, wrote a brief note to "Mrs. Lieutenant-Colonel Mosby." In it he said: "I enclose your husband's commission with my congratulations." He also made brief reference to the generous aid Mosby was giving the Confederate transportation service—"Tell him his horses are doing finely." [5] The promotion had been sought for Mosby by both Stuart and Lee, and was referred to several times in their indorsements of his reports.

Mosby returned from Richmond late on the afternoon of the 18th. He had visited briefly at the capital, and on his way back had stopped along the Rapidan to talk with Stuart. There is no record of what went on at this meeting. It was their last.

The sun had set when the raider rode up to the Joe Blackwell home near Piedmont, recognized as his headquarters since repeated Yankee invasions had driven him away from the Hathaway place. The owner of the new hangout, a big-bodied planter affectionately called "The Chief" by Rangers, had lost his entire collection of slaves soon after the Federals took over Northern Virginia. He now had only one farm hand, a toothless Irishman and former road-crossing flagman named Lat Ryan. This rheumatic-stricken native of Limerick, Ireland, spent most of his time fussing at Mosby's Negro Aaron, who in turn was preoccupied day and night by fears that the Yankees considered his capture next in importance to that of his master. Mosby had had much trouble with the old servant since the first year of the war. His chores were confined almost exclusively to care of the raider's horses, but Aaron definitely was not a military-minded slave. When a shell wrecked a tree above his head in late '62, he fled all the way to Lynchburg, and it took months to get him back. More recently, two Rangers had turned his hair a shade whiter by dashing into the barnyard with pistols blazing, shouting to high heaven, "The Yanks are coming!" Aaron cleared a fence on the bare back of one of his master's best steeds. It was hours later, well after dark, when his cautious tap sounded on the back door.

The leader's return was followed by two fights in quick succession. At Blakeley's Grove, climaxing a running battle that lasted for hours, the Rangers routed a large force of Federals from Cole's command at Harper's Ferry. Two days later, Mosby concealed his band near Dranesville and fell upon a part of the Second Massachusetts Cavalry with such force that some of the enemy riders galloped into the near-by Potomac and were drowned. Mosby lost two men—J. Pendleton Chappelear, native of Upper Fauquier, killed on his first ride with the battalion, and Baron von Massow, out with wounds for the remainder of the war.

Something portentous to Mosby's men occurred in the ranks of the enemy on March 10. In a steady rain, a shabby man with a cigar half buried in his black beard rode up to General Meade's headquarters and alighted. It was Lieutenant-General Ulysses S. Grant, a soldier the Federal army had heard much about. He had come as another organizer of victory to take command of all Union forces. For the present he would remain with the Army of the Potomac.

There were other changes in Federal leadership at this time. Pleasanton was relieved of command of the cavalry corps and sent west. In his place stepped Major-General Phil Sheridan, about whom men in the ranks knew next to nothing. He was a Westerner, a division general of infantry, a short-legged, long-armed man with bullet head and black eyes. His uniform was worn, his hat deplorable. He was one man who did not wear his military prowess on his sleeve.

These were the men on whom the North pinned its newest hopes for quick annihilation of the South during '64. They were experienced leaders, well trained, accustomed to exerting powerful force and drive against the enemy. But before the year was out they would look over their shoulders, alarmed at the activities of a fearless band at their rear.

For instance, a few weeks after the new commander came into power, Burnside's troops were moving southward toward the Rapidan and Germanna and Ely's Ford, where Confederate eyes were watching for the first major action to begin. As the Federal column passed through Centerville, Mosby's band watched curiously from a point a mile off. Later in the day, some distance west of the Orange and Alexandria railroad, a small force of Federal cavalry suddenly awakened to the fact that Rebel horsemen were coming up fast on their heels. Someone said it was Mosby, and the blue-clad riders spurred their mounts frantically in an effort to get away. Capture is bad enough at the hands of any foe, worse when mere mention of the name of the foe strikes fear and paralysis in the heart of the captive.

It was a warm spring day, lovely to ride in even in time of war. The ground had dried from recent rains, and underfoot the light soil, made lighter by the winter thawing, pulverized easily and rose up in dust clouds more characteristic of the sizzling days of summer. There was scattered firing from the rear, causing the Federals to sink their spurs deeper into the flanks of their horses. They rode like mad, heads down. It had become a joke the way Mosby made easy prey of the Yankees, rode circles around them, and then outdistanced them with their own horses when they came back in pursuit.

The flight headed directly for the railroad. Forests to the east of the line were heavier, more irregular; roads were fewer, the terrain tougher. Perhaps there would be more chance for escape in that direction. The Blue riders leaped their horses over the tracks at Warrenton Junction and kept going, lying low in the saddle. Behind them, closing up, came Mosby's irregulars, shouting and having fun.

Shortly after the two bands of horsemen passed the junction, the smoke of a train broke the horizon to the north. It chugged along steadily, rocking with the unevenness of the track leading up to the blackened ashes which had been the station before Mosby had tied up with the First Virginia and Fifth New York Cavalry there the preceding May. Near the ruins, the smoke pouring from the stack of the locomotive blackened and swelled in volume, brakes screeched and the wheels of the train came to a grinding halt. On the steps of one of the coaches stood a small, black-bearded man with a stub of cigar protruding from his beard. He held to the rail with one hand and shaded his eyes against the glare of the east with the other.

"What is that cloud of dust?" he asked of an overalled rustic squatting in the sun at the junction.

"Mosby—chasin' Yanks," answered the countryman.

The man on the steps waved to the engineer and the train carrying Grant from a conference with Lincoln back to put his army in motion for the campaign of '64 pulled ahead. Had its arrival at Warrenton Junction been only a few minutes earlier, events now written in history as a part of America's civil war might have been changed. The train was a special, without guard.[6]

Late in March Mosby rode through the valley on reconnaissance. Among things he learned was that Milroy had been placed in command at Harper's Ferry. Moreover, citizens along the way informed him it was their impression a movement up the valley was contemplated. This information he passed on to Stuart for what it was worth, making no mention, if he knew, that it was hint of a master plan then taking shape in the mind of the new commander of the Union army. Grant was laying the foundation for the complicated campaign by which he hoped to wind up the war. General Franz Sigel, according to his scheme, would sweep down the valley, clear it of Confederates and cut the Virginia Central railroad somewhere around Charlottesville. At the same time, General Crook would advance from the Kanawha Valley into Southwest Virginia and destroy the Virginia and Tennessee line below Lynchburg. Meanwhile, in the eastern part of the state, General Butler would move up the James, cut communications south of Richmond and threaten that city. And as a final stroke, Grant himself would advance on Richmond from the north, cross the Rappahannock above Fredericksburg and hammer at Lee until the Army of Northern Virginia was destroyed.

After Mosby's return from the valley, the command met at Paris and organized Company D. In the customary election of officers, Montjoy, the Mississippian who was setting an enviable record as a fighter, was named captain. The slate of other officers remained intact only a short while. Scarcely had it been chosen before word came of the death of William Trundle, third lieutenant, killed while scouting near Martinsburg.

There is no accurate record of the number of men Mosby had at this time. The customary minimum company enrollment was sixty and, on this basis, the four units of his command would have given him approximately 240. Perhaps there were more, and it is just as likely there were fewer. It is reasonable to believe that, even if he had this many, only a portion of them ever were on hand for an assembly. Mosby and his lieutenants frequently asserted that all of the Rangers never got together at one time. But the North never could clear its uncertainty regarding the strength of the Forty-third Battalion and variously overestimated it. Colonel J. W. Fisher, searching for Rangers with 234 men from the Thirteenth Pennsylvania Cavalry, gave up as he neared the mountain passes beyond Aldie because he had come to the conclusion that "we have not sufficient cavalry forces attached to the division to drive Mosby out of the country." [7]

Toward the end of April a woman rode into Washington with a lock of sandy hair for Abraham Lincoln. She said it had come from the head of Mosby. He had cut off the hair himself, she related, asking that it be presented to the President with notice that the Partisan leader would be in the capital shortly to make Lincoln's personal acquaintance. She said he also asked her to tell Governor Pierpont that he was obliged to him for liber-

15

"The Chance was Lost"

———～～～———

SIGEL PUT HIS TROOPS IN MOTION on May 2 and moved toward Winchester and Strasburg, putting Grant's plans in action. Mosby was waiting for this movement. Lee had urged that he coöperate with General John B. Imboden, Confederate cavalry leader stationed in the valley, in the harassment of this column. Two Partisan detachments were sent to do the work and, in the next four days, they struck at several points, capturing both men and horses.

In the meantime Mosby was doing an even better job against communications of General Grant, preparing then to start his own phase of the offensive against Lee by crossing his army at Germanna and Ely's Fords. Near Belle Plain in King George County, the raider fell on one of Grant's ambulance trains and brought off forty prisoners and seventy-five horses and mules. It was a highly successful maneuver. Coming up on the string of vehicles in the dusk after burning several bridges, Mosby counted ten wagons from the rear, sent Lieutenant Grogan to turn them off at a side road and directed Ben Palmer, with another detail, to circle through the woods to the head of the train and capture the remainder. Grogan and Palmer moved away. Mosby, following the train with a few men, noticed at last that the rear wagons had taken a road to the left. Soon a Federal officer rode back.

"Who the hell turned those wagons off?" demanded the officer in the twilight.

"Colonel Mosby," quietly answered a Ranger, advancing to take the Federal's side arms.

Sigel was having major difficulties on his advance down the valley. Imboden, McNeill and other Confederates were at his heels and the victory march he had planned was not working out. He could maintain no effective guard against these bands that were constantly leaping at him without warning, allowing him no time to prepare for their blow. He pushed on, past Strasburg, past Woodstock, Edenburg, Mt. Jackson. During the 14th and night of the 14th-15th, there was cavalry skirmishing at Rude's Hill and New Market. On the morning of the 15th, two miles below New Market, Sigel stopped. Facing him was General Breckinridge with two brigades and a battalion of infantry, as well as the cadet corps from the Virginia Military Institute, saved by Lee for just such an emergency. There was spirited fighting, tempered on the Confederate side by the valor of the few hundred beardless cadets, and Sigel gave way in a rout similar to those Stonewall Jackson had created in the valley in '62. The Federals retreated to Strasburg and drew up behind Cedar Creek. While they waited, Sigel was replaced by General David Hunter.

In the midst of their celebration over the Confederate success, bad news came to Mosby and his men. It was several days old when it finally worked back into their mountain hideouts. A bullet from the revolver of an anonymous Federal sergeant had cut the Partisan chieftain's main tie with the regular army, had taken the life of the man who had been his champion from the start. The golden-voiced, brown-bearded Jeb Stuart had been mortally wounded in battle at Yellow Tavern near Richmond.

Newspaper reports gave notice on the 25th that the infantry troops on the outer Washington defenses had contracted their lines under orders from headquarters. They said that all government property in the neighborhood of Fairfax Court House had been moved, although a brigade of Massachusetts cavalry still was on duty there. Two days later they announced that as troops were removed "guerrillas stepped in to renew their depredations." [1]

June arrived, and its early days brought more news after the
fashion of May 11, the day Stuart fell. Near Port Republic on
the 5th, well down the valley, a force of 6,000 Confederates
braced themselves to stop Hunter, who had got Sigel's army
back in fighting mood and now was advancing on Staunton.
The battle lasted all morning and afternoon under a broiling
sun. As night drew on, the Gray army was routed. It had looked
like a Rebel victory as the middle of the day passed; then the
commander of the Southerners indiscreetly ran into the hot-
test of the fight to rally some of his troopers. He cursed violently above the tumult and fell in the dust, dead from a bullet
that allowed no suffering. Like Stuart, another of the South's
great cavalry leaders, Grumble Jones had gone to his reward
in the heat of battle.

Little attention was given a dilapidated farm wagon, partly
filled with hay, that rolled one day during the middle of June
through the environs of Alexandria. On the driver's seat, cluck-
ing to the team of thin, emaciated horses, sat an aged farmer,
wrinkled and stooped, signifying plainly by the gray of his head
his exemption from service as a fighter. Pickets let him pass. He
told them he wanted to sell his hay, and there was proof enough
of need for the few pennies it might bring.

Slowly toward the heart of town the vehicle creaked. It
was forgotten by the Federal guard the moment it rolled out of
sight. To them it was too harmless a contraption to be connected with war.

It took a business street farther along and threaded its way
among larger and more prosperous vehicles without creating
more than passing attention. The driver sat with elbows on
knees, occasionally flecking the flanks of his animals with a
small willow switch. Amusing to those who noticed was the
chatter he kept up constantly between stops. It was a jumble
of thoughts: "Git on here, Lucy, an' you, Elmira. Behave
yo'selves. ... You gotta perk up now folks is a-lookin' at you.
Alexander's a right piert town. ... This here's King Street we're
on. We're rollin' fine now, gittin' 'long toward the river. ...
Them's the ruins of the newspaper office, burned when the war

fust broke out, an' we're a-comin' to the Ramsay house. Some say hit's the oldest place in Alexander, an' I reckon 'tis. That high buildin' next the river thar is the City Hotel, where most visitors stop."

The wagon rolled and jolted over the rough, dusty street, casting a strong shadow in the warm sun. A block or two farther on, in front of the building identified as the hotel, the driver clucked to the horses, straightened slowly and raised an arm as if he were stretching.

"This here's the City Hotel. Used to be a fine place, much nicer'n 'tis now. I hear tell thar's whar Guvner Pierpont is a-stayin'. . . . Giddap, Lucy. Quit yo' foolin', Elmira. Move 'long now."

Late that afternoon Mosby, riding alone out of the dusk, met thirty-five picked men from his battalion in a body of pines near Alexandria. He swung agilely from his horse and dropped to the soft needle floor. Rangers gathered around him. He had worked out his plans at last, he announced. He and a few companions would drive the next night to a picket post on the outskirts of Alexandria in a covered market wagon. There would be three detachments after they got inside the town: the first, under his leadership, would go after Pierpont; another would visit General John P. Slough, military governor, and the third would go to the stables and round up all available horses. Next day they hovered in the pines, waiting, excited and impatient. It would be the biggest stroke since Stoughton. How Virginians would laugh when they heard the bogus governor who had set up domain within the state's borders had been kidnapped from his bed.

But this plot was not for execution. Toward night a civilian of Rebel sympathies, apprised of the raiders' presence, returned from Alexandria with incredible news: the Federals in some manner had learned of the plan to capture Pierpont and had fortified each guard detail strongly.

Mosby was keenly disappointed. He had enjoyed mental pictures of Pierpont and Slough riding together through the night as prisoners. But in the face of the unexpected development, he bowed to wisdom. He ordered his men back to Fauquier and, before setting out after them, gave the civilian this written message handed to Pierpont the following day:

"You did not see the farmer who rode by your hotel on a wagon yesterday, did you, Governor? My driver pointed out your window, and I marked it plain. It's just over the bay, and I'll get you some night, mighty easy." [2]

Now, with the summer campaign fully under way, attacks by Mosby's raiders came in rapid succession. On June 24, a scouting party of Sixteenth New York Cavalry was surprised while eating cherries from a tree near Centerville and all but a few taken prisoner. Five days later, with a little mountain howitzer brought in as successor to the piece lost at Catlett's Station, Mosby captured and burned the little military depot of Duffield Station on the Baltimore and Ohio railroad a few miles from Charles Town. This was accomplished without firing a shot after a demand for unconditional surrender had been sent in under flag of truce. The guide on this expedition was John S. Russell, slim, twenty-year-old Irish youth thoroughly acquainted with the Shenandoah Valley. His arrival in the ranks of the Forty-third Battalion filled out a scouting staff already made up of three brothers, John, Sam and Bush Underwood, experts on the area around Washington, and Walter Bowie, authority on Maryland.

Federals on lookout at Harper's Ferry the last of June spied a cloud of dust along a road leading to the Shenandoah River and were unable to determine its origin. A strong detail was sent to investigate. It learned the dust came from a drove of captured Union horses on the way to Mosby's Confederacy. Pursuit was pushed furiously, but was of short duration. The trail ended at the river, directly across from a high, steep cliff.

Into a group of Rangers loitering at Rectortown the afternoon of July 2, Hugh Swartz of General Early's quartermaster department trotted with a cheering bit of news. Early had stopped Hunter at Lynchburg, and now both armies were on their way north, the Federals by way of the Kanawha River basin and the Confederates directly up the valley. The Rebel move was another of Lee's feints. If Early could spread terror in the North, Grant would be forced either to detach a large part of his army for the defense of Washington or to attack Lee in the hope of compelling the recall of Early.

Acting in sympathy with Early, Mosby struck with 150 Rangers and a twelve-pounder Napoleon at Point of Rocks on the Potomac two days later. In a fierce attack that continued along the bank of the river and up the mountain side above the town, he routed the entire Federal battalion on duty there, estimated at 250 men, including two companies of Loudoun Rangers. Store houses and a canal boat were burned, and a train approaching from the west was fired on and driven back.

Mosby's presence across the river caused much confusion. Next day, while enemy reinforcements were racing from Washington, he kept a part of his men on the Virginia side of the Potomac riding in a circle over the brow of a hill and back around behind it out of sight of the Point to give a false appearance of strength. That night he retired, but not to rest. He heard that 100 men from the Second Massachusetts Cavalry and fifty from the Thirteenth New York Cavalry were out searching for him under command of Major William S. Forbes, one of the best fighters opposing the Rangers. Mosby met this force the following day at Mount Zion Church. He still had ninety Raiders with him, sixty having been sent back from Point of Rocks with five wagons of plunder.

Mosby acted with extreme caution when he came in sight of Forbes. Sam Chapman was ordered to roll the artillery piece to the front of the column, and a few men with carbines were stationed beside it, to check with long-range firing the advance of the enemy until it could be placed. In this order they slowly proceeded, advancing for a fight under prescribed methods of warfare instead of by the guerrilla tactics they preferred. The ground over which they passed was that on which Mosby had called the first rendezvous of his original fifteen-man command on January 28, '63.

Forbes' troops waited in excellent order. The first two squadrons were formed and ready. The third squadron and rear guard were not in formation, but nearly so. In the first few seconds after the Rangers halted, scarcely a movement could be seen in the enemy ranks. Then Forbes ordered his first platoon to open with carbines. A roar of gunfire followed, strengthened by a few pistol shots from the second squadron. Bullets rained around the Rebels. Rangers fingered their weapons impatiently, looking toward Mosby. He sat his horse at the front, motionless, the plume hanging from his hat as still as if poured of bronze.

In the breathless moment following the gunfire was the tiniest reaction among the Federals. Mosby saw it. Noise of gunfire had frightened the horses, more accustomed to the click of sword on scabbard than to the roar of carbines. Forbes understood their nervousness. It would be better if his men were on foot. He gave a quick order: the first platoon would move by the right flank and dismount. This was what Mosby was waiting for; it was then he signaled for the charge, giving a shrill blast on a silver whistle he carried on a cord around his neck. Forbes' men, caught off guard while the platoon was executing its flank movement, were thrown into general confusion and scattered.

"I have only to report a perfect rout and a chase for five to seven miles," reported Colonel Lowell after his investigation of the affair.[3] Mosby gave his own losses as one killed and six wounded, listing that of the enemy at sixty-nine killed, wounded and captured. His victory also brought him more than 100 horses. "These horses were well drilled, and of great value to the government," lamented the *Star's* correspondent at Annandale. "Our cavalry had Spencer's repeating rifles, which will also be of material service to Mosby."[4]

Federal reports on the affair could not veil the embarrassment it had caused. "This has been Mosby's bravest and largest capture," wrote one observer. "There is something about it almost unaccountable when we know how efficient this cavalry force has been heretofore, the numerous times they have sought Mosby the past year, and the number of captures we have made." Lowell, the man who had engineered the disastrous expedition, frankly admitted the tables had been turned: "I think the chance was an excellent one to whip Mosby and to take his gun. I have no doubt Major Forbes thought so, too. ... The chance was lost."[5]

16

Berryville Wagon Train Raid

Y OUNG MEN AND WOMEN OF WASHINGTON planned a picnic for July 9 to forget for a brief period the nervous tenseness of the capital. Across the long bridge over the Potomac, up past the fine mansion pointed out as the home of Confederate General Lee, rolled their carriages during the vigorous cool of morning. Near Falls Church they stopped, taking particular care to remain inside the outer defenses, for rumors were growing that Early was advancing on the city. In a shady nook baskets were set out to await the hour of lunch, and games and dancing were started, the more to whet the appetite. But thought of food was banished completely a few minutes later by the appearance of twenty-five horsemen who rode suddenly out of the trees, a majority of them dressed in the flashing gray uniforms and turned-up hats of Mosby's men. Women screamed and men stiffened in a surge of fright. But fears quickly subsided. The Rebels, telling the picnickers not to be afraid, got down and danced a set with the ladies, proving themselves as accustomed to the ballroom floor as to the saddle. Next they turned to the baskets and had their fill. The repast over, they bowed low in gracious appreciation: then rode away as mysteriously as they had come. The male picnickers would have rushed to the near-by forts had not the women, much smitten by the gallantry of the Partisans, shamed them into silence.[1]

The incident was not recorded as an official movement of the Forty-third Battalion. Mosby at the moment was preparing for action of much broader scope. Scarcely had his men cleaned their guns after the rout of Forbes when Henry Heaton, Loudoun County member of Company D, rode in with a message that put them on the warpath again. Acting on his own initiative, Heaton had visited Early, under whom he had served as a staff member in '62, and had been entrusted with a request for the Rangers to go again to the Maryland side of the Potomac, at or near Point of Rocks, to cut railroad and telegraph lines, to send someone into Washington to ascertain the state of things there, and then to wait at Frederick.[2]

Before recrossing the river, Mosby gave attention to commissary demands.[3] The battalion's supply of corn was low and the large number of horses which had moved back and forth across Northern Virginia during the various campaigns had so nibbled forage that there was little to make up for the deficiency. In such case the raider turned for help to the so-called battalion quartermaster department—"Major" Hibbs and his famous corn detail. It was considered nothing short of uncanny the way this grizzled old blacksmith could find, apparently by instinct, the barns of the neighborhood worth raiding, particularly those of Union sympathizers.

On the 11th, things were ready and a dash was made into Maryland. A few blockhouses were burned on the way to Poolesville and the journey was continued in the hope of surrounding the Eighth Illinois Cavalry camp at Seneca. But the enemy had gone when the Rangers arrived next morning. They destroyed buildings and supplies, returning to Virginia that night.

Meanwhile Early had driven off Wallace and arrived in front of Washington. But his stay there was brief: the Sixth Corps and one division of the Nineteenth Corps pushed out in answer to President Lincoln's alarm and drove the Confederates back. On the 14th, the Rebel army withdrew by way of White's Ford above Leesburg and crossed safely to the south side of the Potomac.

Federal reports trace Mosby's movements after his return from Maryland, announcing in one instance that his men had passed Leesburg with 950 head of cattle and that each man was leading a horse. Mosby gives no account of these particular movements in his own reports, but on the 16th he met Early, then falling back to Winchester and Strasburg, at a point between Snicker's Gap and Harper's Ferry. They parted with the understanding that Mosby would do all in his power to protect any movement Early made up the south side of the Potomac.

In the closing days of July the situation suddenly changed. Early found that the reinforcements sent to Washington to drive him off had been ordered to Petersburg, leaving only General Crook, with the combined troops of Hunter and Sigel, to watch him. Promptly he turned about in his retreat. He attacked Crook at Kernstown, forcing him back to Martinsburg and to Harper's Ferry, and with the way thus cleared struck northward into Pennsylvania.

Mosby continued to coöperate. While his men still were operating in several parties, he called them together at Upperville on July 28 and organized his fifth unit, Company E. Lieutenant Sam Chapman, the adjutant and artillery chief, was named captain, and Fountain Beattie, the soldier who had been with Mosby almost constantly since he had left Abingdon in '61, first lieutenant. There were other appointments. Mosby's brother, William H., was assigned to the post of adjutant, and the artillery detail was organized into a separate unit, with Peter A. Franklin, formerly of Company B, as captain.

Early on the morning of July 30, Mosby put his artillery in position at Cheek's and Noland's Fords. A part of the command was kept in reserve and the remainder spread out into lower Maryland on a raid. Telegraph lines were cut and picket posts were attacked, netting seventy-five horses and between twenty and thirty prisoners. Federal officers were deeply chagrined over the expedition. "It is evidently the intention of Mosby to continue his raids upon the railroad when stealing will not pay him better," observed Brigadier-General Tyler, commanding the line along the Monocacy. Major-General Augur sent an exasperated wire from Washington to Major J. M. Waite, commanding at Muddy Branch: "I wish you as fast as possible to get those thieves and marauders out of Maryland."

To headquarters about this time came a message with a lot of good advice from an old Indian fighter—Colonel H. M.

Lazelle, commanding at Falls Church. His theories, he explained, were based on "plain common sense, some little experience in Indian maneuvers, which bears a certain analogy to this warfare," and his own observation.[4] He advised setting up a secret picket line extending out in ambuscade along all roads and paths leading toward the Washington outposts. The old Indian fighter said he could see only two ways in which to cope successfully with "this wily and almost intangible enemy" —occupy the whole country with a commanding force in every district or fight him after his own fashion.

Lazelle's suggestions, given in detail, were tabled for the moment. Something had happened meantime that was hailed in Federal quarters as all that was needed to exterminate Mosby: Grant, in a surprise alteration of command and over the protests of President Lincoln and Secretary of War Stanton, had placed the hardened and bullet-headed fighter, Sheridan, in charge of the cavalry operating against Early.

Sheridan arrived at Washington August 4 and was ordered to report to Grant, who had hurried from the Richmond front to Monocacy Junction because of a dispatch from Lincoln expressing disgust with the confusion along the upper Potomac and indicating the presence of the commander-in-chief was badly needed in the area.[5] Grant ordered the new cavalry chief to concentrate all his available forces without delay in the vicinity of Harper's Ferry, to drive Early out of the territory, detaching at the same time sufficient troops to look after Mosby. "Bear in mind," said Grant, "the object is to drive the enemy south; and to do this you want to keep him always in sight. Be guided in your course by the course he takes." The instructions were clear and reasonable as they applied to Early, but they were confusing in their application to Mosby's raiders, even then lurking on the outskirts of Sheridan's newly-organized command and waiting their chance to attack.

On August 7, the day after he took command, Sheridan's worries started. Reports came in placing the Rangers in several different localities, where it was said they were causing damage and threatening outposts. The 8th passed with more confusing reports. The 9th was quiet, and at 8 o'clock that night

Sheridan wired Augur: "Have heard nothing from Mosby today." But the situation changed before morning. A telegram from Lieutenant-Colonel Wells at Alexandria arrived announcing that "Mosby attacked about sixty of the Sixteenth New York Cavalry near Fairfax Station and whipped them badly."

Lazelle was grossly embarrassed over this repulse of his troops by a Rebel force he learned was outnumbered nearly three to one. "I have nothing to report except disgraceful mismanagement and consequent complete rout of our men," he wrote. "A board of investigation has been called." [6]

On August 10 Sheridan advanced his army from Harper's Ferry toward Early, lying along the west bank of the Opequon and covering Winchester. Next day he moved to secure the fords of the stream between him and the enemy, a step designed to further his march on Winchester from the southeast, thinking Early could be brought to a stand at that point. But Early was not satisfied with the location. He fell back down the valley and took position behind a line of earthworks between Strasburg and Cedar Creek.

While Sheridan was directing these movements, circumstances possibly saved him from the embarrassment that was Stoughton's. Mosby advanced stealthily with a small party one night to the house that had been converted into the Federal general's headquarters.[7] He crawled almost to the ring of campfires around the building and halted until one of his men in Federal uniform, John Hearn, could be sent to learn the strength of the guard. Hearn was challenged by a sentinel and in a hand-to-hand tussle took the fellow's musket away from him. Noise of the scuffle awakened six soldiers asleep on the ground near by and the Ranger narrowly escaped, bringing with him the Yankee's gun. Mosby returned to Fauquier that night.

On the 12th Sheridan sent the Eighth Illinois Cavalry into Loudoun County to search for the Rangers. This was futile effort. The trail there was cold, for Mosby at the moment was moving through Snicker's Gap toward the valley.

At 10:30 A.M. that day the vanguard of a 525-wagon train rolled out of Harper's Ferry in the direction of Sheridan's army. Near the front, in command, rode John R. Kenly, brigadier-general of volunteers. He had one thing on his mind—a para-graph of the orders given him earlier that morning: "It is of importance that the train should reach Winchester as speedily as possible. Commanding officers will be held responsible that no unnecessary delays occur. Should the train be attacked, or any serious obstacle intervene to its march, regimental com-manders will transmit the intelligence promptly to the briga-dier-general commanding, and give to each other support and assistance as may be needed." [8]

Kenly's brigade consisted of three small regiments—the Third Maryland and the 144th and 149th Ohio National Guard. Alto-gether there were around 3,000 men. In the lead marched two companies of Marylanders, followed by the remaining Mary-land companies at intervals of every twenty wagons. Next came the 149th Ohio, distributed on a basis of a company to each thirty wagons. The 144th Ohio stationed two companies behind the rearmost wagon and spaced the remaining units at intervals of twenty wagons, counting from the rear.

Gradually the train got under way. It was in five sections, carrying in order supplies of the Sixth Army Corps, the Nine-teenth Army Corps, the Army of West Virginia, the Second Brigade of the Cavalry Corps and the Third Brigade Cavalry Reserve. Some delay occurred at first in starting the wagons, and then there was difficulty in keeping them closed up. More-over, a herd of cattle plodding along at the rear chewed their cuds and stubbornly refused to hurry. By mid-afternoon, a long, lazy cloud of dust crawled over the road toward Berryville. It hovered for two and a half hours at a given point, and at the end of that period it seemed to deflate over the fields in a broad belt of yellowish-orange.

Noise made by this great shipment of military supplies echoed for miles. It came as a throaty roar of thudding hoofs, squeaking leather and clattering metal. Mules brayed up and down the line. Wagons rumbled and axles knocked. Officers and teamsters, threatening penalties, swore violently in a futile effort to make their charges move faster. Then, if never before, it was learned that a string of 525 wagons can not be made to roll at a uniform speed.

Kenly, not so encumbered as the officers farther down the line, pushed on, now and then sending couriers to learn why the train could not be kept closed up. The sun grew hotter and wagons moved slower. Men and horses were coated with dust. Dark streaks of caked mud marked the trail of perspiration down face and flank. There was no relief from the road or the weather. The dust cloud shut in the heat around the wagons, and there it hung and stifled and roiled.

Sundown arrived, and both the guard and teamsters began to wonder when a halt would be called. Kenly gave no indication of his plans. He rode steadily forward. This was a great responsibility under which he strained. Sheridan lay between him and Early, but somewhere out there in the dark might be lurking Mosby and his bloodthirsty raiders. Newspapers had been notified by their correspondents at Harper's Ferry that his band was hanging on the rear of Federal columns and annoying them by picking up stragglers and information. The nearer Kenly got to the Army of the Shenandoah the better he felt.

Nine o'clock came and the wagons still rolled. Another hour passed. The head of the train was on the last lap to Berryville. At 11 o'clock Kenly stopped at a small creek a mile from the town and ordered the train to go into park long enough to water the animals and make coffee for the men. Steadily the wagons rumbled in and followed each other to a halting place. The Sixth Corps section parked on the right side of the road, that of the Nineteenth Corps on the left. Kenly pointed out where the others were to stop as they arrived.

Soon a myriad of campfires blazed between the lines of vehicles. The smell of water wafted up tantalizingly from the creek bed to dry, dust-coated nostrils. Hot tongues rasped in sticky foam and a great uproar told of the temper of the hungry, thirsty animals. They stamped and bellowed and shook off white beards that clung to their chins like molasses. Time passed and more wagons arrived. As they rolled in in ever increasing numbers, the din was magnified until it sounded like the granddaddy of infernos.

Between midnight and 1 A.M., the Sixth Corps section moved out, even before the cavalry train appeared. As the wagons began to rumble off into the darkness, Kenly rode back to Captain J. C. Mann, quartermaster of the First Division, Nineteenth Army Corps. "I consider this the most dangerous point in the route," he announced. "I desire you to remain here, therefore, until every wagon has passed." [9]

By 2 A.M., the Nineteenth Corps section had gone and that of the Army of West Virginia was beginning to move. Some time later, the chief wagon master reported to Mann that the cavalry trains had come in, their wagons had been unhooked and their stock was being fed. There had been much delay on the road, he said, because of the inexperience of the drivers and the newness of the mules to harness.

Time and again strings of the animals were led down in turn to drink from the now much-addled creek . . . 3 A.M. passed . . . The uproar was fading . . . 4 A.M. . . . . A premonition of danger came over Mann. He rode toward the cavalry trains, found the officers in charge and told them to hook up their teams.

"Start immediately," he ordered. "We're in danger of attack." [10]

The grayness of dawn had begun to filter through the vehicles. It hung there feebly, pushed back by a dense morning mist that extended up from the creek bottom and thinned out only as it reached the overlooking hills. On all sides Mann could see the exhausted teamsters and guards asleep on the ground. He realized suddenly no pickets had been established.

The thoroughly alarmed captain began to circle about among the wagons to hurry the teamsters. He came to the Reserve Brigade train and swore violently when he discovered it was not being hooked up. This train carried five days' rations for 2,250 men, forage, subsistence stores, and the various regimental and headquarters supplies. Frantically he rode about, calling for the officer in charge. No one could help him. No one seemed to know who was in charge. He searched next for the wagon master. That individual, too, had been lost in the mist. In desperation, Mann dismounted and awakened the drivers himself, one by one, ordering them to get their teams ready to move. By this time the sun had begun to rise.

After what seemed an eternity to Mann, the first wagons of

the Second Brigade train swung out of the park, worked their way slowly through the ford at the creek and disappeared on the other side. Sight of the rolling wagons made him feel better. Kenly by this time, it occurred to him, must be within a few miles of Winchester. He remounted and urged his horse into a trot, shouting loudly to hurry the drivers of the reserve train. Most of the lead and swing mules had been harnessed to the wagons, while the wheel mules were in the act of being hooked up.

All at once Mann froze in his saddle. A shot from a light howitzer sounded from a hill close by, and a cannon ball dropped out of the sky and knocked off the head of a mule. It was followed a few seconds later by another that crashed into a wagon; and then, quickly afterward, by a third. General confusion broke loose. The guard stampeded, many of them leaping from the ground where they had been sleeping and rushing off without their guns. Saddle drivers mounted their mules, already saddled, and fled. Mules brayed and horses neighed, nervous and panicky over the situation into which their masters had brought them.

At the second shot Mann galloped toward the commander of the guard. This officer was trying to rally his men and form them in line. Mann, shouting it was impossible to move the train into corral, asked for instructions. The commander, a lieutenant-colonel, gave no answer, and the captain set off around the hill.[11] As he galloped madly away, he saw Rebel cavalry come charging through the mist. They seemed to be clothed mostly in blue and were led by a man in civilian dress. According to his distorted mental image, they wheeled into line from sets of fours and commenced firing with carbines as they advanced.

The eyes of E. L. McKinney, captain and commissary of subsistence, gave him a more accurate picture. The attackers to him seemed a small number of mounted men, charging as foragers. They were dressed in gray uniforms and carried only revolvers, which he concluded they used with more noise than precision.

In its beginning, this attack by the Forty-third Battalion met with unexpected opposition. Under direction of Mosby, whose intelligence regarding the wagon train had come through Scout John Russell, the howitzer had been brought up at a gallop and unlimbered on a knoll commanding the pike. But before the gun could be placed in position, a swarm of angry yellow jackets, living up to their reputation as home rulers, poured out of a hole in the ground and began a stinging protest against invasion of their territory. The hardened artillerymen who could face shell fire without a quiver fled in all directions. Mosby's horse reared up on hind legs and made him feel, in his own words, "a good deal like Hercules did when he put on the shirt of the Centaur and couldn't pull it off." [12] There were a few moments of indecision and almost panic. Off to the left waited a squadron under Richards; to the right, another under William Chapman; and to the rear, as a reserve, Company E and Sam Chapman. Three shots from the gun had been agreed on as a signal for simultaneous attack. But this was a helpless feeling: their signalling device had been captured by an enemy too small and too numerous for the Rangers to rout with their lead-spouting revolvers. The day was saved finally by A. G. Babcock, dauntless first sergeant of artillery. Flailing the air madly with his hat, he rushed in, grasped a chain on the gun and lunged with it a few yards down hill. Then the crew, keeping a wary lookout against the vengeance of the fierce little insects, took over and fired the signal shots.

At no time in their history had the Rangers created more disturbance than followed around the wagon park and along the creek bottom during the next few minutes. The howitzer roared until its carriage gave way, rendering it useless. Horses and mules dashed wildly about in the road. Wagons were upset by their frightened teams. A body of Federals formed behind a stone fence and remained there until the Rangers under William Chapman drove them out. Lewis Adie of Leesburg, young member of Company D, was killed in the charge. Another Federal force took refuge in a brick church near Berryville and kept up a murderous fire until they were dislodged. Richards' squadron routed them in a successful but somewhat costly affair. Welby H. Rector of Middleburg, member of Company A was mortally wounded, and another Rector of the same unit, Edward, worthy lieutenant of Major Hibbs' corn detail, was wounded.

All this time Mosby was back at the park directing men in burning the wagons. One of the vehicles nearest Berryville had been dashed against a tree and most of its contents, including a battered chest, thrown out. They lay on the side of the road unnoticed until Major William E. Beardsley, who had rallied a few of the guard, drove off a party of Rangers applying the torch. The chest was taken up on horseback and rushed away by the Federals. It contained $112,000 in payrolls.

A black cloud of smoke rose from seventy-five burning wagons as Mosby led his men away on the return through Snicker's Gap a few minutes later. With them they carried more than 200 prisoners, including seven officers, between 500 and 600 horses and mules, nearly 200 beef cattle and many valuable stores.[13]

Burning of the wagon train was like a stab in the back to Sheridan. It had come just one week after he had taken over command of the Army of the Shenandoah, just as he was trying to make a showing to prove to the authorities at Washington that Grant's choice of him had not been a mistake. There must have been some embarrassment when he opened an is-this-true telegram from Halleck,[14] who had no detail on the attack. In his answer Sheridan was as accurate as his own information would permit. He gave the partial picture at hand and concluded: "It was said everything was recovered except six wagons, but this was not true." [15]

On August 15 he fell back to Halltown, the base he had left on the 10th.

17

Worrying Sheridan

WORD WENT OUT FROM FEDERAL HEADQUARTERS at Martinsburg August 14th, the day after the wagon train attack, that no reliable news had come from the direction of Sheridan's army. One report went further: "Several of our scouts here say they cannot get through to Sheridan, Mosby having driven them back." [1]

The North's new field commander along the Potomac knew this condition existed. He knew that his orders and reports were not getting through on schedule, even though their place of origin and their destination were in territory under Union control. So, with the ruins at Berryville as a reminder, he prepared to correct the evil, writing Grant that he would "destroy all the wheat and hay in the country (there is nothing else) and make it as untenable as possible for a Rebel force to subsist." [2]

This ruthless destruction was carried out as his army moved back toward Halltown. Soldiers burned and pillaged in a scourge of the countryside that complied to the letter with Grant's instructions given at the time Sheridan took over the cavalry: ". . . it is desirable that nothing should be left to invite the enemy to return. Take all provisions, forage and stock wanted for the use of your command. Such as cannot be consumed, destroy." [3]

But now came more drastic orders from Grant: "If you can possibly spare a division of cavalry, send them through Loudoun County, to destroy and carry off the crops, animals, Negroes, and all men under fifty years of age capable of bearing arms. In this way, you will get many of Mosby's men. All male citizens under fifty can fairly be held as prisoners of war, and not as citizen prisoners. If not already soldiers, they will be made so the moment the Rebel army gets hold of them." [4]

This followed an order that had gone out two hours earlier from a much angrier Grant: "The families of most of Mosby's men are known and can be collected. I think they should be taken and kept at Fort McHenry, or some other secure place, as hostages for the good conduct of Mosby's men. When any of Mosby's men are caught, hang them without trial." [5]

The sentence pronounced by Grant embraced no new penalty for Ranger activity. Constantly since the preceding year it had been understood there would be no official aftermath when a Mosby man was shot down in cold blood.

Change of Federal cavalry commanders seemed to be having no effect on Mosby's activities. No day passed without report from some source of an attack accomplished by him with minor loss, if any. Among these accounts was one that was too mysterious to be logical: a Federal party told of chasing some of Mosby's men near Harper's Ferry until they rode to the bank of the Shenandoah River and disappeared without leaving a trace. Observed a newspaper: "Our scouts are on the alert on the hills, valleys, and through the dense woods, but are unable to catch these picket-shooting assassins and marauding highwaymen." Further comment came a day or two later: "About the only aggressive enemy in the Middle Military Division [6] is Mosby, and the only dangerous place appears to be the rear of our army on its line of communications with this point." [7]

On the 17th Sheridan made a surprising report to Grant: "Mosby has annoyed me and captured a few wagons. We hung one and shot six of his men yesterday. I have burned all wheat and hay, and brought off all stock, sheep, cattle, horses, etc., south of Winchester." [8]

On Mosby's trail at this date appeared a man who from all appearances was the answer to Union prayers concerning the raiders. He was Richard Blazer, hardened Indian fighter who looked on the Confederate independents as fighters of a class with the red men he had chased on the plains. He appeared at Sheridan's headquarters while the furore still raged over the wagon train attack at Berryville and was given an attentive ear. With 100 men, each armed with Spencer repeating rifles, he would clear the country of Rangers, he promised. Sheridan immediately wired military authorities at the capital: "I have 100 men who will take the contract to clean out Mosby's gang. I want 100 Spencer rifles for them. Send them to me if they can be found in Washington."

Mosby at the moment was operating in the valley with three separate detachments. At one point, a Fifth Michigan Cavalry picket was killed by William Chapman in an exchange of shots. The Federal's commanding officer was heartless young George A. Custer. This impassioned fighter summoned his lieutenants and ordered that the homes of five Southern families in the vicinity be burned in retaliation. While the burning was in progress at one of these mansions, a party of Rangers under Chapman rode up out of a ravine and blazed away with their revolvers while they shouted "Take no prisoners!" When the raiders trotted back into the ravine, eighteen of the enemy lay dead.

Three warning shots from pickets along the Fairfax Court House road alarmed the Federal stockade at Annandale at thirteen minutes to 5 o'clock the morning of August 24. Immediately afterward, in quick succession, three shells from a Confederate artillery piece burst out of the dense fog blanketing the lowlands. And after this, scores of Gray horsemen charged up to the entrance to the fort and, without checking speed, deployed to the south and east. But the strong logs of the stockade were too impregnable a barrier for Mosby's raiders. They tried twice unsuccessfully to get a surrender under flag of truce and then bombarded the stronghold for nearly an hour, finally withdrawing to avoid reinforcements rushed from other Washington outposts at sound of the firing.

Mosby accomplished little on the expedition to Annandale. One worthwhile outcome developed through the arrest of Augustus Klock, estimable Falls Church citizen of known Union leanings. Klock was released with instructions to inform Union authorities of retaliatory steps Mosby planned unless two of

his men held in confinement were paroled. A Federal investigation followed and in short time the prisoners were back with
their command. Mosby's Rangers frequently throughout the
war were denied parole and were imprisoned until Mosby could
file protest, usually through Robert Ould, Confederate agent
of exchange.

From his headquarters in the saddle, Mosby at this time
addressed a lengthy report to General Lee in which he gave a
brief account of each major skirmish since March. Lee gave a
summary in his indorsement: "Attention is invited to the activity and skill of Colonel Mosby and the intelligence and courage
of the officers and men of his command, as displayed in this
report. With the loss of little more than twenty men, he has
killed, wounded and captured during the period embraced in
the report about 1,200 of the enemy and taken more than 1,600
horses and mules, 230 beef cattle and eighty-five wagons and
ambulances, without counting smaller operations. The services
rendered by Colonel Mosby and his command in watching and
reporting the enemy's movements have also been of great
value. His operations have been highly creditable to himself
and his command." Lee also wrote Mosby a personal letter
commending him on his success. This letter was captured by a
Federal officer and published in a Washington newspaper.

As days went by, attacks occurred with increasing frequency
along the Washington outposts. Fairfax Court House had a
fright when the Rangers galloped past the town. Alexandria
got panicky and tightened its defenses against a raid it was
positive would come. Pickets at Annandale, Fort Buffalo, Falls
Church were ridden over, captured or killed. Lazelle strengthened the posts, dismounted the entire line except non-commissioned officers and directed each post to build a cribwork of
fallen trees so that men on duty could entrench themselves by
day and prevent their being charged over by mounted Rebels
at night.

A heavy rain set in September 3 and within a short time
streams were badly swollen. Early in the morning, Sheridan's
army moved out from Halltown to take up a new line from
Clifton to Berryville. Simultaneously, Mosby rendezvoused at

Rectortown and divided his command into two squadrons. One of these he sent to operate in the vicinity of Berryville and the other he led toward Charles Town and the rear of Sheridan's moving troops. Near Kabletown next day, after dividing his squadron at Myers' Ford, he and six Rangers directed a Federal ambulance train into a side road and began unhitching horses. Some of the drivers succeeded in escaping and rushed back to warn another ambulance train close behind, badly stampeding it. Subsequent Federal investigation resulted in a conclusion that "the affair was disgraceful." [9]

Bad news awaited Mosby on his return to Myers' Ford. There he learned that the Rangers he had left behind had been surprised by Blazer and his 100-man detail armed with repeating rifles and had been routed.

On Mosby's trail meanwhile was riding Colonel H. S. Gansevoort, with 210 dismounted and sixty-three mounted men from the Thirteenth New York Cavalry. His object was to proceed through the country quietly, much on the style of Lazelle's plan, and to capture or kill Mosby in any way possible. He got word that the Partisan had been at Piedmont organizing a new unit to his command—Company F—and was raiding in Fairfax County, towards Falls Church. Promptly the Federal officer dispatched five troopers to the Centerville road to lie in the rain and wait. A little later, three of them rode back to report. They said they had had a fight with three Rangers and that one of them, before escaping, had been seen to throw up his hand and give signs of pain. This Rebel, they added, was Mosby or a person resembling him.

Gansevoort promptly learned more exact details: Mosby had been wounded by a bullet that struck the handle of one of his revolvers and glanced off into his groin. A search was organized. Rumors of where the raider was hiding grew. It was said he was at Centerville, at Aldie, at Upperville, that he had crossed the bridge at Rapidan Station, that he was safe at Lynchburg. The Federals wore themselves out searching. Some of them concluded he had died of his wound and ceased to debate the matter. But even if he had been killed, his spirit continued to disturb them in the shape of his hard-riding followers.

18

"Hang Them Without Trial"

⸻

FEDERAL BRIGADIER-GENERAL GEORGE H. CHAPMAN got orders to "make arrangements" for the capture of such of Mosby's gang as he could find in the country along the Shenandoah River and beyond. This move was intended primarily to stop John Mobberly, detached scout of White's command, whom the enemy thought a Ranger. Accordingly, at 10 P.M. September 15, the day Mosby was wounded, Chapman started with 400 men from brigade headquarters in the valley. The evening air was pleasant and there were no military units on the road to deter him.

During the early hours of morning they reached the Shenandoah and crossed at a ford near Snicker's Gap. There Chapman detached fifty-five men under Captain Compson of the Eighth New York Cavalry to proceed up river and across into Ashby's Gap. His own route would be through Snicker's Gap and along the eastern base of the mountains to Paris. The two forces, according to his plans, would meet during the early afternoon in Snicker's Gap, which Compson would reach by a path down the ridge of the mountains.

They separated in the dark with no noise except that of cavalry on the move. Chapman was in a hurry. There was much ground to cover, many details to investigate. He rode into Paris shortly after sunrise. Above him on the surrounding heights of the little settlement he noticed small parties of enemy horsemen. They were at safe distance and they gave him an ominous feeling. But he anticipated no trouble: their numbers were too small.

In a few hours he trotted towards Snickersville, arriving around 2 P.M., much fatigued. The day had become uncomfortably hot, and the men were in need of rest. He called a halt for an hour, sent forward one squadron to meet Captain Compson and to hold him in Snicker's Gap until the others arrived. He had seen no more of the enemy who had haunted him at Paris.

Compson was waiting in the gap when the squadron came up. A breeze picked its way along the slope of the cut, feeling out the hollows, bringing pleasant respite from the heat. With it came the odor of sunburned grass, daisy pollen, and a faint tinge of shaded fern. Its softness harmonized perfectly with the setting—leaves yellowing, but not yet brown . . . the ghostly sound of nuts falling from careless squirrels . . . yellow-shafted woodpeckers hammering against time. The single road through the gap, where countless Blue and Gray troops had marched back and forth, where the refuse of war still lay and rotted, was nature's bid for peace.

The Federals dropped their packs, their hats, their bodies. An hour elapsed. They took no notice of time. Some slept; some nodded; some droned over jokes and adventures. But this lapse from the military suddenly was interrupted by a sound that had come to be a symbolical part of the war—the Rebel yell, the nauseating scream of excited humans, abundantly punctured by gunfire.

Behind their peaceful front the leaves, the squirrels, the yellow-hammers had hidden a secret. During the last few minutes of the hour the Federals had been in the gap, sixty men, dressed in gray, had stolen along the ridge of the mountain, along the same path Compson's party had come. Dismounting as they neared their unsuspecting prey, they led their horses to the brink of the gap, their hands on the animals' muzzles. They looked down on the restful scene below for a few moments and then got ready for the charge.

It was a concerted affair. Each man, one foot in the stirrup, waited for the leader's signal. It came, and the riders swung

into the saddle as their mounts, already poised for action, dug
their cleats into the sod and raced down an easy slope upon
the enemy. Confusion paralyzed the Federals. Many of the
sleepers were captured before they fully realized what had
happened, and the South's horse supply was boosted appre-
ciably. All the enemy mounts were taken except a few that
broke away and galloped toward the eastern entrance of the
gap, along with several Union soldiers. Rounding up their captures, the Confederates disappeared quickly in the direction
they had come. At their head rode William Chapman, in command of the Forty-third Battalion during the absence of
Mosby.

On the 19th of September, Sheridan attacked Early, and the
Confederate general withdrew his forces to Fisher's Hill. There
he stopped temporarily before falling back to Winchester,
trailed by the enemy. This movement of the two main armies
in the valley was another development in favor of the Forty-
third Battalion. It meant that Sheridan was advancing farther
from his base, widening the gap over which messages and supplies had to be carried.

Immediately the Union predicament over its line of communications became more severe. Sheridan in distress asked
Augur to send to Winchester without delay all available troops,
even to the number of 4,000 or 5,000, to relieve the men guard-
ing his supplies there.[1]

Still greater was the alarm of Stevenson at Harper's Ferry.[2]
Couriers sent out failed to get through, and two parties with
duplicate dispatches were picked up at widely separated points
the same evening. He notified Secretary of War Stanton that
the country between Sheridan and him seemed alive with
parties of Rebel guerrillas and cavalry, and added that there
were no organized enemy troops in the valley that side of
Staunton "except Mosby's guerrillas." Colonel Edwards of the
Third Brigade estimated that no escort could get through with
fewer than 500 cavalry.

It is good that war does not indicate to soldiers in advance
the horrible fates which sometimes await them. In such case,
battles would be fought with less aggressiveness and with more

concern for self-preservation. It was particularly merciful that no premonition was connected with the expedition that began when Sam Chapman and 120 men rode away from Piedmont on September 22. Chapman's object was to strike a picket post of the Sixth New York Cavalry he had heard was stationed in Chester Gap. That night near Front Royal he learned his information was unqualified, that no Union guard was on duty in the gap. He bivouacked, slept soundly and before dawn rode with two men to a shelf overlooking the valley. As light began to filter into the great bowl of land between the two mountain ranges, he spied something that made his pulse quicken: rolling down the road toward Front Royal was an ambulance train escorted by what seemed about 200 men.

The divinity student hastened back to his command and divided it into two parties. Forty-five raiders under Captain Frankland were instructed to surprise the train guard in front, while Sam, with the remainder, moved to strike in the rear. Preparations were quickly made. The front ambulances were nearing the town. Unless the attack was carried out immediately the chance would be lost.

Suddenly Chapman, moving to get in the rear of the guard, realized he was sending his men into a death trap. A short distance behind the train and now clearly in view moved a long line of cavalry—the Reserve Brigade of Merritt's cavalry division. This he had failed to notice while reconnoitering, but he might have suspected its presence had he known that at Milford twelve miles to the south Fitzhugh Lee's cavalry had encountered the Union troops that morning and driven them back. The dejected Blue soldiers were in no mood to be tampered with, especially by a band of independent Confederates.

Chapman acted in a flash. He instructed Lieutenant Hatcher to take his portion of the command toward Chester Gap while he hurried around in an effort to keep Frankland from attacking. But all his quick perception and haste were not enough. Before he could stop it, Frankland charged and drove the escort back on the ambulances.

"Call off your men!" Chapman yelled as he came up. "You are attacking a brigade!"

Frankland, in the excitement of battle, did not understand. "Sam, we can't stop now. We've got them whipped!"

Chapman waved his arm in a circle. From every direction Blue cavalry was closing in fast, guns out, sabers flashing. Only one avenue of escape remained—they must shoot their way out.

The Rangers fell back, got their directions from Chapman and dashed away. They found an opening in the enemy ranks, headed for it, firing rapidly, and got through somehow. But there was more fighting ahead. The Second U. S. Cavalry had gone off on a tangent, found the Chester Gap road and doubled back. A part of this force was still in front, waiting to block the Rebels. The Rangers struck the Union horsemen, pushed them back, rode through them, and kept going.

When the dust cleared, strewn about were several dead and wounded Federals. But attention of those who came to clear the field of casualties were centered on the body of Lieutenant McMaster, lying prone in the road, dusty, ridden over, riddled with bullets. There were conflicting stories as to the manner of his death. Some said he was killed after he had surrendered; others that he died fighting at the head of his detail in an attempt to cut off the enemy's retreat. In their defense, the Rangers contended that he got in their path, was run down and slain. Explained one of them: "Lieutenant McMaster was killed in the excitement of a fight, by men who were seeking to escape from a superior force and who were fighting for their lives. It is hardly possible at such time to say whether he had an opportunity of surrendering, for the affair was only of a few moments' duration." [3] The tales are open to argument and all may be wrong. At any rate, when Brigade Commander George Custer rode up he could see the incident only from the evidence at hand—McMaster's body, bloody, bruised and riddled.

Custer was in no mood at the moment to rule on the fairness of guerrilla tactics. Mosby's activities had become a drain on the young brigadier's self-esteem. Rangers had captured carriers bringing him messages, and only the day before his orderly, bearing a sheep presumably for the general's mess, had fallen into their hands. This was mockery of a type Custer could not stand. Derision hurt and ridicule disparaged. It was not within his power to lose gracefully in open battle, let alone in the small skirmishes of independent warfare. The repulse that morning at Milford had injured his pride; the sight of McMaster infuriated him, and in the back of his mind was the haunting memory of the house-burners he had sent to their death.

Grant and the authorities at Washington had clamored for extermination of Mosby's battalion. Its leader, whom Custer thought an uneducated brigand, already had been killed or grievously wounded. Now was the time to take such drastic action against his followers that the band of cutthroats would cease their operations through fear, if for no other reason. Six of the Rangers who had attacked the wagon train that morning had been captured. Custer ordered them executed. Supporting him in this extreme measure were Grant's written words: "Hang them without trial."

People of Front Royal never forgot the scenes enacted around their town that morning. Those who dared to peep out at what went on gathered details which burned into their memories and stayed there like raw, cankerous sores. Wrote one eyewitness, a girl: "The 'dark day' of 1864 is indelibly photographed in my memory. I have often wished I could blot it out, for it clouded my childhood." [4]

Most citizens knew something out of the ordinary was happening when a band paraded slowly through town playing the dead march. This was a preliminary gesture to create effect: the public as well as members of Mosby's command must be convinced that the time had come for independent operations in Northern Virginia to stop. Then a noisy mob of soldiers moved along a street and stopped at a church. There the din grew louder and reached a peak after several shots had been fired. When the crowd dispersed, the bodies of two Rangers, David L. Jones and Lucian Love, lay in pools of blood near the back of the church yard.

More shouting sounded to the south of town where Thomas E. Anderson of Mosby's artillery company stood beneath an elm tree until felled by bullets. Pretty soon the uproar became louder. Two horsemen rode through the principal streets, dragging between them, roped to their saddles, a seventeen-year-old school boy of Front Royal, Henry C. Rhodes. This boy had borrowed a neighbor's horse to take part in the attack on the wagon train, hoping to mount himself so he could ride with Mosby. The horse he had borrowed had broken down in the retreat and its rider had been captured.[5] Rhodes was almost unconscious when his fellow townspeople saw him. He was unable to cry out, and some said he scarcely recognized his widowed mother when she rushed in, fighting the soldiers like a wildcat, and tried to free him. This execution, too, was recorded by an eyewitness: "Rhodes was ... dragged in plain sight of his agonized relatives to the open field north of our town, where one man volunteered to do the killing and ordered the helpless, dazed prisoner to stand up in front of him while he emptied his pistol upon him." [6]

The first four executions had not been carried out in exact compliance with Grant's instructions: the victims had been shot, not hanged. Now the method of slaughter was changed. Two Rangers were left—William Thomas Overby, a large-bodied Georgian, and a younger man, Carter, whose surname no one remembered. These men were marched off at the head of a riotous crowd. "Well do I remember the picture: Overby, with head erect, defiant, and Carter overcome and weeping," a woman resident wrote. "And as they moved off the band played a dirge. . . . The song played over and over was 'Love Not, the One You Love May Die.' " [7] Another resident reported the scene: "They bore themselves like heroes. . . . One of them was a splendid specimen of manhood—tall, well-knit frame, and a head of black, wavy hair floating in the wind. He looked like a knight. While I was looking at them, General Custer, at the head of his division, rode by. He was dressed in a splendid suit of silk velvet, his saddle bow bound in silver or gold. In his hand he had a large branch of damsons which he picked and ate as he rode along. He was distinguished looking with his yellow locks resting upon his shoulders." [8]

Beneath a tree midway between the town and the Shenandoah River, the two men were halted and their hands were tied behind their backs. Repeatedly they were asked the loca-

From a photograph taken during the war

Samuel F. Chapman

The Fight at Miskel Farm

Dislodging the Enemy at Warrenton Junction

tion of Mosby's headquarters and each time Overby, spokesman for the pair, shook his raven locks. "We cannot tell that," was his only reply.[9] Promise of freedom brought no change in his answer. When ropes were adjusted around their necks, Carter asked to pray. He was given permission and bowed his head in silence. Overby remained erect beside him. Just before they were hoisted on horseback and the horses whipped from beneath them, the Georgian spoke in a defiant tone—one sentence, uttered through gritted teeth: "Mosby'll hang ten of you for every one of us." [10] Whips cracked on the words.

A haunting silence, the silence of a death watch, hung over Front Royal after the Federals disappeared. Dusk settled, night came on, and the stars which later stole out of the darkness were afraid and unfriendly. Citizens huddled and waited miserably behind closed doors and windows, trying to blot from their minds the doleful echoes of the dead march. Before dawn, aged men, daring consequences, slipped out with wheelbarrows and brought in the bodies of the four Rangers who had been shot. A sheet was draped mercifully over that of Rhodes before it was delivered to his mother.

At sunrise, several of Mosby's men rode cautiously into town. They talked with residents long enough to learn details of what had happened the day before and then made their way to the tree from which dangled, side by side, faces swollen and blinded eyes bulging, the bodies of Overby and Carter. On a placard around Overby's neck, crudely scrawled, were the words: "This will be the fate of Mosby and all his men." [11]

CHAPTER

19

Mosby Retaliates

———✦———

MOSBY RETURNED TO HIS COMMAND September 29. On his face was a two-week growth of beard, sandy like his hair. He indicated it was to stay there, and his men cautiously reserved their comment. The North had heralded his approach. Union scouts reported that he had been seen in Culpeper walking with a cane and next that he was at Rectortown. While absent he had made a brief trip to Richmond and Petersburg, chiefly to talk with General Lee. As he alighted from an ambulance at headquarters, he spied Lee talking with General Longstreet only a few yards away. Before he could hobble up on crutches, the gray-haired Lee advanced to meet him. "Colonel," Lee said as they walked to where Longstreet was waiting, "the only fault I have ever had to find with you is that you are always getting wounded." [1]

Much discouraging news awaited Mosby on his return. First of all, there were the hangings at Front Royal. And only a few days past, the home of Joe Blackwell, in which were concealed reports, correspondence and other valuable papers pertaining to the command, had been burned by the enemy. Moreover, up in Maryland lay the remains of Lieutenant Walter Bowie, one of his staff of scouts, killed while leading an unsuccessful expedition to capture the governor of the state.

But one bit of information put sparkle in Mosby's eye. It was news that the Federals planned to rebuild the Manassas Gap line from Manassas Junction westward. This step had been under consideration more than a year as part of Union occupa-

212

tion of the area, and the Partisan leader was determined it should not be carried out. Two purposes would be served by the line. It would give Sheridan's army better communication with Washington and it would enable troops, when the time came, to move by rail from the valley to Manassas Junction and thence to Charlottesville.

Since Early's army had fallen back from Fisher's Hill, developments in the valley had looked pleasing to the Federals. Grant sent Sheridan a message of encouragement—"Keep on and you will cause the fall of Richmond"—a telegram worded from his prayers, for the commander-in-chief hoped to invade the Confederate capital before winter arrived.[2] He wanted the cavalry to gain a foothold at Charlottesville and to come at Lee from the west. He calculated addition of Sheridan's troops then would enable him to attack with such force as to extend his lines beyond the Southside railroad, main Rebel artery south. But in this dream he overlooked one stumbling block— Mosby's Rangers.

Crews already were at work on the railroad when Mosby arrived. At some points along the approximately sixty-mile route, the track would have to be reconstructed completely; at others, more inaccessible to the destroying hosts, little work would be necessary. But an omen of disaster was in the air. While laborers leveled the grade, laid new ties and placed iron rails end to end, riders in gray haunted them from vantage points, sitting their mounts motionless, watching so steadily their stares seemed to bore into the backs of the men sweating over pick and shovel. This may have been partially the reason Sheridan notified Grant the day Mosby came back that it would be exceedingly difficult for him to carry his troops over the mountain and strike at the railroad around Charlottesville, explaining that he could not accumulate enough stores to do so. He thought it best, he said, to take some position near Front Royal and operate from there, which was not at all what Grant wanted.

Other leaders agreed with Sheridan on the danger of trying to go too far. Halleck, explaining to Grant the difficulties of keeping up his line of communication with the valley, wrote that it would be necessary to send south all Rebel inhabitants and to clean out "Mosby's gang of robbers." He suggested that Sheridan accomplish this object before he was sent elsewhere, recalling that the Thirteenth and Sixteenth New York regiments in Fairfax had been so often cut up by Mosby's men that "they are cowed and useless for that purpose."

Mosby let nothing sway him from his depredations against the railroad. He sent in his calling card at Salem on October 5. Two howitzers were posted quietly on top of a hill south of town, and firing opened with a terrific outburst of both large and small arms. Federal guards and workmen fled toward Rectortown in great confusion, littering the route with weapons, tools and clothing. Lee promptly commended Mosby: "Your success at Salem gives great satisfaction. Do all in your power to prevent construction of the road."

More raids came in quick succession. The Federal camp at Rectortown was shelled at intervals throughout one entire day. The engine "Grapeshot" was wrecked in Thoroughfare Gap. A doubleheader crashed into a gap in the rails near The Plains, killing among others the assistant superintendent of the railroad. Union newspapers called the incident a "guerrilla outrage."

Federal troops drove desperately through the area, striving to catch the raiders. Blazer supplied information that caused them to redouble their efforts. He sent word that Mosby's wound forced him to ride in a buggy. This report overshadowed stories that had come out of the deep South about a Confederate cavalry general named Forrest who had dared direct his army from such a vehicle. It was hard to believe that the captain of a band whose safety depended on its quick getaway would risk his neck with so slow a mode of transportation.

Near Piedmont one day a Ranger rounded a curve and found himself only a few yards from a Blue trooper who was rifling the pockets of a dead Confederate. He shot quickly, and the Federal dropped across the body of the Rebel. Riding to the spot, he dragged the Union soldier's body to one side and turned over the man in gray. It was "Big Yankee" Ames, eighth officer of the Forty-third Battalion to be taken by death. The *Star*, describing him as "a most notorious and lawless man," said he was trying to take an important message through the lines for Mosby.

Partisan warfare on the railroad continued. Cars were fired into, rails torn up and construction parties scattered. Some trains were so molested they were given an infantry escort to walk alongside from one destination to another. Augur warned the road "must be literally guarded the whole way." Crews started building small stockades along the track in sight of each other and prominent Rebel sympathizers were forced to ride on the trains, exposed so they would be subject to enemy fire. As a still more drastic step, Secretary of War Stanton ordered destroyed every house within five miles of the road, except those of friendly persons. Printed notices posted throughout the area announced that civilians found within five miles of the tracks would be considered robbers and bushwhackers.

Sheridan at last put an end to the problem. Through his influence, the railroad-building project was abandoned.[3] He had opposed it from the start. He knew a large force of infantry would be required to keep the road in operation. His cavalry would be weakened. It was possible also that he would have to leave such a large part of his command in the valley that he would have an inadequate force to prosecute a campaign against Richmond. He notified Grant that he would have preferred sending troops to the main army via the Baltimore and Ohio. At the same time, he explained to Halleck that he had been unable to communicate with Washington more frequently because of the operations of guerrillas in his rear. "They have attacked every party, and I have sent my dispatches with a view of economizing as much as possible," he added.

So, while quartermaster crews worked to clear away timber and other shelter along the tracks, orders came through signifying that the project had been abandoned. In a little more than two weeks, Mosby had forced Grant and Sheridan to revise completely their programs in Northern Virginia.

At 9:15 P.M. October 13, a Baltimore and Ohio passenger express pulled out on schedule from Baltimore. It was made up of a locomotive, an Adams Express Company car and nine well-loaded coaches. One coach was filled with German immigrants on their way to take up homesteads in the West. Whispers went about that U. S. Army paymasters with considerable money were on board. But Conductor Shutt, questioned by curious passengers, threw up his hands and shushed at such "absurd" rumors.

The train made good time. It rattled through the dark past Relay House, Monocacy, Point of Rocks. Midnight came and went while the night flyer rolled westward along the curve of the Potomac. Before it came to a stop at Harper's Ferry, many of the passengers had had their fifteenth nap. From there on to Martinsburg the road lay through guerrilla country, but there was little fear. Sheridan had kept Mosby too busy along the Manassas Gap line of late for him to expand his activities to the B. & O.

The engineer up front yawned in his glove after a few minutes at Harper's Ferry. He got a signal from the conductor, released the brakes, drew out the throttle. There was a moment's confusion of chugging, bell ringing and hissing of steam, and then the locomotive got under way, rolled on more smoothly, and the station fell away in the darkness.

The night was clear and there was the tang of the harvest season in the air. Farmers by rights should be happy at this period of the year, but not now: warmongers had taken over their fields and their crops and had left them and their stock to starve. Passengers on the express, struggling along tracks several times destroyed by the opposing armies, closed their windows tight against the chill. Sometimes they pressed their foreheads to the panes to decipher all the news they could drain from the flickering camp fires along the way. Most of the time they kept their eyes closed, trying unhappily to sleep. The roughness of the roadbed and the terrific clanging and banging of the coaches made their backs, their hips and their tempers sore.

Brown's Crossing slid past in the faint glow from the win-

dows. Up ahead the engine, coughing and purring, blasted
forth a long, hoarse whistle and rumbled faithfully on beneath
a stream of sparks. It rounded a curve and straightened out in
a deep cut. The high banks, jutting well up above the top of
the locomotive, forced smoke and cinders into the coaches.
Drowsy passengers stirred restlessly in protest against this
added discomfort. Then came a great din. It seemed all the tin
pans in the world had been piled in the engine's path. Coaches
jammed violently against each other. People were thrown out
of their seats. An explosion and loud hissing added to the confusion, and above the uproar sounded the staccato bark of
gunfire.

Uniformed men dropped down the steep slope of the banks
and spread out along the train.[4] Each had two guns and waved
them threateningly. Some stood back as guards. Others leaped
up the steps and entered the coaches. From the passengers rose
cries of "guerrillas! guerrillas!" To add to the pandemonium, a
few bullets spattered through the windows from the outside.
Men and women, some thrown into the aisles when the engine
left the track, crouched low and waited. From the locomotive,
now tilted against the slope of the cut, the engineer and fire-
man, scalded slightly, crawled and raised their hands in surrender.

The boarding party took charge. Into the ends of each coach
burst gray-clad soldiers, now in the rôle of bandits. Some of
them had the flush of youth in their cheeks. Others looked out
from countenances lined and weatherbeaten, typical veterans.
But they all answered the questions of the frightened travelers
with the same word—"Mosby."

The Rangers worked rapidly. Kearneysville was only a short
distance to the west; Duffield Station still closer. Passengers
were ordered out of the cars and up the banks of the cut. One
of the Rangers emerged from a coach and climbed to the point
where Mosby stood, pivoting impatiently on the foot sprained
at The Plains.[5] "That coach there," said the Ranger, pointing.
"It's filled with Germans who won't get off and they don't
understand English." Mosby was brusk. "Set fire to the car and
burn the Dutch if they won't come out," he snapped.[6] A stack

of New York *Heralds* from the express car was scattered along
the aisle of the coach and set afire. This was a gesture more
easily understood by the Germans, who had held their seats
under the conviction that they had bought tickets which entitled them to passage straight through to their destination. As
the flames spread, the immigrants scurried out into the night,
a confused mass of babbling foreigners.

A group of passengers from another coach struggled up the
incline toward Mosby. He hobbled nearer the edge to lend
some of the women a hand. "General Stevenson will not guard
the railroad and I am determined to make him perform his
duty," he said apologetically.[7]

The cars were cleared of people and of such valuables and
plunder as the Rebels chose to take.[8] A Union soldier among
the passengers slipped out along a fence, took off his uniform
and, in shirt and drawers, walked boldly back among the raiders
and asked for clothing.[9] Louis Cole, general ticket agent of the
Baltimore and Ohio, was forced to give up $19 and a gold
watch.[10] An officer resisted, attempted to draw his gun, and
Charley Dear killed him. This man's body was brought out before the wooden coaches were fired, but somehow a soldier's
body in the express car, en route home from a camp, was overlooked and left to burn. So was a chest containing nearly
$6,000.[11]

As flames spread over the pitch-soaked cars, Charley Dear
and West Aldrich strode up to Mosby. They displayed a satchel
and a tin box filled with greenbacks they said they had taken
from two U. S. Army paymasters on board.[12] Mosby detailed
Charley Grogan and a small party composed of Dear, Aldrich
and Jim Wiltshire to take the money across the Blue Ridge to
Loudoun County and there to await arrival of the remainder
of the train wreckers.

Now all the Rangers were gathered on the south bank above
the cut. They found their horses, packed their plunder behind
their saddles and rode away in the dark. The train had crashed
at 2:15 A.M.; it was nearly 3 A.M. when they departed.

Among the prisoners taken away by the Rangers was a young
German lieutenant, newly commissioned, on his way to join his

regiment in Sheridan's army. His uniform—fine beaver-cloth overcoat, high boots and hat with gilt cord and tassel—attracted the attention of Mosby, who liked himself to dress in such colorful finery. He rode beside the captive and they engaged in conversation.

"We have done you no harm," said Mosby. "Why do you come over here to fight us?" [13]

"Oh, I come to learn the art of war," replied the lieutenant.

Later, in the course of the ride toward the Blue Ridge, Mosby became worried over danger of an attack. He moved to the front of the column and presently was joined there by the German. Such a change had come over the fellow that the Partisan leader scarcely recognized him. His fancy overcoat, boots and hat had given way to a mixture of Federal and Rebel uniform. The lieutenant was furious.

"Didn't you tell me you came to Virginia to learn the art of war?" asked Mosby.

"Yes," replied the German.

"Very well. This is your first lesson."

Near Bloomfield, the train wreckers met the four-man detail with the captured money. In line they waited until it could be counted and they could be given their proportionate shares— $173,000 divided into eighty-four parts, affording each about $2,100. Mosby would have none of it. Seeing that their insistence would not sway him, his men made up a purse and bought him "Croquette," a thoroughbred he had spied in a pasture at Oatland, later his favorite horse.

The attack on the train had a telling effect on the Federals at Washington. Fear for the safety of the railroad was general, and for a time transportation along the B. & O. came to a virtual standstill. This had been due partly to a raid conducted on the 14th by William Chapman. He dashed into Maryland, destroyed several canal boats, plundered store houses, scattered the Loudoun Rangers and returned safely to Virginia while enemy troops were waiting to ambush him at a ford higher up the river.

The greatest evidence of fear over Mosby's activity came from Paymaster Ladd. He telegraphed Washington from Mar-

220 RANGER MOSBY

tinsburg under great stress: "I have my funds in the parlor of the United States Hotel here guarded by a regiment. . . . I shall make no move until I can do so with safety and, in the meantime, await orders from you." [14]

Mosby returned from the Greenback Raid, as the train-wrecking expedition came to be called, to find that the enemy had been busy in his confederacy during his absence. The Thirteenth and Sixteenth New York Cavalry and two companies of the Fifth Pennsylvania Artillery had carried off all his heavy ordnance. The guns—a three-inch ordnance piece, twelve-pounder howitzer and two small mountain howitzers, with limber of caissons—had been concealed in a thicket on the crest of the Cobbler mountains, extending through Fauquier County. A guard of nine men was captured with the ordnance.

Another commander had been away from his men at this period, but a far more serious situation than that Mosby found awaited him when he returned. Sheridan came back to Winchester the afternoon of October 10 to find his army nearing demoralization. It had been surprised by Early and driven back a mile and a half north of Middletown. Sheridan's appearance stemmed the tide. The Federals rallied and drove the Confederates to a strong position at Fisher's Hill and then to New Market, in a battle that practically ended the valley campaign.

Mosby had a distasteful task to deal with on the 19th. In his command, which had grown to six companies, not including the artillery unit, was an element of what he termed "military dead wood"—soldiers of good character and eligible for membership in every way except that they did not have the quality as fighters he demanded. Other undesirables were classed as deserters from the regular army, a status he had learned of after admitting them. Acting relentlessly, he checked his rolls and marked off these members, sending them to the regular army.[15]

This mood for efficiency was noticeable next morning at a rendezvous near Rectortown.[16] About him loitered a group of civilians and soldiers who seemed to hang on his words. He was all business, abrupt, impatient. One after another complaints

were heard from residents of the neighborhood. Someone had
lost a prize cow. A barn had been burned. Two teams of horses
were missing. He listened and made his disposition promptly,
deciding some cases to the satisfaction of complainants, leaving
others to await developments. Presently a man with guns
strapped around his waist edged into the circle and said something in a voice inaudible to bystanders. The thin, restless
figure of the Partisan leader straightened, his piercing eyes
snapped, and the muscles of his face rippled above his beard.

"You are a skulker and no soldier," he said in a high-pitched
voice. "You can go where you please, but you can never ride
with my men again."

The man slunk away without argument.

The 24th found Mosby in the valley. He rode leisurely toward Winchester until a two-horse light spring wagon, rolling
rapidly east, caught his attention. William Chapman and Lieutenant Grogan were sent with details to capture it. They came
back bringing as a prisoner Brigadier-General Duffie, the fiery
Frenchman who had chased Jeb Stuart out of Middleburg during the Gettysburg campaign. Duffie's capture was one of the
most important for the Rangers since Stoughton's unpleasant
awakening.

More and more as the closing months of the war passed,
Mosby's men began to realize that their most formidable enemies were the Eighth Illinois Cavalry. As one Ranger replied
in later years to his younger son's query whether Yankees were
not cowards strapped to their horses, "nobody who fought
against the Eighth Illinois could ever think of them as anything
but brave and gallant soldiers." [17] Captain Frankland, supported by 106 raiders, struck the trail of 200 riders from this
unit on October 29 and made the mistake not only of going
at them with inferior numbers, but without the advantage of
surprise. The Rangers were routed in a fight that ranked in cost
with the Warrenton Junction and Loudoun Heights repulses.
Four Partisans were killed, five wounded and nine captured.

Five weeks had passed since Mosby's men were executed at
Front Royal and there had been no move at retaliation. Fed-

erals considered the matter closed, and members of the Forty-
third Battalion began to wonder what was wrong. Their concern had been increased meanwhile by still further cause for
Rebel vengeance. During October, Brigadier-General William
H. Powell of the Army of West Virginia gave notice he had
hanged a Ranger and had placed a placard around his neck
with this message: "A. C. Willis, member of Company C,
Mosby's command, hanged by the neck in retaliation for the
murder of a U. S. soldier by Messrs. Chancellor and Myers.'"[18]
The two men accused of killing the soldier were described as
"members of Mosby's gang of cutthroats and robbers." Powell
also revealed that he had sent a detachment to destroy the
residence, barn and all outbuildings and forage on the premises
of Chancellor, as well as to drive off all stock of every description. The brigadier failed to mention in his report that the
U. S. soldier had posed as a Confederate and had visited farms
of the neighborhood in which he was killed to spot cattle and
horses for Federal raiding parties.[19]

Mosby had not been unmindful of the injustices to his men.
Throughout the period of waiting he had pondered and sorted
—carefully picking over and identifying each of the Federals
brought in by his men. On October 29, he dated a letter to
General Lee and sent it to Richmond by his brother:

"I desire to bring through you to the notice of the government the brutal conduct of the enemy manifested toward citizens of this district since their occupation of the Manassas
(Gap) road. When they first advanced up the road, we
smashed up one of their trains, killing and wounding a large
number. In retaliation they arrested a large number of citizens
living along the line, and have been in the habit of sending an
installment of them on each train. As my command has done
nothing contrary to the usages of war, it seems to me that some
attempt at least ought to be made to prevent a repetition of
such barbarities. During my absence from the command, the
enemy captured six of my men, near Front Royal; these were
immediately hung by order and in the presence of General
Custer. They also hung another lately in Rappahannock. It is
my purpose to hang an equal number of Custer's men whenever

I capture them. There was passed by the last U. S. Congress a bill of pains and penalties against guerrillas, and as they profess to consider my men within the definition of the term, I think it would be well to come to some understanding with the enemy in reference to them. The bearer of this, my adjutant, will give you all the information you desire concerning the enemy in this country. Of course I did not allow the conduct of the enemy toward citizens to deter me from the use of any legitimate weapon against them, but after throwing off the train they guarded the road so heavily that no opportunities were offered for striking any successful blow, and I thought I would be more usefully employed in annoying Sheridan's communications...." [20]

Lee attached this indorsement to Mosby's letter immediately: "I do not know how we can prevent the cruel conduct of the enemy toward our citizens. I have directed Colonel Mosby through his adjutant to hang an equal number of Custer's men in retaliation for those executed by him." The letter moved up the official ladder and when it reached Secretary of War Seddon it was still further indorsed: "General Lee's instructions are cordially approved. In addition, if our citizens are found exposed on any captured train, signal vengeance should be taken on all conductors and officers found on it, and every male passenger of the enemy's country should be treated as prisoners."

A captain of Custer's command had orders to catch up with a wagon train moving out of Front Royal and to accompany it down the valley.[21] Unaware of the retaliation Mosby was planning, the officer rode hurriedly off on his mission, trailed by a Negro unofficially attached to his service. Near Newtown south of Winchester during the afternoon, he came within sight of the train, winding painfully along in a great cloud of dust. The wagons rolled on ahead of him, cleared the town. Some time later he trotted along through it, still considerably outdistanced. On the far side he encountered a small party of men eating cakes and apples in front of a store beside the road. They were in blue uniforms and their caps bore the Greek cross of the Sixth Corps. No sabers could be seen, but on their saddles were fastened Spencer rifles, a reassuring item, for it was generally known that this most modern of small arms was restricted to Union service. The captain took the soldiers to be members of the rear guard of the train and spoke to the non-commissioned officer in charge.

"Good morning, Sergeant. You had better close up at once. The train is getting well ahead and this is the favorite beat of Mosby."

"All right, sir," replied the sergeant, saluting. He nodded to his men, and they mounted and followed the captain.

As they galloped along, a feeling of distrust in these cake and apple eaters grew in the Negro. He cocked his ears with a keenness for self preservation common to his race. Gradually and without creating attention he urged his horse to the side of the captain. "Secesh sure, massa. Run like de debbil," he whispered.

The captain looked around to find the Negro's fears were well founded. He stared into the barrel of the sergeant's revolver.

"We closed up as you directed, Captain," the sergeant said, smiling. "I hope our drill was satisfactory."

The captain flew into a rage. "All right, sergeant," he flared. "Every dog has his day, and yours happens to come now. You have sneaked upon me in a cowardly way, disguised as a spy, and possibly my turn may come tomorrow."

"Your turn to be hung," commented the sergeant.

They rode on, the captain fretting. He learned from those nearest him the man he had taken to be a sergeant was C. F. Whiting, Clarke County boy riding with Mosby. This fellow led the way toward the mountains. Darkness came on, and a cold silence with the snap of November settled over the land. Somewhere in the blackness the leader found a path and wound mysteriously up through the heavy forest. For hours there was slow riding and then, shortly after a gray dawn filtered in from across the mountain ridge, they threaded through the trees into the dense shadows of a glen off Ashby's Gap. In its center, waiting quietly beside their horses, was a group of half a hundred men in mixed uniforms. At one side the captain saw an officer he identified as Mosby by his plume, collar ornaments and scarlet cape. Later he gave newspapers this partially-correct description of the Partisan, terming him "the great modern highwayman":

"He stood a little apart from his men, by the side of a splendid gray horse, with his right hand grasping the bridle rein, the forearm resting on the pommel of his saddle, the left arm akimbo, and his right foot thrown across the left ankle and resting on its toe. He is a slight, medium-sized man, sharp of feature, quick of sight, lithe of limb, with a bronzed face, of the color and tension of whip-cord; his hair a yellow brown, with full but light beard; a straight, Grecian nose, firm-set, expressive mouth, large ears, deep-gray eyes, high forehead, large, well-shaped head, and his whole expression denoting hard service, energy, and love of whiskey. He wore top boots and a civilian's overcoat—black, lined with red—and beneath it the complete gray uniform of a Confederate lieutenant-colonel, with its two stars on the sides of the standing collar, and the whole surmounted by the inevitable slouched hat of the whole Southern race." [22]

When Whiting reported and produced papers taken from the prisoners, Mosby examined them carefully and turned toward the Federal officer. "Good morning, Captain," he said with a note of satisfaction. "There is but one man I would rather see than you and that is your commander. Were you present, sir, the other day at the hanging of six of my men as guerrillas at Front Royal?"

The Union officer made no answer, and Whiting was ordered to search him. A gold watch and chain, several rings, a set of shirt studs and buttons, some coins, a Masonic pin and about $300 in currency were placed in a pile on the ground. The leader picked up the pin, then selected three men to assess the value of the remaining loot. The watch brought a top valuation in Confederate money of $3,000. To the collection was added the Federal's boots, appraised at $650. Finally the Negro was given a value $1,000 short of that of the watch. In the end the total was divided equally among the men who had brought in the prisoners.

Mosby called the captain to one side and returned his Bible, letters, pictures and pin. "You may as well keep this," he said of the pin. "It may be of use to you somewhere." Then he added: "Your people greatly err in thinking us merely guerrillas. Every man of my command is a duly enlisted soldier. They are picked men, selected for their intelligence and courage. We plunder the enemy, as the rules of war clearly allow. 'To the victors belong the spoils' has been a maxim of war in all ages."

At Rectortown later that day, twenty-seven Federal prisoners were placed in line and made to draw slips of paper from a hat. Seven of the group opened the folded slips to find them numbered. But one of the seven was identified as a drummer boy and, after consultation between Mosby and some of his men, was released. A second drawing was held to fill his place. With this over, holders of the marked slips were sent under guard to be hanged as close to Custer's headquarters as they could be taken in safety. It was Mosby's way of retaliating, what he described as the most loathsome act of his career. He explained it was one he had delayed as long as practicable and now executed solely because it was the only method by which he could force the customary considerations of war for members of his command when they were taken prisoners. Significant in comparing Mosby with Custer is the fact that the latter stood by while the executions were under way at Front Royal, while Mosby, a cutthroat in the eyes of the enemy, witnessed the drawings and then rode in a direction opposite that in which the condemned victims were taken to their death.

Night came on, dark and rainy, as the condemned men were conducted toward Custer's headquarters, and one of them managed to escape in the darkness. This caused plans to be changed. A halt was called near Berryville on the Winchester turnpike and three of the Federals were hanged. It was slow work—"too damned slow work," commented one of the executioners. The remaining three were placed in line. Three Rangers raised their revolvers. Two explosions sounded, followed by shouts and the sound of running feet. The Federal at whom the third gun was aimed had freed his hands during the ride.

From a photograph in the Library of Congress

Mosby in Richmond, Early in 1865

The sword and the landscape backdrop are obviously studio furniture. Mosby never wore a sword, and it is unlikely that he would have taken binoculars with him on a train trip to town.

Mosby in the Last Months of the War

In a flash he raised on the balls of his feet, knocked the weapon aside, struck the Confederate on the head, jumped over him and fled into the dark.[23] After the confusion had quieted, this note prepared under Mosby's eye was attached to one of the bodies dangling from a tree:

"These men have been hung in retaliation for an equal number of Colonel Mosby's men, hung by order of General Custer at Front Royal. Measure for measure." [24]

Mosby did not know the two men had escaped when he later called before him Scout John Russell. It would have made no difference. "I was really glad to hear it," he afterward commented, "for it increased the moral effect of the act. They (the escaped men) could relate in Sheridan's camps the experience they had with Mosby's men." [25]

Mosby asked Russell if he could get through to Sheridan's headquarters.[26] The frail young scout, more familiar with the Shenandoah Valley than any other member of the Forty-third Battalion, nodded. "You must be careful," Mosby warned. "On the way you will pass near Custer's camps and possibly will encounter some of his men on the road. If they capture you, they may show you no quarter."

The scout listened stoically. Mosby handed him a letter and directed that he place it in Sheridan's hands.

Late the next day, Russell stood before Sheridan at Winchester. The scout had been fired at while he waved a flag of truce, had been threatened by Custer with hanging, and had moved to headquarters blindfolded. Through it all his defense had been that Mosby was holding 100 prisoners who would be put to death if a hair of his head was harmed. Sheridan waved him toward a seat before reading the message he had brought:

November 11, 1864.

Major-General P. H. Sheridan,
Commanding U. S. Forces in the Valley.

General: Some time in the month of September, during my absence from my command, six of my men, who had been captured by your forces, were hung and shot in the streets of Front Royal, by the order and in the immediate presence of

Brigadier-General Custer. Since then another (captured by a Colonel Powell on a plundering expedition into Rappahannock) shared a similar fate. A label affixed to the coat of one of the murdered men declared that "this would be the fate of Mosby and all his men."

Since the murder of my men, not less than 700 prisoners, including many officers of high rank, captured from your army by this command, have been forwarded to Richmond, but the execution of my purpose of retaliation was deferred in order, as far as possible, to confine its operation to the men of Custer and Powell. Accordingly, on the 6th instance, seven of your men were by my order executed on the Valley turnpike, your highway of travel.

Hereafter any prisoners falling into my hands will be treated with the kindness due to their condition, unless some new act of barbarity shall compel me reluctantly to adopt a line of policy repugnant to humanity.

Very respectfully, your obedient servant,

John S. Mosby.[27]

20

Sheridan Puts the Torch to Mosby

―――――

OWARD NIGHTFALL A FEDERAL SCOUT lying in underbrush near North Mountain saw two Confederate soldiers enter a glen and set a strange flag against a tree. He waited while they made plans for the night. Presently one of them went in search of water, and the scout sprang on the other Rebel, tied him, tore the flag from its staff and made his way safely back to his own lines. The flag thus captured inflamed the North. It had a single star on a black field, with the word "Winchester" inscribed beneath. But the feature that caused greatest resentment was two other words—"no quarter." Immediately the emblem became a black flag, denoting enemies of all mankind, outlaws who took no prisoners. In time it was linked with the Forty-third Battalion, even while investigation definitely was fixing the ownership on two of Early's men.

One result of the general rage the flag created against Mosby in civilian quarters of the Union was the appearance of a succession of infamous and diabolical caricatures of him in Northern journals. No denunciation was too vile. But no matter how great its wrath, the Federal populace could not overcome its curiosity. More details concerning his identity were demanded, and newspapers called on their correspondents nearest his scene of action for biographies.

While the North was trying to find out more about Mosby's background and habits, the raider was busy with growing problems. Early's defeat at Cedar Creek in October and his subsequent withdrawal far down the valley left Mosby with the responsibility of watching the area west of the Blue Ridge, as well as that around Washington. In a letter to Lee on November 6 he reported indications that the larger portion of Sheridan's army would be transferred to Grant.

The weather through the opening weeks of November continued cold and fair, further stripping Virginia of its golden brown leaves, scenting the air with the tang of wood smoke and apple cider. It was the post lull of the harvest season. But little harvesting had been done in the northern tip of the state, where Sheridan's troopers rode the highways and tramped the brush in search of the raiders.

It was an exasperating struggle. From Richmond came definite evidence that the Confederate States had not much longer to live. Yet, up around Washington, where the Rangers still showed their heels to the Middle Military Division, the opposition met by the Federals seemed to strengthen daily.

From Harper's Ferry November 19 Stevenson sent a tragic sequel to Sheridan's wire announcing the organization of Blazer's outfit. Worded nearly three months later to the day, Stevenson's message stated: "Two of Captain Blazer's men came in this morning, Privates Harris and Johnson. They report that Mosby, with 300 men, attacked Blazer near Kabletown yesterday about 11 o'clock. They say that the entire command, with the exception of themselves, was either captured or killed." [1]

With a few variations, that was the story. Blazer, during his entire career as an independent scout on the trail of Mosby and his band, had never been a serious threat. He had failed to prove Lazelle's theory that the way to get rid of the Forty-third Battalion was to give it some of its own medicine. Rangers recalled that they never had heard his name on Mosby's lips until November 15, the day word came that he had ambushed a party of raiders near Berry's Ferry, killing two.

Mosby was not feeling well when this news was brought to him. A troublesome cold had all but disabled him, the first time since the war started that he had been laid up by anything less than a serious wound. He called Dolly Richards to his side and told him to take A and B companies, the units surprised by

Blazer at Myers' Ford in September, and to "wipe him out." Richards trailed Blazer to Kabletown, concealed one company, feigned retreat with the other and, when the Federals rushed into the trap, turned upon them with both units in a crushing blow. Blazer fled with part of his men toward Myerstown. Hard on his trail rode four Rangers—Sam Alexander, Syd Ferguson, Cab Maddux and Louis Thornton Powell. But it was Ferguson —the Rev. Sydnor G. Ferguson of Fredericksburg, Va., in later years—who clubbed Sheridan's captain of scouts over the head with a revolver and captured him.

Meantime more violent things had been happening back at the battle scene. John Puryear, young Richmond warrior recognized by Mosby as one of his best fighters, had ridden down Lieutenant Cole, second in command to Blazer, killing him even after he had surrendered. The youth had his reasons. He had been captured by Blazer's men the day before and had been roughly treated. Cole wanted to know the location of Mosby's headquarters, and had tried unsuccessfully to get the information from the young prisoner. As a last resort, he ordered him swung up by the neck. Three times Puryear was pulled into the air at the end of a halter, and the last time lost consciousness. Cole gave up after that, but a glance at the youthful Confederate would have told him the matter was not ended.[2]

Blazer's defeat drove Sheridan to a use of extreme force against Mosby. Since August, Union cavalry details had been dispatched at frequent intervals to sweep certain sections of the country. They had operated individually and in combinations, a strong array, but they had been better armed than trained. Invariably they came back with only a handful of prisoners or with some drastic tale of disaster to themselves. In his experiments, Sheridan had tried hanging, and the rope metaphorically had slapped back and lassoed some of his own men. He had met guerrilla tactics with guerrilla tactics, and the 100-man force assigned to the task had been gobbled up almost in toto. Now, to sweep Loudoun Valley clean of Rebels, he sent out the strength of the Middle Military Division.[3]

As a military leader, Sheridan had reason to take action.

There had been considerable embarrassment in the loss of
Blazer. His capture had come only a few days before Grant
had appeared in Washington on an official visit, and it was not
unlikely that some of the conversation the commanding general
had while in the Federal capital concerned Mosby's most recent success. Perhaps it explained a telegram Sheridan received
from Halleck on November 26: "I understood from General
Grant when here on the 23rd that he did not intend to order
away the Sixth Corps so long as you thought it should be retained in the valley. It seems to me that before any cavalry is
sent away, Mosby's band should be broken up as he is continually threatening our lines." [4]

Sheridan answered immediately:

"I will soon commence work on Mosby. Heretofore I have
made no attempt to break him up, as I would have employed
ten men to his one, and for the reason that I have made a
scapegoat of him for the destruction of private rights. Now
there is going to be an intense hatred of him in that portion
of the valley which is nearly a desert. I will soon commence
on Loudoun County, and let them know there is a God in Israel.
Mosby has annoyed me considerably, but the people are beginning to see that he does not injure me a great deal, but
causes a loss to them of all they have spent their lives in accu-
mulating. Those people who live in the vicinity of Harper's
Ferry are the most villainous in the valley, and have not yet
been hurt much. . . ." [5]

Sheridan's arrogance and confidence on paper failed to extend to the field of action. Always present was the fear that
Mosby might spring another of his surprises such as the wagon
train attack at Berryville. So, at the same time he prepared his
reply to Halleck, he sent this warning to the commanding officer at Charles Town and Summit Point: "Look out for Mosby
tonight. He is reported to be about." [6]

Mosby's cold had bothered him much of late and he had
projected no action of moment since the elimination of Blazer.
True, he had crossed the Blue Ridge on the 24th, Thanksgiving
Day, but the expedition had been fruitless and Mosby had had
a narrow escape when the horse he was riding became unman-

ageable during pursuit of a wagon train. Only prompt assistance from two of his men saved him and, after that, he decided
to take things easy for a few days.

While Mosby was incapacitated, tragedy stole in to rob the
command of another of its veteran members. In a running
fight with the Loudoun Rangers near Leesburg, Montjoy
pushed to the front. Suddenly a Federal wheeled a quarter
way round, threw up his revolver and fired. The dark, handsome fighter from Mississippi raised in his stirrups, fell forward,
slumped like a sack of corn, and dropped from the saddle. Comrades who hurried up found a gaping hole in his forehead. He
was the third company commander lost to the battalion through
enemy bullets, and his death was one of the severest blows to
date. Under his excellent leadership, Company D had come to
be looked on as the best behaved of the Ranger units.

Sheridan informed Major-General Couch at Cumberland the
night of November 23 that there was no danger of a guerrilla
raid in the Cumberland Valley. On the tail of this bit of information, he added: "If you have arrested spies, hang them; if
you are in doubt, hang them anyway. The sooner such characters are killed off, the better it will be for the community." [7]
But the most important communication that went out from
Sheridan's headquarters at this period was intended for Brevet
Major-General Wesley Merritt, commanding the First Cavalry
Division, the mounted arm of the Federal troops in Northern
Virginia.[8] Dated November 27, it instructed him to proceed at
7 o'clock next morning with two brigades of his division
to the east side of the Blue Ridge. Going through Ashby's Gap,
he was to operate against the guerrillas in the area bounded
on the south by the Manassas Gap railroad, on the east by the
Bull Run range, on the west by the Shenandoah River and on
the north by the Potomac. Mosby's Confederacy made up
almost the entire northern half of the territory included within
the prescribed boundaries.

Sheridan described this section as "the hotbed of lawless
bands who have from time to time depredated upon small parties on the line of army communications, on safeguards left at
houses and on troops." He said their real object was plunder

and highway robbery and that, to clear the country of them, "you will consume and destroy all forage and subsistence, burn all barns and mills, and their contents, and drive off all stock in the region." He ordered further that the instructions must be "literally" executed, but that no dwellings should be burned and no personal violence should be offered civilians. "The ultimate results of the guerrilla system of warfare is the total destruction of all private rights in the country occupied by such parties," he concluded. "This destruction may as well commence at once, and the responsibility of it must rest upon the authorities at Richmond, who have acknowledged the legitimacy of guerrilla bands."

Merritt was instructed further that his Reserve Brigade should move on the 29th to Snickersville, which would be his point of concentration and of operation. The command was to take four days' subsistence, to gather forage from the country through which it passed, and to return to camp via Snicker's Gap on the fifth day.

At 7 o'clock the morning of the 28th a long line of Blue horsemen swung away from the camp of the First Cavalry Division, U. S. Army, and rode eastward toward the Blue Ridge. It was bitterly cold. Horses and riders suffered extremely from the weather, the first severe freeze of the season. But they rode without halting. Sheridan was angry.

By noon those at the front of the column were passing through Ashby's Gap; by late afternoon, they were burning. At Upperville, clear of the gap, they divided into three parties: one to go north by Bloomfield to the Potomac, one to go south to Piedmont and Salem, and around to Middleburg, and one to go directly to Aldie and there to strike the Snickersville pike. Each group had its task of destruction: they must burn or confiscate everything that would make food and they must rid the neighborhood of guerrillas.

In impudent defiance of this horde that poured through the mountains, Mosby assembled his command that day to organize Company G, seventh unit of his battalion. Most of its members were from the artillery outfit, disbanded after loss of the ordnance. Thomas W. T. Richards was elected captain. To the

surprise of some, Puryear was chosen third lieutenant. His promotion, his comrades knew, was made solely as a reward for
his fighting ability. They were aware the young Richmonder
lacked the judgment necessary to a good leader and that he
placed no value on his life. Fresh in their memory was the time
he had come in from a raid, long black hair whipping in the
breeze, and had been called before his commander. "Puryear,"
Mosby said, "I am going to make you a lieutenant for gallantry." The youth bowed low with royal gesture. "But," added
Mosby, "I don't want you ever to command any of my men." [9]

To the Federals as they rode through Loudoun Valley the
net seemed so tightly drawn that there was no way for Mosby
to get his men out of it. "There will be a grand drive for
Mosby on the east side of the ridge," their instructions read,
"and he must not be permitted to escape.... Connect your
command with pickets along the top of the mountain.... There
must be no failure to be on prompt time." [10]

Another snare was added to the trap. Two regiments were
detailed to march at daylight, one to the crest of the Blue
Ridge, the other along the foot to Paris. They were told to
destroy as they went and to keep up communication with each
other by a line of mounted men. They were cautioned that they
should pay particular attention to securing stock secreted in
the mountains. Two other regiments were sent to Millville and
to Middleburg to complete unfinished work in that country,
as well as to destroy a quantity of pork the Confederates were
believed to have secreted near Millville. The four regiments
were instructed to meet at Philomont and to remain there,
watching the mouth of Loudoun Valley, until the arrival of a
force under General Devin, provided it appeared before 4 P.M.;
then to return to camp. "Let them use every exertion to kill
or capture any guerrillas that may be seen by decoying them
into ambush or in some other way," the orders concluded.

At the end of the first day of Sheridan's vindictive campaign,
night closed over Loudoun Valley in a shroud of uncertainty.
Down into this once peaceful country, many times trodden
over during the last three years, had come close to 5,000 men,
each with a torch and each with official military license to de-

stroy as he saw fit, homes excepted. What damage the Federals would leave behind was a matter of conjecture. Their commander had given an ultimatum that day in a message to Stevenson opening the way for wholesale pillaging: "Should complaints come in from the citizens of Loudoun County, tell them they have furnished too many meals to guerrillas to expect much sympathy." [11]

At a hospitable home near Upperville, several Rangers sat enjoying the comforts of a fireside.[12] They had been there all evening, engrossed in jovial conversation. But their pleasure was shattered suddenly by the host, who rushed in excitedly from a back room. "Boys," he said, "I don't know that there is anything wrong, but I think you had better be out and looking around. One of the black boys says he heard a number of shots out towards Upperville and heard someone calling out 'Halt!'"

The Partisans scurried to their saddles and galloped toward town. Ahead of them in the skies as they rode, a bright glare grew rapidly. They reached the top of a hill and stopped. Before them stretched a view that signified the heart-breaking story of war. Scattered over the terrain were numerous fires, large and small, angry pyres of hay and corn and other items priceless to a war-ravaged people. Flames licked greedily in the night, unhampered, plentifully fed, sending up sprays of sparks toward the shivering stars.

The riders drew together in the glare along the hillside. They talked briefly before parting, each man to speed off on his own path in the blackness beyond the rise.

Toward dawn, while Union pillagers stretched out to rest before resuming their ravage, frightened groups of civilians— men, women and children—prodded cattle, sheep and hogs along back paths to hiding places in the mountains. They were aided by Rangers aroused from their points of refuge by the riders who had separated on the hill.

Daylight of the 29th revealed a black pall of smoke over the entire sweep of valley. But Sheridan did not know. From his headquarters on the other side of the Blue Ridge he wired Stevenson: "Have you any news from Loudoun?" And Stevenson answered: "I have nothing from Loudoun County today."

Merritt carried out his orders in minute detail. Soldiers, whether heartless wastrels or men brought up under the benevolent doctrines of the church, spread in a great fan from the western mountains and went stolidly about their program of destruction. Mills, barns, hay, wheat, straw were given to flames in an alliance of famine. A widow was dragged bodily from the brick smokehouse in which hung her winter's supply of meat, freshly killed.[13] Federals threw out the hams and the side strips and the shoulders, and stood by until the lot disappeared on a pile of burning rails. Even the county almshouse came in for its share of pillaging.[14]

Attention that day was centered on the part of the valley lying south of Little River turnpike. Toward Rectortown, Merritt had sent the First Brigade with orders to divide the command there and to dispatch strong columns to Salem and The Plains. Flankers were kept out constantly, not so much for protection as to lessen the chance of overlooking destructible property. Wherever they moved, horses, cattle and other livestock were herded together and driven toward Snickersville. Mercy was shoved to the background. Families were robbed of table silver, heirlooms and priceless family valuables. Jewelry was loot of the first order.

By nightfall, Merritt was confident at least the lower half of the valley was a veritable desert. Smoke billowed up toward the heavens all along the path his men had followed. Low weeping that came on the wind was from people who that day had lost all but their land and the roofs over their heads; from children tired after a day in which they had wept bitterly over loss of some pet, animal or fowl, and had cried out from the folds of their mothers' skirts a hatred they could not understand. Sleepers, where there was sleep, tossed restlessly and bemoaned their fate in troubled dreams. Outside the cold night breezes fanned dying embers, embers which flamed in the blackness and sank into oblivion, as helpless as the population that had felt the wrath of Sheridan.

There had been ample evidence during the tortuous hours of the 29th that the Rangers still were in the neighborhood. To begin with, the roundhouse at Piedmont, important railway point at the foot of the mountain grade, had been destroyed by thirty men in gray. Stores there had been looted and a culvert near by suddenly had burst into flame. At Bloomfield, the advance guard of Merritt's Reserve Brigade was fired on by Partisans. The Federal invaders in many instances were distracted by small parties of Confederates who leaped upon them and then fled, leaving behind dead and wounded. One Rebel, mistaking a Union officer for Custer, dashed up close and fired, inflicting a mortal wound.[15] As usual, there were conflicting reports of Mosby's whereabouts. One officer placed him seventeen miles from Point of Rocks traveling toward Upperville with 250 men. Other dispatches located him at Berryville. These were given support by an attack on the Twelfth Pennsylvania Cavalry camp in the Shenandoah Valley.

A part of the Ranger activity that day was not in evidence. As Merritt advanced northward late in the afternoon, Mosby's men, working on the theory that there was no reason for the pillagers to backtrack, made plans to shift livestock under cover of darkness into hiding places in the part of the valley already burned.

For five days, from Monday the 28th of November through Friday the 2nd of December, the Federals destroyed unceasingly. Horsemen threaded and rethreaded the rolling country and the forested slopes of the mountains. From barns, fields and hiding places were led horses and cattle. Torches were touched to corn shocks, hay stacks and outbuildings. Only the dwellings remained to make the scenes created different from the horror crusades of Indians in colonial times. Smoke rose in great volumes, volumes so dense Federals who had got up to Point of Rocks on the 30th wired that it was plainly visible from there. At night, terror was engendered by glowing beds of coals, before which stalked the invaders like goblins in the gloom, seeking bodily warmth as well as material gain. As though the elements had sided with the Confederates, not once was there a letup in the weather. Many of the Union cavalry bucked wind and cold during their act of destruction or search for the Partisans and regretted it later when they returned to camp with fingers or limb scored for life by frostbite.

Gradually the fan of blue-clad soldiers closed to the north and drew in on Snickersville. The Reserve Brigade swung around by Purcellville with from 1,500 to 2,000 head of cattle and sheep. Another force arrived at Lovettsville with 900 head of cattle and 150 horses. And Crowninshield, back with the Sixteenth United States Cavalry and twenty-seven head of cattle, leaving in his wake the charred ruins of four barns and four corn fields, reported that his men saw a few Rebels, but found it impossible to catch them.

By the week-end the Federals were back in their camps. Behind them Loudoun Valley lay like an inflamed sore. Merritt reported that his directions from army headquarters had been "literally complied with," listing as fruit of the expedition 5,000 to 6,000 head of cattle, nearly 1,000 head of fatted hogs, and 500 to 700 horses, including mares and colts. But he added that it was found "next to impossible to come in contact with any guerrillas, as they avoided even the smallest portions of the command. By stratagem and hard racing, between thirty and forty of these men were killed or captured. . . ." [16]

The extent of damage would never be known. Even the smallest estimates were enormous. Many old and well-built mills and barns of brick or stone had survived to a degree, but there virtually was nothing left except the homes to reveal the civilization that once had graced this rich little valley. The North had given its residents a cruel reprimand, and the job, so far as it pertained to destruction of property, had been well done.

Despite the drag on the physical aspects of the countryside, there had been a strong element of failure in this expedition: not once had Mosby been seen. Moreover, only a few of his men had been kicked up out of the brush, and these, with few exceptions, were too elusive to be caught or even fired at tellingly after they were seen. Members of the Forty-third Battalion had melted into the countryside with the ease of mountain goats. Rangers who were hellcats on horseback sat it out in the chimney corner as cripples or old men, or scurried to the many hideouts which were so readily accessible to them in their knowledge of the country. General Merritt explained that the entire valley had been gone over, but that the guerrillas were exceedingly careful to avoid any encounter with any of the parties. "Efforts were made to run them down or capture them by stratagem, but these in most instances failed," he added. "The sides of the mountains bordering Loudoun Valley are practically throughout their entire extent for horsemen, and the guerrillas, being few in numbers, mounted on fleet horses and thoroughly conversant with the country, had every advantage of my men."

While but an insignificant part of the success they had pictured, Federals prided themselves on an achievement near Harper's Ferry. While wandering among the ashes of a building burned near the Shenandoah River in that area, a soldier's horse crashed through a charred trap door. In a tunnel below could be seen a stairway winding down out of sight. With the aid of torches, a party descended and found a cavern large enough to conceal between 200 and 300 horses. Crude stalls had been laid off along its straw-covered floor and at the far end was a narrow opening. Here was one of Mosby's principal hiding places. The mouth of the cave was so narrow only one horse could enter at a time, and then only by wading through nearly three feet of water. On the outside, the opening was concealed by bushes and rocks, and above it towered a high cliff, directly across the stream from the point where Rebel raiders frequently had disappeared so mysteriously.[17]

Mosby had not assembled his command since the 28th for the simple reason that he realized such a move would be foolish at such a time when he was completely surrounded by an overwhelming enemy. A few hundred men congregated in one body, or even in two or three bodies, could not check thousands who were numerically strong enough to spread in force over the entire countryside. It was beyond his power to keep Loudoun Valley from learning there was a God in Israel.

Mosby's elusiveness in the face of the Federal effort to bottle him up had one direct and important effect on Sheridan. When the little general took over as head of the Army of the Shenandoah, its forces consisted of three divisions of the Sixth Corps, commanded by Brigadier-Generals David A. Russell, George

W. Getty and James B. Ricketts, one division of the Nineteenth
Corps and two divisions from West Virginia, all infantry. Plans
were made at once to bring Torbert's division from the Cavalry
Corps of the Army of the Potomac as the mounted arm and,
when it arrived, Torbert was made chief of cavalry and Merritt
was named to succeed him as division commander. There was
talk, after withdrawal of Early down the valley, of sending the
Sixth Corps to the Army of the Potomac. Grant, while in Washington November 23, had seemed in no hurry to order this
recall and had left the matter in Sheridan's hands. Halleck had
wanted the troops retained until Mosby was broken up, as
revealed in his telegram of the 25th, but Sheridan as late as the
28th opposed him and announced that he would commence
sending off the Sixth Corps on the morning of the 30th.

When dawn of the 30th arrived, Sheridan's information from
Loudoun County was not pleasing. Mosby's men not only
eluded capture, but were able to conceal themselves in the
very neighborhood through which the Union cavalry was riding. This bespoke a dangerous force, if not numerically, at least
potentially. Before Merritt returned to camp, Sheridan changed
his plans concerning the Sixth Corps. Russell and Ricketts'
divisions took to the road, but Getty's remained behind.

21

A Single Shot in the Dark

SOLDIERS AND CIVILIANS GATHERED at the railway station in Richmond the evening of December 5 stared with interest at a smartly dressed officer who stepped off the Virginia Central train from Gordonsville. Many things about his appearance set him apart from the average soldier. Beneath his drab hat, decorated with ostrich plume, gold cord and star, was a lean, muscular face given an extra touch by a partially-full beard. A heavy, black beaver cloth overcoat, with cape lined in English scarlet cloth, hung from shoulders unnaturally bent for the man's years. It half covered a gray sack coat bearing on its collar the stars of a lieutenant-colonel. As he walked along with rapid step, the skirts of his great coat swung open and gave bystanders a view of legs encased in long cavalry boots and in gray trousers with seams set off by a narrow yellow cord. To many of those who saw him disembark he remained a mystery until the *Whig* announced next morning: "Colonel Mosby arrived in this city last night. When he leaves Richmond, the Yankees will hear further of his whereabouts."

Newspapers, like the Federals, had been at a loss during recent weeks to keep up with Mosby. Only a few days earlier, the *Whig* had informed its readers that "we are unable, at all times, to hear from Mosby through Confederate sources for the reason that he and his men are generally too busy to write either the authorities or the newspapers, and hence frequently we have to depend upon Northern accounts, which we always take—and suppose our readers do the same—with very many grains of allowance." [1] Following this had come three accounts, all taken from the Philadelphia *Enquirer,* of successful raids of Mosby's men on Federal parties in the Shenandoah Valley. "It seems that Mosby is not idle," the Richmond paper observed. A day or two later, in praising the work of Forrest, it stated: "We would as soon expect Mosby to be foiled in a raid as that Forrest could be whipped by any force the Yankees can possibly concentrate against him." [2]

Mosby, leaving his command in charge of William Chapman, had set out for Richmond with several things on his mind. First of all, he went to see Secretary of War Seddon and asked authority to divide his command into two battalions, each to be commanded by a major. "The scope of duties devolving upon me being a much wider extent than on officers of the same rank in the regular service," he explained in his formal application, "but small time is allowed me to attend to the details of organization, discipline, etc." He turned next to Petersburg. There he wanted to learn from General Lee himself, whom he had not seen since September, what the future held for the South. On the eve of his departure from Loudoun Valley, a message had reached him announcing that Army Headquarters was sending a representative to that section to collect and bring out available cavalry arms captured from the enemy. The letter had added: "Our numbers are largely increasing, increasing daily. Many of our men are without proper cavalry arms, and many of them have no guns at all." Parts of this correspondence, when coupled with reports on the stability of the Southern lines which had seeped into his confederacy, did not make sense.

But the most urgent topic to be discussed with the commanding general concerned his own operations during the months immediately ahead. Merritt's destruction of crops created a problem that needed prompt attention. Forage had been so generally burned or carried away that little in the way of either grain or long feed remained to quarter throughout the winter the hundreds of horses belonging to the Forty-third Battalion. Seddon, in answer to complaints from citizens of the Northern Neck that marauders from gunboats of the enemy were committing many heinous deeds in that area, had suggested to Lee in June that Mosby be ordered down the peninsula with a portion of his command. Lee was sympathetic toward the idea, but objected to its execution on the grounds that the raider's presence on the Northern Neck would be betrayed and his retreat too easily cut off. But now seemed the time for at least a part of the Rangers to quarter in that section of the state which had not been overrun by moving armies.

Mosby was back in his confederacy on the 20th, ending a highly successful journey. The War Department had given its permission for him to organize his command into two battalions and, on December 7, had given official notice of his promotion to the full rank of colonel. His operations for the winter months also had been worked out. While together at dinner in Petersburg, Lee had proposed that he retain as many of his men in Loudoun Valley as he saw fit and send the remainder to the Northern Neck.

Back with him he brought news of still another development. En route to Lee's headquarters he had stepped off the train at the little railroad stop of Chester and had spied in the crowd of soldiers and civilians waiting there a familiar face. It was that of Aristides Monteiro, seventh son of Francis Xavier Monteiro de Barros and the student whose name had appeared just above his own when he first enrolled at the University of Virginia in 1850. They had not seen each other since college days and recognition was not mutual. Monteiro was deceived by Mosby's beard and had to be told the identity of its lean, sunburned wearer, several years his junior. The medical man had heard of the independent band operating in Northern Virginia under a crafty leader named Mosby, but never had connected the name with his student days at Charlottesville. "Of all my university friends and acquaintances," he said, "... (Mosby) would have been the last one I would have selected with the least expectation that the world would ever hear of him again." [3]

In the few minutes they talked at Chester, Mosby learned that Monteiro was surgeon of the Twenty-sixth Virginia Regiment, Wise's Brigade. "You're the very man I want!" the Partisan leader exclaimed. "My surgeon, Will Dunn,[4] is too fond of fighting. I want one that will take more pride in curing than in killing." [5] Monteiro was interested, but not optimistic. He gave his consent for the change, personally convinced that no argument from Mosby would be powerful enough to shatter army red tape. But on this score he was to receive a surprise that increased his respect for the younger man. An order came to him within a few days directing him to report to the Forty-third Battalion.

Mosby put his reorganization into effect at once. His battalion commanders were of his choice—William Chapman, promoted to the rank of lieutenant-colonel, and Dolly Richards, raised to a majority. In the battalion under Chapman were placed Companies C, E, F and G, while the more experienced fighters of Companies A, B and D were assigned to Richards.

A few hours after he rode back from Richmond, Mosby suspended business for matters of a social nature. Jake Lavender, his ordnance sergeant, and Catherine Edmonds were to be married that evening. Mosby set out for the nuptials dressed just as he had appeared at the Confederate capital, except that from his shoulders swung a gray cape, lined with scarlet like the overcoat. His spirits were high. While on his trip, he had received praise at every hand and had heard from the mouths of the military leaders themselves their elation and great pride in his activities.

But festivity was not for him that night. Scarcely had he reached the home at which the wedding was to take place when one of his scouts brought word that a body of Union cavalry was advancing on the Salem road a few miles away. Motioning to Tom Love, near at hand, the Partisan slipped off to the stables without attracting attention. Avoiding roads as much as possible, he led the way rapidly across field toward the east. A cold drizzling rain had started earlier in the day and, now that dusk was settling, was freezing into a solid coating of sleet. Near the Salem road he and his companion stopped to listen for the sound of cavalry, but noise of the icy rain pellets and of icicles dropping from trees limited their hearing. They rode on. Presently two horsemen came out of the forest ahead, followed by others, and began firing. Suspecting they were flankers for a cavalry force, the raiders fell back to an eminence and from there watched the enemy move toward Rectortown. Later they saw camp fires blaze up near the village and were confident the Federals had gone into bivouac for the night.

Mosby sent a Ranger from a neighboring farm house to tell Chapman and Richards he wanted the camp attacked about daybreak next morning. Then he set off in the opposite direction, still accompanied by Love. It was his plan to round up additional men and to have a strong enough force on hand before dawn to assure victory.

Night had fallen by this time and they rode in complete darkness, allowing their horses to pick the way. Near Rector's Cross Roads, lights of a home gleamed through the blackness. The pair applied their spurs: old Ludwell Lake, most Rangers knew, was a friend of the South and set a mighty fine table, even for war times.

At the front gate, Love suggested that he remain outside on guard, but Mosby objected. "It wouldn't do any good if you were out here in the cold," he said. "There is no danger. Get down."[6] They slid to the ground, leaving their revolvers in the saddle holsters, looped the reins over the front fence and entered the gate.

Lud Lake, short, stout gentleman farmer, bald and jolly, was seated at late dinner with his two daughters, Mrs. Landonia Skinner, called Dona by the family, and Mrs. Sarah Smith. An excited clamor ran over the room when a servant swung back the door of the modest home. Always there was a place for Mosby's raiders at its table; one of them, Ludwell Lake, Jr., had come from beneath its roof. The two men walked in, their boots thumping with hollow sound on the uncovered floor. There was no formality. Acting as members of the family returned, they shook the icicles from their hats into a fire of blazing logs on an open hearth. Wrappings were laid aside, Mosby dropping his plumed felt, overcoat and cape in a corner. Distinctly noticeable on the collar of his gray sack coat as he sat down were the stars of his new rank.

The warm room was a sharp relief from the icy weather

through which the visitors had been riding. In the center of the table a tallow light cast a yellow glow over the white cloth, the dishes, clothing and faces; it was a flickering illumination that seemed to take courage from the flames licking greedily and independently at logs in the fireplace.

It was close to 9 o'clock and most of the food had disappeared when horses' hoofs sounded above the talk across the table. Mosby arose, panther-like, and cracked the door of the dining room that opened on the back yard. Outside, in the dim reflection from the windows, he could see horsemen and could hear them talking loudly, too loudly for Rebels stealing their way through the country. He whirled and motioned for the light to be doused. One of the women extinguished it with a single puff. Then came a hushed movement as they pushed away from the table, followed by an ominous silence, so noticeably intense that it strengthened the noise of men and horses trampling the icy crust in the yard.

Mosby closed the door and slipped toward a bed chamber at one side of the dining room. His footsteps were quick, silent as a cat's, but there was no shutting out the flickering glow from the fireplace. As he stepped into the doorway a revolver shot rang sharply from the outside and a bullet crashed through a window pane.[7] The Partisan leader crumpled to the floor. For a flash he lay still, stunned, then stirred and wriggled out of sight, dragging his body over the floor of the darkened bedroom.

The Federals who poured in through front and back doors a moment later found two frightened women, a stout, baldheaded man and a soldier in gray uniform. They stood with hands raised, dark but not belligerent figures. Someone lit the tallow light. In the adjoining room, prone in a pool of blood, the intruders stumbled on another Confederate, coatless and in long cavalry boots. His face and hands were bloody, and beneath his butternut shirt they discovered a gaping bullet hole in the abdomen, two inches below and to the left of the navel.

The Union troops were a raiding party from the Thirteenth and Sixteenth New York Cavalry. They had left Fairfax Court

House in search of Mosby on the 17th and had started once more over the country so often threshed for signs of the Forty-third Battalion's leader. Near The Plains they had surprised Lieutenant Charles Grogan of Company D and had gravely wounded him as he attempted to flee to his horse. Now they were on their way back to camp and, because of the keenness of Corporal Kane, leader of the advance guard, had come upon two horses tied to a fence in front of a house near the road. It was the corporal who had spied the figure of a soldier through the window and had fired.

When the main body of troops came up, Major Douglas Frazar, in command, was told by some of his men who emerged from the house that a Rebel lieutenant had been shot. The major crawled unsteadily from his horse. The severe weather, in his opinion, had called for a stimulant, and he had imbibed too freely in the dark. But this gave him no embarrassment. About him were other officers and men equally unsteady.

Inside the house, Frazar knelt over the wounded man. "What's your name?" he asked. The Confederate, apparently in great agony, groaned faintly: "Lieutenant Johnson, Sixth Virginia Cavalry." [8] The major opened the victim's shirt and pants. A wound met his eyes that convinced him the man was dying—a sizeable hole through which blood was pouring freely. Other officers, Major Birdsall and Captain Brown included, were of the same opinion.[9]

There was no further delay. They had skirmished some during the afternoon with a handful of Rangers who had taken on the appearance of the advance guard for a larger body and they were behind schedule. This was foremost in Frazar's somewhat befuddled mind. He ordered all out of the room, pronouncing as a benediction over the prone Confederate that he would not live twenty-four hours.

With them as they rode away the Federals carried Tom Love and the long cavalry boots of the wounded man. Somewhere in the dark along the column, a soldier clung to a plumed hat, a gray overcoat and a gray cape.

On arrival at Middleburg that night, Frazar reported to his superior, Lieutenant-Colonel D. R. Clendenin, that he had

wounded a Rebel lieutenant. To both it seemed a trivial incident: lieutenants were plentiful and their capture was not considered of great moment. But later, when the camp fires were
lit, Frazar had cause for doubt. Someone brought him a hat,
dressed with gold cord and star, and said it had been found
at the home where the wounded man lay. Frazar gazed at the
gray felt in amazement: the hat he held was that of a field
officer. He hurried with it to the part of the camp in which
were held captive eight men taken in as Rangers during the
raid. They shook their heads. Frazar insisted: there was nothing to conceal; the man who had worn the hat was dead. They
still shook their heads. In the morning the hat was shown to
Clendenin and to "Yankee" Davis, who had served as guide on
the expedition. They could offer no help. Meanwhile the long
cavalry boots had been found identical in make with a pair
taken from the Joe Blackwell home at the time it was burned
the preceding fall.[10]

Expanding rumors began to circulate rapidly during the next
few days, but the Christmas season, as well as other confusing
reports concerning Mosby, delayed official action until December 27. That day notice went out from Washington giving
positive information that Mosby had been wounded and ordering parties to search for him. Gamble wired from Fairfax Court
House that he was sending Frazar and 300 men on a night
march. A few days later, on the basis of this investigation, he
forwarded a longer dispatch in which he laid blame for the
uncertainty concerning the wounded Rebel directly on Frazar:

"Major Frazar did not search the officer for papers, nor inquire who he was from the people in the house; and, although
two ambulances and a medical officer were with the command,
the wounded Rebel officer was not examined or brought in; all
of which, in my opinion, any good officer should have done.
I am also informed that Major Frazar was too much under the
influence of liquor to perform his duty at that time in a proper
manner." [11]

Reports on the 28th were more cheering to the Unionists.
Colonel Wells at Alexandria relayed information from Fairfax
Court House of the death of Mosby. Sheridan also predicted

the Partisan leader's demise. The little general's dispatch, addressed to Stevenson, was based on intelligence brought in by Torbert who, in order to search for the wounded Rebel, had turned aside on his return march with 5,000 troops from a raid in the direction of Gordonsville. Torbert had failed to find the victim, but he reported he had obtained unimpeachable authority for the statement that the wound was mortal.

In the New York *Tribune* appeared a delayed dispatch: "The pleasant intelligence that the pest Mosby was shot near Piedmont and killed was brought here tonight by a soldier." [12]

But Stevenson warned: "The story of Mosby's death is not true, but given out to prevent his capture while wounded." [13] He had heard the Rangers were spreading false rumor to discourage the Federals in their search.

Major Frazar started late in the afternoon of the 28th for the vicinity of Middleburg with a scouting detachment of 300 men. He questioned thoroughly the Lake daughters, threatened them with imprisonment if they withheld the truth, and came away as baffled as on the start. A severe snow storm began on the morning of the 31st, locking the countryside in a deep blanket and closing the roads to travel. Federal searching efforts came to an abrupt close, involuntarily, and it seemed just as well. Sheridan that day had wired from Winchester: "I have no news except the death of Mosby. He died from his wounds at Charlottesville." [14]

22

Final Punches

IN A MODEST HOME NEAR MCIVOR, VIRGINIA, well up in the Blue Ridge Mountains surrounding Lynchburg, a graying mother bent over her diary and wrote with painful hand. It was New Year's, a bleak Sunday, and Virginia McLaurine Mosby's recordings were taken up largely with the Lord's day as it affected her home life. But there was one entry that stood out in sharp contrast to the others. It read: "Hear by the papers today that John is recovering. We feel intense anxiety about John. No tidings from John." This was followed two days later by another entry: "This evening . . . John arrived safely."

Mosby's fight against death was phenomenal. A ghost of the dead could have brought little more surprise to the face of the Lake women and their father than did this wounded Rebel when he staggered out of the bedroom after the Federals had left the night of December 21. A strong constitution had kept him alive, but it was his presence of mind and possibly the whiskey beneath the belts of the enemy that saved him from capture. Even as Union officers leaned over his prostrate form he could see through partly closed lids, drooped to feign approaching death, the coat that would have changed in a flash his significance as a potential prisoner. It lay beneath a washstand where he had shoved it. That had been next to his last act before the Blue soldiers rushed in; the last had been to run his hand, dripping with the blood of his wound, across the lower part of his face and to force out saliva with the rattling gurgle of a dying man.

Mosby, too, thought his end had come.[1] On emerging from the bed chamber, he wavered in the faint glow from the fireplace, bootless and helpless, waiting for the Lakes to collect themselves enough to act. It was Dona who showed the greatest presence of mind. While she and her sister stretched the now docile leader of the fierce Loudoun Valley raiders on the floor and tore up petticoats to swathe his wound, the corpulent parent waddled out through the weather after an ox cart. The Lake family never forgot the harsh exchange of words that passed between old Ludwell and Mosby when a Negro slave took up the reins to drive to the Acquilla Glasscock home.[2] This time, with a disadvantage, a far different disadvantage from that at the Miskel farm, the Partisan was fighting with his back to the wall. There was a bounty on his head, and he was convinced the path chosen by his ebony-skinned driver would lead directly to the camp of the enemy. But the cold, tortuous ride ended as Lake had planned.

Mosby's men soon gathered around him. Vedettes, carefully spaced, guarded the roads in all directions. In front of the Glasscock home at all hours stood an ambulance with horses attached, ready to dash off to the mountains at the slightest alarm. For more than a week this constant watch was maintained while Mosby passed through his crisis, attended by the fighting Ranger surgeon, Dr. Will Dunn, and by physicians of the neighborhood. Then, in the face of a threatening snow storm, he was borne along a circuitous route to Culpeper and thence to the home of his parents. There he soon was joined by Dr. Monteiro, who had come directly from Richmond.[3]

On the day Mosby arrived at McIvor, Companies C, E, F and G of his command set out for the Northern Neck. At the front of the column rode Sam Chapman, but their ranking officer was his brother, William, at the moment on his way to Petersburg to receive instructions on their operations directly from General Lee. Back in Loudoun and Fauquier were the other units and Dolly Richards, long weeks and lean weeks ahead.

A week after Monteiro reached his bedside Mosby began to voice impatience to return to the saddle.[4] His medical friend treated the idea coldly. It would be many days, he said, before the wound would be healed.

But on January 28 there was concrete evidence that Mosby was made of stronger stuff than even his physician supposed. That day he visited the Lynchburg *Republican*. He was pale and thin, and moved about with a stiffness that indicated he still was far from complete recovery. But in the course of conversation at the newspaper office, he took the liberty to exaggerate a little, assuring reporters he would be in the saddle again by the first of February. When the Richmond *Whig* heard of this visit it gave prompt notice, adding: "Let the Yankees look out, as he is a military Shylock, and will demand of them the debt they owe him to the last farthing." [5] The Federals already had learned that Sheridan's announcement of Mosby's death was premature. On the 18th, the *Star* had reported that the Partisan was at Lynchburg and that he would be riding again shortly.

Mosby went directly by rail from Lynchburg to Richmond. At the beleaguered capital, where people shook off their fits of depression at sight of a Confederate who still could say he held the upper hand on the enemy, he was given the greatest acclaim accorded him during the war. Here was the man they all would like to be.

His appearance in the halls of the Confederate Congress on the 30th brought prompt recognition. Unanimous approval was given a resolution inviting him to a privileged seat on the floor of the House during his stay in the city.[6] A three-man committee was appointed to wait on him and to escort him into the chamber, and when this was done the House took a ten-minute recess to pay him its respects. With the Speaker performing the ceremony of introduction, members separately approached to shake his hand and were followed by a number of ladies who were in the hall as spectators. During the same day, the Virginia Legislature gave him a fitting reception.[7] Commenting on it, the *Whig* observed that "South Carolina, in the first revolution, was justly proud of her Marion and Sumter, and Virginia today is no less proud of her fortunate son whom the Yankees denominate a guerrilla and a bandit." The Confederate Congress later invited him to a seat on its floor during his stay in the city.[8]

Before leaving Richmond for the last time he was to see it in Confederate hands, the wounded raider journeyed to Petersburg and partook of a meager dinner with General Lee. Their conversation was more on recollections than projections. The gray-haired commander of the Army of Northern Virginia manifested great interest in the visitor's account of his operations, possibly because his own father, "Light Horse Harry" Lee, had been a Partisan in the Revolutionary War. As the 31-year-old leader of independents prepared to depart, Lee repeated previous precautions against unnecessary exposure to danger.

A day or two later Mosby took another journey. Judge Robert Ould, the Confederate agent of exchange, invited him to go down the James on a boat carrying several hundred prisoners to be exchanged. The *Star* heard of the trip and gave its readers an account: "The guerrilla chief Mosby, on the last trip of the steamer *Mary Allison*, which brought down the exchanged prisoners, came down as a passenger, in company with several ladies. He seemed to be quite friendly with some of our officers, but the majority of them did not notice him. He looks quite thin in flesh." [9] One person on board that day rushed to embrace the raider. It was the drummer boy he had saved from hanging during the drawing among Custer's men.

Failure of Mosby to strike with customary frequency caused the press in the North to comment that "his gang since his absence has diminished in numbers, and lost much of its prestige among the Secesh who expect wonderful things upon the return of their chevalier." [10]

The command's activity during its leader's convalescence had been brilliant if not extensive. Richards, in one instance, led a party to the B. & O. railroad and derailed a train of fifteen cars two miles from Duffield Station. It was loaded with rich stores. He next stole with a few men toward the Twelfth Pennsylvania Cavalry camp of Colonel M. A. Reno near Charles Town, wrung the countersign from a prisoner and, with it, managed to steal in and stampede a majority of the horses in the stables. Reno had a speech ready for his command next morning. "With such men as Mosby's, I could go anywhere!" he stormed.[11]

Through Loudoun Valley for weeks a couple of Confederate deserters had been riding in an effort to learn the hiding places of Mosby's men. Near the middle of February, having learned that Ranger Dolly Richards was staying at his father's home near Upperville, they hurried into the Federal lines to report. On the 18th, a force of 228 men, augmented by a staff of scouts and the two deserters, left camp in the Shenandoah Valley. Four inches of snow lay on the ground as nature's contribution toward a successful expedition.

At Paris, the Federals separated into two parties and took divergent routes, one led by Major Thomas Gibson, the other by Captain Henry E. Snow. Throughout the night they rode, intending to meet again at Upperville, but their plans went astray. The detail under Snow, first to come in at that point, uncovered two barrels of liquor and a third of its members proceeded to get hilariously drunk. Failing in his search for Richards and fearing consequences of an attack from the Rangers while such a large number of his troopers were tippling, Snow set out for camp an hour before dawn.

Gibson's party arrived at Upperville after daylight and set out immediately on the homeward journey, harassed continually front and rear by small parties of Rangers. At Paris, hostile fire was trained at them from behind a stone wall. They hurried on, through the village and into Ashby's Gap. With them they carried eighteen prisoners and fifty horses.

At Mount Carmel, their route turned at a sharp angle toward Shepherd's Mill, along a narrow, rocky path that seemed to have been cut out of the mountain side. With soldiers unable to ride abreast in this narrow defile, Gibson called a halt and put things in order to resist an attack. Front and rear were strengthened and the rear guard was placed in charge of Captain D. K. Duff. Ahead of the rear guard and immediately behind the main body were strung out the prisoners and led horses. After these dispositions were in shape, Gibson rode to the head of the column and turned around to view the effect. It was a beautiful picture. Blue uniforms standing in strong color against the white background of snow. Sleek animals made sleeker by the fresh morning air. And all of it given a touch of medieval romance by the overtowering crags.

As he surveyed the riders he saw several men waving and making gestures back among the rear guard, which still had not turned off from the main road. Surprised and surmising there was trouble, he ordered troops near him to be on the alert and to move the captives and horses into the midst of the extreme advance.

"No sooner had I issued these commands than I saw Captain Duff and his party at the rear of the small party who marched in the rear of the led horses," Gibson later stated in a report in which he pleaded for investigation by a court of inquiry.[12] "Captain Duff's command was coming at a run. I saw Rebels among and in the rear of the party, charging. I ordered the command forward, fired a volley and ordered a charge, which the men did not complete. Captain Duff in the meantime was trying to rally his men in the rear of my line. Before his men had reloaded their pieces, I had fired another volley and ordered a second charge. All the prisoners and led horses had not yet entered the path. The charge was met by one from the enemy and the command was broken. The men had no weapons but their carbines and these were extremely difficult to load, and inefficient in the melee that ensued."

This fight was one of the most brilliant encountered by the Rangers and was a fine reminder of the wisdom of Mosby's decree that revolvers should be the weapons of the Rangers. Thirteen Federals were killed; many were wounded. Sixty-three, including several officers, were taken prisoner and ninety horses were captured. The Partisans had but one casualty.

Such a setback from an enemy the high command considered fairly well scattered might have been sufficient cause for severe reprisal. Sheridan had said in November that the Forty-third Battalion must go, and it had been his intentions during the winter lull to carry out that aim. But as he weighed the matter, Grant set the wheels in motion for his spring campaign to capture Richmond. He wrote Sheridan on the 20th to move toward Lynchburg as soon as he could travel, to head the streams in Virginia to the west of Danville and to push on to join with Sherman, then "eating the vitals" out of South Carolina.[13] "Sufficient cavalry should be left behind to look after Mosby's gang," cautioned the commander-in-chief.

Mosby got back to his command just as Sheridan was starting for Lynchburg, leaving General Winfield S. Hancock in command of the Middle Military Division. The march down the valley was hurried, and it ended as Grant had planned. Early was defeated near Waynesboro, Charlottesville was captured, and 20,000 more troops were ready to close in on Lee's lines at Petersburg.

Blustery March brought rains and high streams. As the month advanced, Hancock sent a force to Loudoun County under Colonel Reno to do intense scouting work. It was a combination of foot soldiers and horse—1,000 men. Hancock had high hopes for its success.

The pass through the Blue Ridge into Loudoun by way of Clarke's Gap followed a long defile for miles between high mountain walls and then, at Hillsboro, opened on rolling terrain stretching toward the rich, well-tended farms of the Quaker settlement around Hamilton. It was just clear of this gap on the 21st that some of Mosby's scouts got sight of Reno's column. To all appearances it was a supply train on its way to the Washington outposts—a long line of covered wagons rolling between a guard of cavalry flankers. But the Rangers had suspicions that proved correct. Peering from cover along the route, they got glimpses of bristling guns in the hands of infantrymen wedged into the innocent wagons.

The road south out of Hamilton for some distance took an eccentric course. It stumbled half a mile past farm houses and open fields and little patches of wood, then turned abruptly westward for a few hundred yards, took another sharp turn, over a hill and past a larger body of wood, and kept on southwestwardly toward the little hamlet of Lincoln. This last body of trees fell away from the road into a dell-like depression, well concealed. In this hiding place waited 120 men from the Forty-third Battalion. Loitering at Hamilton were Mosby and a hand-ful of well-mounted Rangers.

When Reno's cavalry advance came into Hamilton, it spied the small group of Graycoats and gave chase. Down the eccen-tric road the pursuit continued, past the farm houses, the fields, around the sharp curves, over the hill and into the range of the men waiting in the wood. Out of cover at this moment rode the concealed Rangers, and the flight turned sharply about and headed back toward Hamilton. The Federal advance was driven back on the wagons with a loss of twenty wounded and killed.

As a cold, disagreeable wind whipped up the last strong blow of March, a courier from Gordonsville found Mosby and delivered a message from Lee: "Collect your command and watch the country from front of Gordonsville to Blue Ridge and also Valley. Your command is all now in that section, and the general will rely on you to watch and protect the country. If any of your command is in Northern Neck, call it to you." [14] The dispatch told Mosby much that he had tried to find out while in Richmond. The end was nearer than he had supposed. There was no comfort in the realization that a battalion of fewer than a thousand men was all the South had to defend the wide expanse of country west of Gordonsville.

The winter months had seen new faces ride in almost daily to join the Rangers. As commands went to pieces in the regular branch of service, Confederate soldiers took advantage of the opportunity to get into detached operations. During Mosby's absence, Dolly Richards looked over the best of these pros-pective Partisans and told them to find a boarding place in the vicinity. By April, more than half a hundred recruits were wait-ing to be taken in, and on the 5th of the month Mosby banded them together as Company H, his eighth unit. These additions brought his muster to 800 effectives, a promising force with which to carry on his campaigns now that spring had opened.

The new company was headed by a young man who already had established himself as an outstanding fighter in the regular service—George Baylor, native of Jefferson County, Virginia, and formerly of Ashby's Brigade. What success may have been in the cards for him as a unit leader under Mosby got only an embryonic reflection. His first expedition was against the camp near Halltown of the Loudoun Rangers. It resulted in the capture of nearly all of these old enemies of the Forty-third Battalion. Stevenson got word of the affair and passed it on in a brief message that began: "Mosby surprised camp of Loudoun Rangers near Keyes Ford and cleaned them out." When the telegram came to General Hancock, he read it and tossed it aside with the terse remark, "Well, that's the last of the Loudoun Rangers." [15]

Mosby had no time to rejoice over extermination of his old enemies. There was talk that Lee's lines had broken at Petersburg and that Richmond had been evacuated. Some of this information had leaked out of Washington and it seemed worth investigating. He summoned Ranger Channing Smith, a friend of the Lees, and sent him to learn the truth.

CHAPTER

23

"I Am No Longer Your Commander"

———————

L EE'S SURRENDER AT APPOMATTOX was announced to civilians
living in the area embraced by the Middle Military Division through a circular distributed April 10. This broadside told
of the terms—delivery of all except officers' sidearms and private property, with parole not to take up arms against the
United States—and added: "The guerrilla chief Mosby is not
included in the parole." [1] From the circular the raider got his
most definite information of developments in the principal
theater of war. Reports since Channing Smith set out for Richmond were that Johnston had defeated Sherman in a surprise
coup and was marching to reinforce Lee.

Out of Richmond at this time emanated a move to have the
Partisan leader included in Lee's surrender. Grant approved
the idea. In a letter to Secretary of War Stanton he wrote: "I
think . . . there will be no difficulty now in bringing in on the
terms voluntarily given to General Lee all the fragments of
the Army of Northern Virginia, and it may be the army of
Johnston also. I wish Hancock would try it with Mosby." [2]

The day after Grant dated his message to Stanton, Brigadier-
General C. H. Morgan, divisional chief of staff, took considerable pains with a letter. When completed, it was entrusted,
along with a copy of the circular, to a messenger with instructions that it be delivered to J. H. Clarke, merchant and hotel
proprietor of Millwood, who had advised Union officers he
could contact Mosby. This letter was accompanied by copies
of letters concerning the surrender of the Army of Northern

Virginia and informed the raider he would be offered the same conditions as those granted Lee. Morgan added that an officer of equal rank would meet Mosby to arrange details at any point and time designated by him.[3]

On April 12, Hancock informed Halleck that he had sent the communications, but had received no answer. "It is quite as likely," he wrote, "that Mosby will disband as that he will formally surrender, as all his men have fine animals and are generally armed with two pistols only. They will not give up these things, I presume, as long as they can escape. I will employ the cavalry force here in hunting them down."[4]

Hancock gave new warning on the 13th. Recalling that the circular and the letter to Mosby had gone unnoticed and that depredations by independent bands continued, he advised the people that it would be decidedly more to their interest and comfort to assist him by giving information against the Rangers than to harbor and encourage them longer. "The search for the guerrilla parties will end only when their operations cease and they yield obedience to the laws," he decreed.

Passage of April 13 marked the end of the second day since the message had been sent Mosby. The man who had taken charge of the letter still waited at Millwood. Civilians there relayed reports—authentic and fresh from the Partisan leader, they said—that there was no occasion for the surrender of his command. This exasperated Hancock and he made plans to bring matters to a head. Mosby had had his chance and had let it pass. The Federal officer gave orders for an infantry and cavalry force to move into Loudoun County to meet troops which would be started the following night from Washington. Its objective was complete destruction of the Forty-third Battalion and punishment of inhabitants of the country who had harbored or assisted the Partisans.

But a tragedy the night of the 14th postponed immediate action against the raiders. To the horror and consternation of both the North and South, an assassin, believed to be John Wilkes Booth, the actor, shot and fatally wounded Abraham Lincoln while he sat engrossed in a play at the Ford Theater. At the same moment, another desperate killer forced his way into the home of Secretary of State Seward and stabbed him as he lay in bed recuperating from injuries received when a team of horses ran away with him a day or two earlier.

The Federals by this time had located Mosby. He was reported at Leesburg trying to induce all stragglers to join him. Messages passed back and forth from Middle Military Division headquarters served only to increase suspense as to what Mosby planned to do. This continued to grow until a letter from the raider was brought to Hancock at Winchester under flag of truce on the 15th. In it, Mosby explained that his notice regarding the Army of Northern Virginia had come only through the enemy and that, in his opinion, the emergency had not yet arisen which justified the surrender of his command. "With no disposition, however, to cause the useless effusion of blood or to inflict on a war-worn population any unnecessary distress," he added, "I am ready to agree to a suspension of hostilities for a short time in order to enable me to communicate with my own authorities or until I can obtain sufficient intelligence to determine my future action." [5]

Mosby had prepared his answer after careful consideration. Developments of the last two or three days had brought stubborn proposals from his men. Some wanted to keep the command intact and set out for Mexico, where Maximilian was offering strong inducements to experienced soldiers. But the soundest argument against surrender was Joe Johnston. The fate of his army still was unknown. The most logical step, it seemed, would be to head for North Carolina in the hope of carrying out the movement Lee had in mind at the time he was blocked by the enemy at Appomattox. If this failed, they would be that much nearer Mexico. But in the meantime, until some news concerning Johnston could be obtained, no harm would result from parleying.

Hancock replied through his adjutant immediately that he would agree to a cessation until noon Tuesday provided there were no hostilities from Mosby's command. At that hour, he added, an officer of equal rank would meet the raider at Millwood to arrange the details of surrender.[6] Following this, he quickly spread the word that a suspension of hostilities had been agreed on with Mosby. He was confident the Partisan would come to terms and wrote Halleck he had set a meeting to accept the surrender.

In the midst of Hancock's correspondence came a warning note from Secretary of War Stanton.[7] It said that "in holding an interview with Mosby it may be needless to caution an old soldier like you to guard against surprise or danger to yourself." Stanton explained that his fears were based on the assassination of Lincoln, which he said showed such "astounding wickedness" that too much precaution could not be taken. "If Mosby is sincere, he might do much toward detecting and apprehending the murderer of the President," the Secretary concluded.

To stave off hostilities until a meeting could be held, Hancock ordered a full account of the situation to be sent all officers concerned. He specified that Brigadier-General George Chapman should conduct the interview on the 18th and should permit officers and privates to return to their homes after they had been paroled. "The major-general commanding wishes General Chapman to impress very clearly upon Colonel Mosby's mind the great necessity that with his surrender all guerrilla operations should cease," the notice concluded.[8]

Mosby called his command together at Salem Monday, the 17th. Among the men who appeared were members of the companies quartered on the Northern Neck. They had returned on the 13th, armed with tales of their exploits, the most daring of which was a night raid on Williamsburg. Also present was Channing Smith, newly back from Richmond with a pathetic account of his experiences.[9] At the evacuated capital, he had waited in hiding until dark and then had gone directly to the home of his uncle, General Chilton, at one time Lee's chief of staff. Soon after he was admitted to the residence, a knock sounded on the door. A candle was lighted and the portal opened to General Lee, out on one of the nightly strolls he took for exercise.

Smith imparted his message from Mosby: "What should the Rangers do—surrender or fight on?"

"Give my regards to Colonel Mosby," Lee answered, "and

tell him that I am under parole, and cannot, for that reason, give him any advice."

"But, General," said Smith, "what must I do?"

Lee replied: "Channing, go home, all you boys who fought with me, and help to build up the shattered fortunes of our old state."

Mosby kept his command together only a short time on the 17th. He told his men of developments and cautioned them to maintain the truce on hostilities. He added that those who wanted to accept parole individually had his consent to do so. Before dismissing them, he directed a number of his officers and scouts to meet him at Paris at 10 A.M. the next day.

Hancock wrote Stanton on the 17th that, although he had conferred with two of Mosby's men, he did not intend to meet the Partisan in person "at this time." [10] If Mosby surrendered, he said he would endeavor to ascertain from or through him something concerning Lincoln's assassination and then probably would have an interview with him. "I have now a suitable person engaged in seeking information of that kind from Mosby's men," he added.

Grant was informed that day from Darnestown that a number of White's and Mosby's men had sent word they wished to be paroled. In an indorsement to the Secretary of War, he expressed the view that it would be better to have them in Maryland as paroled prisoners of war than at large as guerrillas. He also advised that each man be required to sign his own parole, instead of allowing officers to sign for the entire group.

The anticipated surrender of the Forty-third Battalion failed to develop on Tuesday. Mosby was late arriving, and two of his men were sent ahead to notify the Federals of his approach. Shortly after noon, he rode up with an escort of fifteen men. The meeting place agreed on was the hotel of the intermediary, J. H. Clarke. In this building, beside a road along which had marched Stonewall Jackson's troops on the way to Manassas, waited with his staff Brigadier-General George H. Chapman, the same whose advance detail had been surprised by William Chapman in Ashby's Gap.

Courtesies were exchanged, during which the Partisan leader and his companions expressed sincere regret over the death of Lincoln. Then they turned to the business at hand. Conversation was abrupt and to the point after Mosby voiced a request for an extension of time, explaining that he still had not been able to contact Johnston's army. The Union officer accepted the proposal calmly and indicated by his questions that he would make as much concession as his authority would permit.

Mosby told Chapman he was unwilling to surrender at once because his command was not in immediate danger.

"I have had no information as yet that would justify my concluding the Confederate cause is altogether hopeless," he added.

Chapman insisted that the cause was lost and the continuation of hostilities could have no constructive result.

"I am anxious to avoid any useless effusion of blood or destruction of property," Mosby told him. "For that reason, I desire to suspend hostilities for a short time until I can learn the fate of Johnston's army. Should that be defeated or surrender, then I will consider the Confederate cause as lost and will disband my organization."

"You will disband your organization?" questioned Chapman.

"Yes, even if the end has come, I do not intend to surrender as an organization for parole," Mosby replied. "I will disband my command instead and let each individual choose his own course. In fact, I have already informed my men that they may go and give their parole if they desire."

"How about you?" asked Chapman.

"I have no favors to ask," Mosby answered, "I am quite willing to stand by my acts, all of which I believe justifiable. But, for that matter, I do not intend to remain in the country."

When the conference ended, a ten-day cessation of hostilities commencing April 20 and ending April 30 was agreed on subject to approval of General Hancock. Mosby was to be notified at Millwood by noon of the 20th what Hancock decided. It was further specified that, if in the interval General Johnston's army should capitulate or be dispersed, the raider would disband his organization.[11]

Chapman immediately sent a copy of the agreement to Hancock with a letter explaining the outcome of the meeting.[12] "I did not give him to hope that this agreement for a ten days' suspension would be concurred in," he said of his talk with Mosby. "I regret that I have not the pleasure of communicating the surrender of this force, but trust my action in the premises will meet with your approval. The interview throughout was characterized by good feeling. Perhaps I ought, in justice to Colonel Mosby and his officers, to state a universal regret was expressed because of the assassination of the President."

Hancock looked to Washington for an answer to Mosby's proposition, and Washington in turn looked to Grant. It came in a terse order:

"If Mosby does not avail himself of the present truce, end it and hunt him and his men down. Guerrillas . . . will not be entitled to quarter." [13]

The harshness of Grant's reply may have been influenced by a report linking Mosby with Lincoln's death. It said evidence showed the Partisan leader knew of the assassination plot and had been in Washington with the assassin, now definitely established as Booth. Warning was given that some of the gang involved in the scheme were trying to escape by crossing the upper Potomac and joining Mosby.

The charge against Mosby was untrue, although it later was found that an ex-Ranger had been Seward's assailant. This attempted murderer was Louis Thornton Powell, twenty-one-year-old youth of powerful physique from Alabama and one of the four Partisans who rode down Blazer. He was the son of a Baptist preacher and had been wounded at Gettysburg before he became a Partisan. After serving a year with the Forty-third Battalion, he deserted and rode into the Union lines at Alexandria, taking the oath of allegiance under the alias of Payne, name of the family with which he had boarded as a Ranger. At Baltimore he came in contact with Booth, stage idol he had met when he came up to Richmond with the Second Florida Infantry at the outbreak of war, and the assassination plot was developed. Jail and the gallows awaited him.

So it was in the midst of this confusion resulting from the

President's death and its resultant diversion from military duties that Hancock sent word to Mosby on the 19th—even while he suspected the Partisan of complicity in the assassination—that the truce would end at noon the following day.[14] He added that an officer would be at Millwood to receive the Confederate's decision. "Unless you then announce your immediate surrender," Hancock stated, "the arrangements will be perfected at Millwood. Truce of hostilities in such case will only refer to that point and be of such duration as only to allow time to prepare and sign the paroles and receive the public property." He concluded with a report that the command had been given "not to offer you or your men terms again" after expiration of the truce.

Hancock followed up this letter to Mosby with dispatches to members of his own military family. The gist of these in all instances was: "Look out for your lines after 12 o'clock tomorrow. Mosby will surrender or the truce with him will end at that hour."

Mosby met designated Rangers at Paris on the 20th and rode away to his final conference as an officer of the Confederate States army. At Millwood sharply at noon, he found Union officers waiting in the parlor of the little hotel. There was still an arrogance about the stooped figure in gray who walked rapidly into the room and took a seat. Mosby was too much of an independent to lay down arms as long as there was a fighting chance to continue operations, and he told the Federals so in the conversation that followed. He was shown a telegram from Grant to Hancock instructing that all Rebel officers and soldiers be given the same terms as Lee, but that those from states that had not passed ordinances of secession would be permitted to return to their homes only on compliance with the amnesty proclamation. Mosby read without comment; then said he was not prepared to surrender, although a part of his command already had disbanded.

"The truce has ended," crisply announced the Federal officer in charge. "We can have no further intercourse under its terms."

As they prepared to adjourn, a gray-clad soldier broke

through the guards and rushed into the room. It was John Hearn, Ranger of Company C. He had been an unofficial member of the party from the Forty-third Battalion and had waited on the outside while the conference was in progress.

Hearn was an illiterate soldier who had been unable to take in the exact meaning of this meeting behind closed doors. While he waited, he had sought to display competitively his skill as a horseman. Union soldiers, huffed by his conceit, took him up, and it was with great pride that the Ranger dashed out into the open in a race that had no goal or purse other than an exhibition of individual adroitness. Their course by chance led into the path of a Union brigade. Sight of the Blue column caused Hearn to pull hard on his horse and head back to town, convinced of something he had suspected all along.

"Colonel," he cried as he burst into the room at the hotel, "the infernal devils have sot a trap for you. I jist now rode out about a mile and found a thousand of 'em hidin' in the bushes. It's a trick to capture us. Let's fight 'em."

Dr. Monteiro, one of the Rangers present, recorded the scene that followed:

"With a look that I shall never forget, Mosby sprang to his feet, instantly grasping one of the murderous weapons in his belt and glaring upon the Yankee officers with an expression that reminded me more of a tiger crouching to spring upon his prey than anything I have ever seen. . . . He said in a loud and sharp voice: 'Sir, if we are no longer under the protection of our truce, we are, of course, at the mercy of your men. We shall protect ourselves.'

"With that inimitable sign and gesture that so often had sent his gallant followers like a thunderbolt into the serried ranks of the foe, he led the way with long and rapid strides to the door. . . . It was a scene difficult to describe, but never to be forgotten. Every Partisan was well prepared for instant death and more than ready for a desperate fight. Had a single pistol been discharged by accident, or had Mosby given the word, not one Yankee officer in the room would have lived a minute. With Hearn's warning voice ringing in our ears, we mounted our horses in silence and Mosby led the way. His only word of command was 'mount and follow me.' We galloped rapidly from Millwood to the Shenandoah River, closely followed by a cloud of Yankee cavalry." [15]

Late that night Hancock reported that Mosby had departed from the meeting at Millwood "very much agitated." [16] But the Federal leader was not worried. "My impression is that everything in this country shows a state of pacification . . .," he concluded. "If Mosby is in Loudoun Valley, I will hunt him out."

Salem had never seen such a gathering of Rangers as assembled there April 21. Some were on hand soon after daybreak, dressed in their finest uniforms, wearing their shiniest brace of revolvers, riding their best horses. It was a dismal day. Rain fell during the early morning; and forenoon was well advanced before oilcloths and raincoats were thrown back to reveal the brightness of rich cadet gray. Many of the horsemen had ridden considerable distances, though a large majority had come from homes scattered over the rolling terrain between the village and the mountains plainly visible on each side.

People were uncertain of the purpose of the assembly. It was rumored Mosby planned to surrender, and they knew of the meetings he had had with Federal officers at Millwood earlier in the week. But residents in the neighborhood of his confederacy, particularly those living in the village recognized as the principal rendezvous of his audacious riders, looked on him as too much of a rebel to capitulate. Queries as to what he had in mind brought no satisfactory answer. The word sent out—last message to be broadcast over his grapevine system— ordered all members of the battalion to report at Salem in full uniform.

The Partisans were not cheerful over developments. Their hopes had been dashed at Appomattox on the 9th. Now, twelve days later, they had been summoned to a meeting that to all appearances would be the windup. It was said Mosby had spent considerable time that morning in the preparation of a document of some sort. The original had been copied and that copy, so talk went, was in the pocket of Adjutant Willie Mosby. Its mystery gave it importance.

Mosby was among the late arrivals. He dismounted near the center of the village and threw the reins to one of his men. He was clean-shaven now, nattily garbed, boots blacked. His men slowly gathered around him, studying his face, listening to his words, trying to draw him out. But Mosby avoided conversation. He turned away and walked, here and there, eyes shifting to entrances of the village and to faces of horsemen who rode in from the distance.

Shortly before noon company leaders were ordered to form their units on the green north of town. At the command, the uniformed assemblage and most of the residents moved out from the crossroads to the designated spot, a wide, open field skirted on the far side by a fringe of bushes and trees.

Scarcely 200 Rangers were present. One by one they found their places in a long line, divisible into eight parts, each representing in order a company in the sequence in which it had been organized. There was no roll call. When the last man had sidled his horse into position, a deep silence fell over the gathering. Eyes were turned toward the leader.

Mosby sat still between the two battalion commanders, William Chapman and Dolly Richards, a few feet behind the adjutant. With the formation complete, he rode to the upper end of the line and slowly moved down the long row of faces. First was Company A, waiting confident like an eldest child. Next Company B, the second eldest; Company C, blessed throughout with faithful officers; Company D, not itself without Montjoy; Company E, the reserve unit because of the rallying ability of its belligerent captain, Sam Chapman; Company F, the troubadour unit whose members carried in the back of their roster book the words of "Seeing Nellie Home"; Company G, born while enemy fires crackled over Loudoun Valley, and Company H, the neophyte.

Exactly what was running through the leader's mind as his horse, with neck arched, paced off the length of the line no one ever would know. Perhaps a thought flashed back over the years to the day he rode into Abingdon as a recruit; over the months since he parted from Jeb Stuart to become a Partisan, at bay, cruel, hardened to the overwhelming odds against him.

Graves now turning green would have marked finis to some of those reflections—

> The circling seasons come and go,
>   Springs dawn and autumns set,
> And winter, with its drifted snow,
>   Repays the summer's debt;
> And song of birds and hint of bloom
>   Are gay and bright, as when,
> Those gallant lads rode to their doom
>   Long since with Mosby's men.[17]

Many faces were missing that had given Mosby his greatest confidence during his turbulent career as a Partisan. Some were absent with excuse—Tom Turner, Whitescarver, William R. Smith, Captain Hoskins, "Big Yankee" Ames, Montjoy and half a hundred others. But the cause for which they had fought now was drawing its final, wheezing gasp. The Army of Northern Virginia had folded; only Joe Johnston's troops were in the field farther south.

Mosby rode back to his position between Chapman and Richards, turned his horse about and waited, motionless. His brother unfolded a slip of paper in the raw, damp air and read slowly—

> Fauquier,
> April 21, 1865.

Soldiers:

I have summoned you together for the last time. The vision we cherished of a free and independent country has vanished, and that country is now the spoil of a conqueror.

I disband your organization in preference to surrendering to our enemies. I am no longer your commander. After an association of more than two eventful years, I part from you with a just pride in the fame of your achievements and grateful recollections of your generous kindness to myself. And now, at this moment of bidding you a final adieu, accept the assurance of my unchanging confidence and regard. Farewell!

> Jno. S. Mosby,
> Colonel.[18]

24

Parole

———◦∿◦———

PEOPLE HEARD SOON AFTER the Forty-third Battalion disbanded at Salem that Mosby's own men were pursuing him in hope of claiming a $2,000 reward offered by Hancock. Secretary of War Stanton believed none of it, and warned the nation to be on the alert. Intolerantly he decreed: "Guerrillas are entitled to nothing but powder and ball." [1]

Federals galloped in larger numbers along paths of Northern Virginia. They were curious, each man individually, to know what had become of Mosby—and so was the *Whig* at Richmond. Many rumors were afloat. It was said he was hovering around the fallen Confederate capital for predatory purposes, and again that he had crossed the James River en route to the Trans-Mississippi.

On the other hand, "more authentic intelligence" reported he had been defeated by U. S. cavalry south of Winchester and had been forced to disband. Advices direct from Winchester went so far as to announce he had surrendered on the 17th. But at Alexandria, paroled Rangers spread word that he and a few of his followers were trying to make their way to Texas. Washington newspapers, thinking he still was harbored by Rebel sympathizers at Salem, scoffed at such an idea. They said his command had deserted him and that some of its members had offered to bring him in for $5,000. This higher reward, the press explained, was demanded because the services of several men would be required to make the capture, and their proportionate share of the $2,000 already posted would be too small compensation for the risk involved. Hancock, with Grant's approval,[2] promptly assured the larger sum would be paid.

The first week of May advanced with more elaborate rumors. Halleck, transferred to Richmond in charge of the Military Division of the James, informed Grant that a squadron of cavalry sent to Lynchburg had returned with a report the city was held by 1,000 of Mosby's guerrillas. He said Sheridan had been sent to bring them in, that he proposed soon to issue an order that all armed men in Virginia who did not surrender by a certain date would be held as outlaws and robbers.

A second week passed. On the 15th, the brigade commander at Lynchburg, who had had no part in the rumor that guerrillas had taken the city, reported all quiet, adding: "It appears that Mosby has gone South with 100 followers. His last remark on leaving his father's house was 'I am an outlaw, and self-preservation is the first law of nature.' "[3]

Halleck prepared to expedite matters. He had not been connected with the reward posted by Hancock, so it was a separate effort when he announced on the 18th that $5,000 would be paid for Mosby's capture if he did not surrender by the 20th.

In the Lynchburg *Republican* of June 14 appeared an item of much interest to the Forty-third Battalion. It said Mosby had come to Lynchburg to surrender and had been in the act of leaving under parole when a telegram ordering his arrest arrived from Richmond. He escaped, the account added, closely pursued.

Mosby's efforts at parole were made nearly two months after his command was disbanded. Leaving Salem, he had set out for Richmond with a few men to seek information as to Johnston's fate. Near the city he drew up in hiding beside the old Lynchburg canal and sent one of his companions, John Munson, to gather late news. A canal boat came along in the meantime and from it those who remained behind got a newspaper that told them Johnston had surrendered. Next morning Munson returned with a plan for the capture of all Union officers quartered in the home from which Jefferson Davis had fled at the evacuation of Richmond. Mosby shook his head at the suggestion. "Too late," he said. "It would be murder and highway robbery now. We are soldiers, not highwaymen." [4]

This was the end. The little band rode back to the home of Robert Walker near Orange Court House and separated, each to take his own route back to the family he had left four years earlier.

Along the way toward his father's home at McIvor, Mosby rode leisurely through Charlottesville.[5] A small cavalry force was on duty there and he passed a lieutenant and a private in the street, but they ignored him and he continued on to the university to visit one of his former professors. His movements were calm and unhurried. But a short while after he left, soldiers appeared and surrounded the campus. Someone other than the Federals had recognized the lean, brown figure, and had talked.[6]

Because of the nearness of the Federal force at Lynchburg, Mosby remained at his father's less than a week; then went to the home of his uncle, John Mosby. It was situated far back in Nelson County, behind what some folks said were "the worst roads God ever let inflict the earth." [7] Shortly after the refugee arrived, the uncle sent an ex-Ranger to Richmond to learn what the Union planned to do with the Partisan leader. Another emissary found that General Lee was waiting to discuss the matter with General Grant.[8]

May passed with Mosby fidgeting to be out of his self-imposed exile. Meanwhile newspapers continued to wonder about his whereabouts and to jog the public in the hope of bringing to a close another chapter of the fratricidal war. But the opening of summer—the warm, restless air and the smell of blossoms—did more to prod the hardened fighter than the people's interest. Early in June, he sent his brother into Lynchburg to confer with Captain Swank, provost-marshal. Swank, unprepared to give a definite answer, promised to make inquiries of proper authorities. On June 12, William Mosby went back into the city and was told his brother would be paroled if he came in and gave himself up.

Mosby rode to Lynchburg the following day, in full uniform,

including revolvers, and stopped at the law office of a cousin.[9] Friends and acquaintances gathered around him. Soon they were joined by Union soldiers, all eager for a view of the mythical raider.

At Swank's office, he found the provost-marshal's duties temporarily in the hands of an officer who knew nothing of previous arrangements. This led to a flurry of official checking, of impromptu consultations, and when the answer was given, supported by a fresh dispatch from Richmond, it called for Mosby's immediate arrest. Surprised at this turn of affairs, the raider slapped the guns hanging at his sides. "There are twelve bullets here, gentlemen, and every last one of them will be fired before you take me," he announced.

The Federals hesitated, and Mosby resorted to the forensics he had used little since he left Bristol. He deserved fair treatment, he argued. He had come into the city in good faith, on assurance of parole from Captain Swank, and he had expected the Union to stand behind its promises. The officers put their heads together, and a few minutes later Mosby rode out of Lynchburg, assured cavalry would not take his trail until the next day. At sunrise, Federal horse rode forth, but even in peace Mosby eluded them.

A second offer of parole, this time supported by a positive promise of protection, was sent a few days afterward. Behind it was General Grant's desire to have absolute peace as quickly as possible, a goal talked over and agreed on in conference with Lincoln and Sheridan in April.

The Washington press announced June 29 that Mosby, "having been paroled on the same conditions as other officers of Lee's army, has returned to Culpeper and opened a law office." [10] It was true Mosby, finally paroled at Lynchburg, was staying at Culpeper temporarily, but it was not in his mind to enter legal practice there. Fauquier County was his choice. He had a feeling, encouraged by the advice of friends, that the course of the Unionists toward him in the neighborhood of his former confederacy would be more kindly after the first excitement of the surrender had passed.

Mosby stepped from the cars at Alexandria the afternoon of August 11 after a hot and dirty ride from Culpeper. He was dressed in trousers of army blue, a dark sack coat and a light soft hat. After four years in the open, he was raw-boned and sun-tanned, in the pink of condition. The Alexandria *Journal* noted in reporting the arrival of "the notorious guerrilla chief" that "his temperament is of the sanguine billious."

Within an hour, news of his presence had spread, and curious people congregated. Wherever he moved, crowds surrounded him. They shook his hands and cheered him, pushing in among Rangers who voluntarily had collected as an unofficial body-guard.

At a store on the corner of King and Royal Streets, his presence brought trouble. The assemblage outside, made up largely of Negroes, grew until it blocked the sidewalk and street. One colored civilian, his image of a fierce Rebel shattered, spoke in profane and deprecating terms of the slim figure in sack coat, uttering words that found an unsympathetic ear. A white man at his elbow slapped him and told him to keep his "damn mouth shut." Commotion followed, and a riot seemed imminent until the slapper was dragged off by the military to the judge of the Freedmen's Bureau.

But the crowd in the street was slow to disperse. At 4 p.m., police followed the simpler of two courses: they removed Mosby instead of the throng. He was arrested and placed in jail to spend two restless nights while the provost-marshal waited for instructions from headquarters.

The ex-raider found a degree of thrill in his treatment at Alexandria, although later confessing he was glad to get away. It was pleasing to know he had been such a thorn in the side of his enemies that they were reluctant to bury the hatchet; and there was some satisfaction in the acclamation he received in public. But it was a depleted wardrobe rather than a willingness to accept balm for his deeds which induced him to permit an admiring Philadelphia tailor to measure him for a free suit of clothes while he lay in jail.

Soon after the journey to Alexandria, a Northern newspaper correspondent found Mosby at Richmond. Out of the incident came a moving account: "A solitary man was seen beside the grave of Stuart in Hollywood Cemetery, near Richmond. The dew was on the grass, the birds sang overhead, the green hillock at the man's feet was all that remained of the daring leader of the Southern cavalry, who, after all his toils, his battles, and the shock of desperate encounters, had come here to rest in peace. Beside this unmarked grave the solitary mourner remained long, pondering and remembering. Finally he plucked a wild flower, dropped it upon the grave, and, with tears in his eyes, left the spot. This lonely mourner at the grave of Stuart was Mosby." [11]

By the last of August the former Partisan nerved himself to return to Fauquier. It was his plan to open a law office at Warrenton, where he reasoned meager facilities would be more than offset by the presence of many of his Rangers.

Early September found his shingle hanging from the California Building, across the street from the Warren-Green Hotel, where he and his fifteen-man detail had stopped in January, '63. From there in a few days he sent a brief, gossipy letter to Monteiro at Richmond. It was the beginning of a correspondence that continued until death. He wrote that he might become almost forgetful of the despotism of Yankee rule if he had the physician at hand to relate an occasional anecdote. Fauquier had been quite gay during the summer, he reported, and suggested that his friend visit him at Warrenton, advising that one of the doctor's old sweethearts "still flourishes like a green bay tree." He recalled his experiences at Alexandria. "The Yankees seemed to look upon me as a sort of menagerie," he related, "and I had to pay the penalty of their inordinate curiosity. They kept me two days under arrest and then released me with an order never to return there or into Fauquier again." In this letter, as in all other correspondence after the war, he left off his military title.

Mosby soon was joined by his wife and children, and, with his home once more organized, he turned seriously to the art of making a living. Real estate was a thriving business in the months following the war, so this was added to his law practice and for a time threatened to surpass it as a source of revenue.

But the violent conditions throughout the state created ample need for legal service. In November, a Washington newspaper observed that the raider had been admitted to the bar in the adjoining county of Fairfax. Shortly afterward, the same journal unkindly announced: "The famous guerrilla, who has probably done more mule stealing than any man living, is associated with Aylett Nicholas, Esq., prosecuting attorney, in the trial of Mr. Styles, internal revenue collector for the district of Prince William County, Va., who is himself on trial for mule stealing." [12]

Mosby's release from prison at Alexandria was not the end of his troubles with the Federals. Early in January, '66, he went to Leesburg on business, planning to return to Warrenton two days later. But his schedule was changed abruptly in a manner beyond his control. He wrote his wife that he was just in the act of starting home when an order came for his arrest and that he still was in the hands of the authorities, awaiting orders from the provost-marshal. "Don't be uneasy," he consoled. "Kiss the children for me." [13]

These surprise impalements of her husband disturbed Mrs. Mosby. Finally, in desperation, she took steps to stop them. While on the way to Baltimore in February with her son, Beverly, she stopped at the White House to see Andrew Johnson. The President had served in Congress with her father, had been a friend of the family, and it had been only a few years—but turbulent years—since he was a guest at her wedding. She expected kind treatment from him, and her visit was made with the confidence of friendship. But Johnson had changed. The reception she got was so cold that even the six-year-old Beverly noticed it and prayed that night for Andrew Johnson to be sent to the devil.

Mrs. Mosby was not a woman to be put off or to be discouraged by rebuff. After a night's rest, she bundled up her son again and went back into government quarters, this time to see General Grant. She was graciously received, as much so as if she had been the wife of a Union officer. Her story found a patient and sympathetic listener. When it was completed, Grant gave her the following statement written in his own hand:

Hdqrs. Armies of the United States,
Washington, D. C., February 2, 1866.

John S. Mosby, lately of the Southern army, will, hereafter, be exempt from arrest by military authorities, except for the violation of his parole, unless directed by the President of the United States, Secretary of War or from these headquarters.

His parole will authorize him to travel freely within the state of Virginia, and as no obstacle has been thrown in the way of paroled officers and men from pursuing their civil pursuits, or traveling out of their states, the same privilege will be extended to J. S. Mosby, unless otherwise directed by competent authority.

U. S. Grant.

This certificate was all Mosby needed while on his ordinary business rounds, but it in no way excused him from the Federal decree that no Confederate buttons or insignia should be worn. So there was only his individual obstinacy to blame for what happened at Leesburg in April.

Union soldiers standing on the main street of the town were astounded by the sight of an individual in resplendent Rebel uniform, buttons and all. This fellow gave them no attention, and passed on until an officer blocked his path and told him to remove his uniform or the buttons. It was an abrupt order, seriously uttered, but the reply it got almost swept the Federal off his feet. The wearer of the prohibited announced in phrases richly punctuated with profanity that there were not enough damn Yankees in Leesburg to strip his uniform of its identification. In that status the matter remained until a squad of soldiers was called out under arms. Ensuing developments were variously distorted by mouth and press. Some reports said Mosby mounted his horse to leave town and was fired at by the pursuing Federals; others that Mosby had fired at the detail sent to arrest him. No matter which was the correct version, Mosby escaped without injury, buttons and uniform intact.

25

Fifty-two Years Too Late

—◆◆◆—

MOSBY FOUND HE HAD MADE GOOD CHOICE in locating at Warrenton. The countryside was beautiful except for the pockmarks of war, and about him were some of the most prominent political and military figures of Virginia. For him, it was the beginning of a new era. He was facing his prime at thirty-three. Behind him were four years of unusual responsibility and experience.

So it was quite within reason that he should attempt to take up civilian life with the same fervor he had turned to military, giving no heed to such wild misstatements as a press report that he was engaged in the manufacture of corn cob pipes at Richmond.[1] By the end of the first year, he was able to write Monteiro: "I am getting on very well in my profession and, if the infernal Yankees will leave us alone, I hope to be able to make my living." [2]

But there was a restless strain in Mosby that seemed never to permit him to relax—that kept alive in him always a belligerent attitude that acted not always to his own good. During February, '67, for instance, the fighter who had been so careful to avoid vulnerability in warfare laid himself open to attack in a letter written to the Richmond *Examiner*.[3] In it was a statement General Rosser of the Confederate army construed as a personal injury. Rosser wrote Mosby for an explanation. Receiving none, he commented in writing to a friend that he "would have supposed that Colonel Mosby would have been one of the first men to repair a wrong inasmuch as he is represented to be quick to resent an injury." [4]

That summer, politics was smothered by the Freedmen's Bureau, the Carpetbaggers and the Federal occupation forces. Richmond papers advocated organization of a conservative party "to be composed of the great mass of those true, noble and gallant Virginians who sympathized warmly with the Confederacy," and urged that all respectable colored voters and original Union men unite with it. [5] Northern journals made fun of the proposal. Some of them reported that many of the late "fighting rebels" desired to ally themselves with the Republicans, in the hope of finding peace and prosperity.

Mosby managed to stay clear of the political field at this period. He added successful cases to his practice, enhancing his legal reputation, and in September bought for $3,700 a house and four-acre lot fronting on Warrenton's main street. On first going to Fauquier after the war, he had boarded until his family arrived and then had occupied a residence a short distance from town.

Washington newspapers buried in their personal columns October 22 an item that would have rated a streamer two and a half years earlier. It was an announcement that Colonel John S. Mosby, late of the Confederate service, was among prominent persons who had arrived at Willard's Hotel. A conference called by trade groups to discuss plans to reconstruct the Loudoun and Hampshire railroad, up and down which his Rangers had galloped with destruction, had brought the lawyer to the capital. The Washington session was followed by a meeting at Leesburg. During this assembly, a newspaper correspondent made Mosby the subject of one of his daily dispatches:

"While the railroad meeting was in progress yesterday at Leesburg, a turning of heads in the direction of an individual at the rear of the hall indicated that he was a personage of more note than his outward appearance indicated; and presently the word 'Mosby' buzzed about the room told the story. The famous Partisan chieftain practices law in Warrenton, and is now attending the court in session at Leesburg. He knows everybody in this part of Virginia, and has a very good practice. It will be remembered that he abandoned law to enter upon his wild military career. In personal appearance he looks the lawyer even less than the warrior. Dressed in careless, easy Virginia style, with white slouch hat, a dust-stained bob-tail coat, milk and molasses colored pants and vest (the latter minus two or three buttons), a badly adjusted false front tooth, a figure of medium size, close shaven, sunburnt youthful face, slouched shoulders, quiet, taciturn, undemonstrative in manner, it was not quite easy to believe that he was the individual whose name and daredevil achievements figured in the papers almost daily during the war." [6]

A month later, the New York *Post* published a news item announcing that "considerable excitement was caused at the Gold Board this afternoon by the appearance in the vice-president's desk of the Rebel General John S. Mosby." [7] According to the report, Mosby had appeared at the door and had sent his card to the presiding officer. In a moment, he was admitted and took a seat beside the official. As soon as some of the members learned the identity of the visitor, they directed a note to the head of the table asking for his withdrawal. The message was read aloud, and Mosby, hat in hand, prepared to leave. But before he could depart, a division occurred. Some members came to shake his hand, while others denounced him as a traitor. "He was also loudly hissed," continued the news item. "The affair caused considerable excitement, which did not subside until long after adjournment of the board."

The following year Grant was nominated for the Presidency and was elected by a good majority. The South stood by and waited impatiently for the March 4 inauguration. It was hoped in this part of the nation that a new face in the White House would bring some respite from the unsympathetic administration of Andrew Johnson.

The change of chief executives was staged with much ostentation. Two days before it occurred, newspapers reported Mosby was at Willard's.

His presence at the inauguration was chiefly in the nature of a vacation from his law books, although there may have been some other motive deep in his mind. Political interest with him had not spread far beyond the borders of Virginia, or even beyond the unhealed war sores of Warrenton. And at the moment, he was greatly exercised over matters at home, particularly activities of the town's military governor, Colonel W. H. Boyd.

Mosby had taken a violent dislike to Boyd from the start. In the months after his return from the inauguration—although national politics was in no way concerned—this hostility grew. In October, it reached the breaking point. The two met while riding horseback along a road near Warrenton and the military officer swung across the lawyer's path. There were sharp words, most of them from the lips of Boyd. He warned the ex-raider to stay out of his way, that if he continued to interfere in his business, he would make it a personal matter.

"I take that to mean you want personal satisfaction," said Mosby.

"Take it to mean what you want, but stay out of my business," replied Boyd.

"Then you'll get it when we return to Warrenton," Mosby snapped.

They parted without further words.

The lawyer's anger grew after he reached his office, and he made immediate preparations to accept the challenge according to prescribed rules. A friend, Colonel Thomas Smith, was called in as a second and sent to make arrangements. With him he carried a note that stated in part: "I now formally notify you of my acceptance of your proposition for a fight." [8] Smith was back in thirty minutes with a reply. In it the governor said he refused to be placed in the position of a challenging party, which would be opening himself to prosecution under the anti-duelling laws of Virginia, and that his words had been meant as a threat and not as a request for satisfaction. Mosby retaliated sharply:

"I wish you to know that as long as the interests of my clients and the people of Fauquier demand it, I shall continue 'to interfere in your business.' I now demand of you satisfaction for the language used by you in reference to myself."

Night came with a meeting on the field of honor as far off as when the two principals parted on the road. Some residents

remembered seeing Mosby down in a ravine near town practicing with a revolver shortly before dark.

Next morning, Boyd answered Mosby's second note with a
curt message in which he hedged and attempted to bring the
matter to an end. He said the lawyer must base his proposition
on other terms than that of satisfaction for words which he
had not even quoted, and concluded: "I deem a further correspondence useless." But Mosby felt differently. He forwarded
another note, his third:

Warrenton, October 3, 1869.

Sir: Your note of the 2d is evasive. If I omitted your offensive
language, it was because I desired no explanation or apology.
My object has been to test whether you would fight as a gentleman; and to remove all pretext for further equivocation, I
now quote your objectionable language. You said that "you
could prove in Pennsylvania that I was a highway robber." I
now demand satisfaction, not explanation or equivocation.

Will you fight? Colonel Smith has full authority to act. Respectfully, your obedient servant,

John S. Mosby.

Boyd never answered this letter, and there the matter ended.

The months of '69 brought charges against Mosby in a letter
published in the New York *Sun* under the heading: "This outlaw hanged five stragglers at Berryville." [9] The lawyer answered
the attack, giving details of Custer's hangings and of his own
in retaliation. "Sheridan acknowledged the justness of the deed
by ordering my men to be treated with the humanities of war,"
he gave as a final defense.

While in Richmond during March of '70, in the interest of
a judgeship for a friend, Mosby met General Lee and his
daughter, Agnes. They were crossing the foot bridge connect-
ing the Ballard and Exchange Hotels. Lee seemed pale and
haggard, and Mosby stopped for perfunctory courtesies. Later
he went to see the gray-haired veteran at his hotel room. During his stay of nearly an hour, they engaged in general conversation, Mosby making a conscious effort to exclude reference
to the war.

As he came away, he met General George Pickett and casually mentioned that he had been to see Lee. Pickett urged the lawyer to return to the hotel with him, explaining he would like to pay his respects, but did not want to be alone with his former commander. Mosby consented, and afterward regretted the move, finding himself in a meeting that was extremely embarrassing. As they left, Pickett spoke bitterly of the Southern leader and referred to him as "that old man," adding that he "had my division massacred at Gettysburg." Mosby, staunch to Lee, commented dryly, "Well, it made you immortal." [10]

The lawyer had one more opportunity to talk with Lee. In July, he went to a home in Alexandria where Lee was visiting. As they were about to part, Lee said, "Colonel, I hope we shall have no more wars." [11] Mosby concluded in later years that Lee reminded him of the inscription on Montcalm's tomb in the Ursuline Convent at Quebec: "Fate denied him victory, but blessed him with a glorious immortality." [12]

The part of Virginia around Warrenton is horse country, and its people, then as now, talk and estimate in terms of racers, trotters and pacers. Mosby had preserved several fine animals from his war string, among them a black horse called The Raven; a big bay, Captain; a fat, dapple gray gelding, Dandy, and his favorite, Croquette. Eventually he became interested in racing, and added several racers to his stable. Two of them were Dewdrop and Red Cloud, young blooded horses, and another was Eugenie, named in honor of the Empress of Napoleon III. But his participation at races was for the sport only: he refused to back up his entries with money. The nearest he ever came to betting was in the fall of '71. On that occasion, he matched his filly, Eugenie, against Mesty, a bay gelding owned by J. H. Rixey, proprietor of the Warren-Green Hotel. The race was for 1,000 yards and repeat. Both heats were won by Mesty, despite the enthusiasm with which Mosby's Negro jockey, Chapman Otey, spurred on Eugenie. A large crowd was present, and newspapers reported that "there was a good deal of excitement on the ground and a considerable amount of money changed hands on the results." [13] Seventy-five dollars of the sum came from Mosby. He learned $150 had been staked on

Eugenie, and he rewarded the loser for his faith by reimbursing him for half the loss.

It was at this period Mosby collected the largest fee of his legal career—$10,000. His client was the Pennsylvania Railroad Company, preparing then to extend its line into Virginia.[14]

Politics during the opening months of the election year '72 was lethargic and unexciting. The only sparkle was created by the gradual evolution of the Southern states from the shackles of military rule to a stage at which they could take on a semblance of political independence. But this quasi-freedom at the polls was too insignificant to buck the powerful Republican rule in the North, especially in view of Grant's excellent chances for re-election. As President, he had shown during his first term marked leniency and consideration toward the South. This captured the heart of some who had sided with the Confederacy, yet failed miserably in shaking the vast majority of the die-hards in Dixie. Defeat had taken from them their principles, but not their party loyalty.

The political pot grew hotter when the Liberal Republican convention at Cincinnati was stampeded toward Horace Greeley, newspaper man and editorial writer who had advocated amnesty toward the South. The Democrats also indorsed him, but many refused to support a candidate who had spent years opposing the principles for which they stood. Among these was Mosby who, on meeting United States Senator John F. Lewis of the Valley of Virginia, commented that the incumbent seemed to be the lesser of two evils, that the South had been fighting Greeley for forty years, while it had fought Grant only four. This remark was carried to the White House by Lewis. Appreciating it, Grant told the senator he would like to meet the raider who had given him so much trouble during the war.

The public read in shocked surprise in the *Star* on May 8:

"A sensation was caused at the White House this afternoon by the appearance of the once famous Colonel J. S. Mosby, who called in company with Senator Lewis, of Virginia, to pay his respects to President Grant. They were admitted to see the President in a few minutes after sending in their cards, and

remained for some time. In his personal appearance Colonel
M. hardly comes up to the popular idea of a guerrilla chief. In
stature he is a little below the medium height. His face is
smooth shaved, and he is apparently about 35 years of age.
He is a pleasant spoken and mild mannered man, and to con-
verse with him one could scarce bring himself to believe that
he is really the man who harassed the rear of our armies in
Virginia during the rebellion, and achieved such a wide reputation as an independent Ranger and bushwhacker. This is the
first time that Colonel Mosby has ever visited the White
House."

Mosby had seen the President once before—at the National
Theater in Washington, in a box with General Sherman.[15] Since
Appomattox, the leader of Partisans had carried a kindly feeling toward the Federal commander-in-chief, and this had been
deepened considerably after Mrs. Mosby's successful trip to
his office. But the one factor that influenced his visit to the
White House more than anything else he later explained in his
memoirs: "When Horace Greeley was nominated, I saw—or
thought I saw—that it was idle to divide longer upon issues
which we acknowledged to have been legally, if not properly,
settled; and that if the Southern people wanted reconciliation,
as they said they did, the logical thing to do was to vote for
Grant. I have not changed my opinion, nor yet have I any
criticism to make of those who differed with me. We were all
working for the same end. Some said they couldn't sacrifice
their principles for Grant's friendship. I didn't sacrifice mine." [16]

Grant's reception of the former raider was informal and
friendly. Immediately after they had been introduced, he
plunged into recollections of the close escape he had had from
capture at the hands of his visitor while returning to the Army
of the Potomac during the spring of '64.

"If I had captured you," remarked Mosby, "things might
have changed—I might have been in the White House and you
might be calling on me."

"Yes," agreed Grant, wryly.[17]

In the conversation that followed, Mosby became convinced
that the President wanted to help the Southern people. He

went so far as to predict Virginia would vote Republican if
Congress would relieve ex-Confederates of their political disa-
bility, and Grant accepted the suggestion.

When Mosby left the executive mansion, he came away with
determination to support the incumbent as the most effective
way in which to aid the crippled states of the South. So ab-
sorbed was he in his new conviction that he failed to get off
the Aquia Creek boat at Alexandria, as planned, and was
aroused only after the bell tolled for Mount Vernon, a short
distance below that point. On board was another staunch Rebel,
General Wade Hampton of South Carolina. Mosby told him
about the trip to the White House and that he thought the
Southern people, by supporting Grant, would have an opportunity to get relief from many evils under which they were suffering. He noticed that Hampton voiced no dissension to these
views.[18]

It was a milepost in the life of Mosby, this decision to back
the man who had headed the conquering forces in the late
war. To all intents and purposes, it was a step as important
as that of January, '63, when he had set out for Fairfax with
the handful of men assigned him by Stuart. From '72 on,
Ulysses S. Grant was the guiding force in the lawyer's activities. "I crossed the Rubicon when I paid my first visit to the
White House," he once remarked.[19]

But the South refused to follow or to sympathize with the
example set by Mosby in this sudden change of faith. Quick as
it was to idolize him as a raider, just as quick now it turned
against him as a politician. As it praised, so it condemned. Pride
in achievement was smothered by censure at inconsistency. The
time would come when party bolting would be accepted with
almost the same complacency as a transfer from one branch of
military service to another. But in '72, with the country still
locked in its worst period of internal hatred and bitterness, it
was political and social suicide.

The wartime hero was denounced by press and public alike;
by people who had been close to him and by those who knew
of him only by reputation; by enemies at large; by many even
of his old command, particularly the dissatisfied coterie. Mosby

accepted this condemnation with the same indifference he had scorned the hatred of the North. He was as partisan in politics as he had been in war.

But the sharp turnabout in his political status marked another change in his life. Again he was on the defensive. For years to follow, a small ivory-handled revolver swung in a buckskin pouch strapped to his right hip.

Grant's second nomination came at Philadelphia the last week in June, and the lawyer immediately began stumping in the incumbent's behalf. Newspapers sympathetic with the administration carried advance notices of the meetings at which Mosby was scheduled to speak. Whenever business made it necessary for him to cancel an appearance, a letter of regret penned by him was read from the rostrum. More than one of these assemblies would have ended in confusion and possibly riot but for the presence of men who, regardless of their own political adherence, stood by, steel-jawed, well-fingered revolvers in their pockets, to see that their old commander was given a fair opportunity to speak his piece.

Mosby's disdain for Greeley caused him to be overbearing toward those who failed to share with him what he considered the wisdom of supporting Grant. One of the men who fell under his ill will was the mayor of Warrenton, Dr. Withers. In a Saturday afternoon gathering at the Warren-Green early in August, some wag remarked that the Greeleyites would not send its trained speakers to answer Mosby in a speech he was to make at Salem, but instead would delegate the mayor, a novice in stump speeches. This quip reached the ears of Mosby and was accepted as an affront. He commented that he would denounce Withers and those who sent him if he put in his appearance. Withers, in time, got wind of Mosby's remark, but not until after the Salem meeting. The mayor waited his chance. Called to speak at Warrenton a few days later, he clambered to the rostrum with eagerness and announced his readiness to meet Mosby on any terms.

The press picked it up. "The well-known character of both parties for playing with the trigger made the timid judge at Warrenton very nervous," commented one newspaper.[20] The judge in this instance was James Keith, whose brother, Isom, had served with the Rangers and whose appointment Mosby had been seeking the day he met Lee in Richmond. Fearing a duel between the two prominent citizens of his jurisdiction, he bound them over to the peace until their friends had an opportunity to investigate the origin of the statement that had put them at odds.

Meanwhile Dr. Withers had been given cause to be happy that the field of honor had not been the rostrum. A correspondent who had attended the Salem meeting wrote his paper that Mosby "speaks as fiercely as he fights. Take him all in all, he is an ugly customer to tackle either in the field or on the rostrum." [21]

Even the Greeley press admitted Mosby's opposition to its candidate was not without its effect and suggested that a number of good canvassers would be needed to overcome it. It was known that he had a host of friends throughout the country and that many people shared his indignation over the way those who disagreed with him misconstrued his motives. One paper took it on itself to bring out that Mosby was the owner of a marble quarry situated on the left bank of the Potomac. It charged that he planned to use his friendliness with the administration as a means to obtain a contract to furnish from this quarry tombstones for the national cemeteries. Mosby stemmed this rumor with an open letter in which he termed the statement "a lie from beginning to end" and said it was known to be such by "the cowardly slanderer who wrote it." [22]

As early as the middle of August, Mosby gave assurance that Virginia would be carried by Grant. His conviction was strengthened when North Carolina voted Republican the last of the month. Virginia's election was held November 5. When the ballots were counted, it was found the lawyer's foresight was correct. He wired Grant November 7: "Virginia casts her vote for Grant, peace and reconciliation." [23] It was the first time the Old Dominion had gone Republican.

Now the White House door stood farther ajar to the cavalryman whom its chief inmate would have hanged by the neck without trial just seven years earlier. Many times Mosby went

Mosby's Men Returning from the Greenback Raid

Railroad Iron on the Fire

A pile of bent and twisted railroad iron across a heap of smouldering
ties was often the only indication found by the Union soldiers that
Mosby had paid them another visit.

Attack on Sheridan's Wagon Train at Berryville

to the executive mansion during the next four years, and only once did he fail to see Grant. The President on that occasion was in the hands of a dentist.

Early one morning a few days after the election, Mosby's business took him to the Treasury Department where he waited in an ante-room for the arrival of the Secretary. Suddenly a door opened and in walked Grant.

"I heard you were here," said the President, "and came to thank you for my getting the vote of Virginia." [24]

Mosby was a visitor at the White House on December 18. He was there again in February, this time accompanied by the Attorney General. They were among the few persons admitted by the President that day. Next morning, Mosby called at the Attorney General's office, upon request, and that afternoon newspapers revealed the purpose of the visit. They said the lawyer had been tendered a position of a professional nature in a Western state, but had declined on the ground that his accepting the appointment might lead his friends to infer that his support of Grant in the recent campaign was based on a desire to be rewarded by a government job. The history of this offer went back to December. Grant had said then that he would like to give Mosby an office, but Mosby objected, explaining that he could have more influence by taking nothing for himself.

His refusal to share in election spoils any more than he had partaken of the rich loot from the Federal army did not end his trips to the White House. He was there shortly after Grant's second inauguration. Three days later, he was back again. Next, he was reported at the office of the Postmaster General and other high government officials. The motive underlying these numerous interviews at the capital was manifested a few weeks later when newspapers took note of the fact that many of Mosby's friends were tasting of the political plum. Among them were some of his Rangers, the more prominent of whom were the Chapmans. His sister was named to a clerkship in the Patent Office.

The solicitude Mosby had for the welfare of others was characteristic of a kindness and humanness about him no one understood. It was this quality noticed in him at Stuart's grave. It came out when he was around his children. Nothing was too good for them, in his estimation, and he liked to have them near him at all times. This accounted for his habit of taking his elder son with him on most of his trips to neighboring county seats.

The Mosby at home was far different from the Mosby in the saddle. When each day's work was done, he took to the habits and appearance, domestically, of a country squire. Relaxing, he quaffed a glass of lager beer or, at dining table, sipped a bit of claret. It was the extent of his bibulousness. He was not a teetotaler, but he shunned strong drink and he never smoked. One of his greatest failings as he advanced in life was an absent-mindedness he could not overcome. It was this that caused him to fumble abstractedly with a key in the front door of the Warren-Green Hotel until Beverly timidly reminded him that his office was across the street.

He played no musical instrument, nor was his voice tuned to song, although he was fond of good vocal music. Often in the evenings his sisters, Lucy, who made her home with him for years, and Blakely, both of whom had good voices, entertained him at the piano. Games to him seemed a waste of time. He refused to play cards, and he boasted that he never had witnessed a baseball match.

Mosby's family had grown to six—two sons and four daughters. John S., Jr., the war baby of the group, was now nearly ten years old and the youngest child was two. Over those who were old enough to read, the father watched carefully, directing them to certain volumes in his growing library. For each book they completed, he paid them an attractive fee, explaining he would much rather they learned by reading and had the money than that it should be paid out to someone to teach them. During the preceding winter, his two eldest children, May Virginia and Beverly, aged fourteen and thirteen, had been sent to school at Montreal, Canada, result of their plea that they be permitted to accompany some of their wealthier playmates.

With the state election coming up, the political pot in Virginia during '73 began to simmer early. The Republicans, expecting an easy victory on the heels of their Presidential triumph the preceding year, started to boom Colonel Robert W. Hughes of Abingdon for Governor. Against him the old time Whigs and Democrats, who merged under the name of the Conservative Party and claimed they were an independent faction to keep the white people in control, pitted James Lawson Kemper of Orange County, major-general in the Confederate army. With the field thus drawn, the campaign buckled down to a fight between the Radicals and the Conservatives.

In June, the Washington correspondent of the Richmond *Whig* found Mosby at the capital and learned that he was making a successful fight against the Radicals, including members of Congress, over a vacant office. "His friends here claim," said the reporter, "that, while supporting Grant, he has no love for the Radical managers in Virginia and that they have little for him." But the correspondent was dubious. "We shall see what we shall see," he quipped.[25] Before the month was out, Mosby verified his stand with the Conservatives, repeating, however, that he still thought Grant the ablest man in the country.

Politics became more heated as the election approached. Fights were common between both political speakers and the electors who made up their audience. Using the powerful medium of fear, the Republicans in a last-minute move whispered that Federal office-holders, among them "Mosby's men," who did not remain true to the party from which they had received their spoils, would have their official heads chopped off. But these individuals ignored the warning, and a Conservative press encouraged them.

Ballots were cast in the election after a riotous windup. Kemper was elected, and sympathetic papers screamed the news with such headlines as "Glorious Victory!" "Republicanism Meets Its Sedan!" and "The War Carried Into Africa!"

Kemper's closest advisors during his political campaign were Mosby and James Barbour, lawyer of Culpeper, both favoring close coalition with the Grant administration. Hoping to bring about this friendliness between the President and a state formerly hostile to the Republicans, they worked quietly to accomplish their end before those who opposed the purpose learned of it. In December, Barbour went to Orange County to peruse and criticise the inaugural address that Kemper would deliver in January. On returning to his home next day, he wrote Mosby to come to see him at once. Mosby made the trip and was asked to go to Washington to tell Grant of the content of Kemper's speech, to tell him that Kemper and the Virginia Conservatives were preparing to join him, and to arrange an interview for Kemper.

One benefit expected to come out of this coalition was more Southern control over a third Civil Rights Bill then brewing as part of a drive to give the Negroes more privileges. Mosby was in Washington the first week of January, visiting both Grant and Alexander H. Stephens, former vice-president of the Confederacy and then member of the House of Representatives. The trip brought two results. The Civil Rights Bill, at Grant's request, went to sleep in committee for more than a year, and the way was opened for Kemper to visit the President.

But Kemper never visited the White House. Mosby went from Washington to Richmond and met Kemper at a hotel. The Governor was much upset. The secret of Mosby's trip to the capital had leaked out, the politicians immediately had set to work on Kemper. Prominent Democrats in Washington telegraphed him to abandon his plan, and a committee was dispatched to argue with him in person against the step. They insisted the President had a political motive for wanting the Virginia Governor to visit him, and that if Kemper accepted the invitation he would be sacrificing his self-respect as a Virginian and a Conservative. Under this pressure, Kemper gave up the coalition plans and Mosby's friendship. Feeling he had been duped, Mosby never spoke to Kemper after that.[26]

Mosby's law office was adjoined by that of General Eppa Hunton, member of Congress and a Confederate leader during the war. They were good friends, often working together on legal detail, often discussing politics. So there was something of friendly rivalry involved when Mosby talked early in '74 of opposing Hunton in the forthcoming congressional race. A local newspaper took him up on the proposal immediately and commented that he was "in the hands of his friends," adding: "We are satisfied of one thing—that if Colonel Mosby were returned to Congress he would be of much more real service to this district and the Southern people than any other man we could select." [27]

The press soon announced that Mosby would run as an independent, "swooping down on his opponents unexpectedly and defeating them while detached, after the most approved style of the military art." [28] It was said he had assurances of the warmest support from Grant and would base his chances on a platform of accord between the Conservative Party of Virginia and the administration. "Mosby would undoubtedly have much influence in Congress, as he is a great favorite with General Grant, who finds in his former troublesome foe a kindred spirit and valuable supporter," observed one paper.[29]

The campaign grew hotter with the weather. An indication of the gravity with which issues at hand were taken appeared in a Baltimore paper early in June.[30] It announced that an altercation had occurred at Salem between Mosby and B. F. Rixey, ex-state senator, in which a cane and a carriage whip were freely used. Politics, the article stated, was being discussed before the gladiators came to blows.

A tragic incident in July took Mosby's attention temporarily from politics. On July 15, death came to a seventh child—born the preceding August, a son named George Prentiss after the famous lawyer of Mississippi—S. S. Prentiss—for whom Mosby had great admiration. The funeral was held Sunday, and the press announced it was one of the largest ever witnessed in the town.

When August arrived and the time drew near for political action in convention, Mosby realized more and more that it would be useless for him to continue the congressional race. First of all, he was not a politician. Added to this was the malice many voters of the district held toward him because of his support of Grant, whom they looked on more in the light of an enemy military leader than as the nation's chief executive. Under such circumstances, the lawyer began to seek a substitute who would hold his friend Hunton's feet to the fire.[31]

The logical man seemed to be Barbour of Culpeper, and now, at Mosby's direction, political stooges began to prepare for an emergency. They spread the word for as many supporters as possible to get themselves appointed to the pending convention at Alexandria and to back Barbour in case Mosby had insufficient strength.

At this period the lawyer again took to his guns. Argument most used against him was that he favored a third term for Grant. This he ignored through respect to the President and because he actually was in favor of breaking the two-term precedent. But when charges of duplicity and deceit, allegedly contained in a certificate in the handwriting of Captain A. D. Payne of Warrenton, one-time commander of Black Horse Cavalry, were aired, his reserve snapped. He boarded a train for Warrenton Junction, stopped there long enough to send a challenge to Payne by Barbour, and then went on to Washington. This affair of honor would be fought across the river from Alexandria, in Maryland. That night he was arrested by capital detectives and held for Virginia authorities. The challenge meanwhile had brought acceptance and terms: the duel would be with squirrel rifles at forty paces. But police and the law had the matter in hand by the following afternoon. Mosby was under bond to await requisition from his home state, and Payne and his second were at Warrenton under a heavier bond to keep the peace. Taking advantage of this forced lull in hostilities, Hunton and Judge Keith got busy and drew up an agreement settling differences by apologies on both sides.[32] Thus ended the affair—without so much as the snap of a trigger from the squirrel rifles.

The press and the public at large, influenced by Democratic leanings, were not sympathetic with Mosby in his latest challenge. One newspaper brushed him off with compliment and then booted him with invective:

"We are rather inclined to think well of Colonel Mosby's idea of settling his political differences by the enemy enthyme of the duello. That is the only kind of logic likely to be conclusive with him, and he needs convincing—in fact needs to be suppressed or abated. It is allowable to wish, but impossible to hope, that a firebrand of his sort can be quenched in any ordinary way. Some men are like fleas; no half-way measures will suffice with them. It is either torture to you or death to them. During the war, when Mosby haunted the hills of Loudoun County, he was as irritating as a cantharides blister and as irrepressible as a Minnesota grasshopper. He infested the Federal skirts like a flea in a beggar's gabardine; he was as pervasive, as annoying, as incurable as the proverbial seven-year's itch. Now that the cruel war is over, he is bestowing upon the unhappy Democrats of Virginia the same sort of attention precisely that he gave Grant and Meade, Sheridan and Banks, Wright and McDowell. His attacks, now as then, are made by preference upon the rear. . . ." [33]

As anticipated, Mosby votes were lacking at the August convention and Barbour was selected to finish the race against Hunton. But Mosby's name was never abandoned as a campaign weapon. It was noted in September that the busy little lawyer made two trips to the White House in one week and that several appointments to government jobs followed for people in his district. An Alexandria newspaper decried Hunton's claim for the vote when Mosby really had represented the constituency. "Within the last three weeks," it said, "we have had six ladies and gentlemen appointed to office, solely through his (Mosby's) influence, besides the many before. This, too, not because General Hunton has not tried. He has tried repeatedly, it is said, but invariably without success." [34] Despite this and other favorable argument, the Mosby ticket was defeated, although it carried Fauquier, the home county, and a major part of the lower end of the district.

Late in November, the stage was set for one of the biggest social honors Mosby could have asked: Grant indicated acceptance of an invitation to visit the lawyer at Warrenton. Plans were made by the host for a big reception. But at the last minute, Grant had trouble in the preparation of his annual message to Congress and it was only after some delay that he managed to get it ready at all. In the rush, the Warrenton trip was abandoned.

The next year passed without happenings of unusual moment

to Mosby, but the twelve-month period that followed brought its share of gloom. In March, '76, was born an eighth child, given the name of its paternal grandfather. Pauline Clarke already had been weakened by her average of a child every two years, and the arrival of still another spelled her doom. She died May 10, a devout woman, even more beautiful in character than in face. A few weeks later, she was followed in death by the infant.

To lighten the burden of his sadness, Mosby plunged more completely into law and politics. He announced when the Presidential campaign arrived that he would support Hayes, choice of Grant, and not an eyebrow flickered. Once during what developed into a lively political battle, he turned aside to pen to a former Confederate comrade a lengthy epistle explaining why he would not vote for Tilden, the Democratic nominee.[35] One paragraph of the long letter epitomized his political sentiment:

"The sectional unity of the Southern people has been the governing idea and bane of their politics. So far from being the remedy for anything, it has been the cause of most of the evils they have suffered. So long as it continues, the war will be a controlling element of politics; for any cry in the South that unites the Confederates re-echoes through the North and re-kindles the war fires there. Thus, every Presidential canvass becomes a battle between the two sections, and the South, being the weaker, must be the losing party."

In this letter, Mosby used the phrase "the solid South." Some sources have given him credit for being its originator. Regardless of its source, it quickly was picked up by the press of that date.

The New York *Herald* hailed the letter as "an able political manifesto" and admitted it was surprised to find in Mosby, whom it had always known as a cavalryman and guerrilla chief, "a writer of peculiar piquancy and power." [36]

Late in '76 Mosby received a telegram from Wade Hampton asking him to use his influence to aid South Carolina, then in severe political turmoil. Hampton was waiting to be inaugurated as Governor of the state and promised peace and quiet after he took office. But in the meantime there was possibility of Carpetbag violence and Federal intercession. Mosby hurried to the White House to solicit Grant's help, making the mistake along the way of confiding his mission to a fellow passenger. This wayfarer turned out to be a friend of the editor of the Alexandria *Gazette* and promptly spread the information. When the paper printed an account of Mosby's visit, the Democratic press was at Hampton's throat in a flash. Better would it be, irate editorialists wrote, for South Carolina to be damned under Negro rule than to get relief through the turncoat Mosby. A few days later Hampton apologized to his constituents in an open letter, explaining he had not known how odious Mosby was to the Virginia people. The lawyer tucked the incident away in his memory, personally censuring himself as one who had been used and then abused.[37]

But the deluge had been started. Bitterness developed into a rage against Mosby, obliterating the American right of political freedom. Succeeding months served to pour oil on the fire, and Grant watched the wave of animosity with increasing fear for the welfare of his Rebel friend and champion. One night in '77 as Mosby stepped off the train at Warrenton, someone took a pot shot at him out of the dark. Grant heard of it and became more convinced that an alarming situation was at hand. He appealed to his successor, President Hayes, who had taken office in March. In time, it was announced that John Singleton Mosby, lawyer of Warrenton, would be the next consul to Hong Kong.[38]

So the independent who had spent his life at law and raiding turned next for an occupation to the protection of American merchants and seamen. For seven years, from '78 to '85, he was a resident of the British crown colony, and in that period it is doubtful that he ever left the island. He never liked China. To describe his opinion of the country, he pointed to a line of Tennyson's *Locksley Hall:* "Better fifty years of Europe than a cycle of Cathay." [39]

The brightest spot in the period came in '79 when Grant, then on a world tour with his wife and son, Fred, visited Hong

Kong. At breakfast one morning, the ex-President told of a trip by donkey from Jaffa to Jerusalem.

"That was the roughest road I ever traveled," he said.

"General, you traveled one rougher road than that," reminded Mosby.

"Where?" asked Grant.

"From the Rapidan to Richmond."

Grant chuckled. "I guess there were more obstructions in that road," he agreed.[40]

Mosby accompanied the Grants to the vessel by which they were to proceed along the China coast. At the ship's side, with guns in the background firing salute, they parted for the last time.

Once while in Hong Kong, Mosby was haled into court by a man who turned to the law a jump ahead of the lawyer. The consul compiled evidence against this individual, a boarding house operator suspected of helping American seamen to desert ship, and made the statement that if the practice were not stopped an arrest would follow. The threat was carried to the keeper of boarders by his runner. Shortly afterward, Mosby was summoned to answer to a charge of slander. He served as his own counsel at the subsequent trial, and made such a masterful and humorous speech in his defense that the judge chewed a handkerchief to keep from laughing and the three-man jury let him go scot free.

China was fully conscious of the identity of the slim little American, and Li Hung Chang, premier, once sought to take advantage of the consul's military ability. China and France had become involved in an irregular war. Li sent Mosby an invitation to enlist the services of 300 of his fellow Confederates from the United States and to fight with the Chinese. His premise for this action was Frederick Townsend Ward and Charles Gordon, two generals from abroad who had brought remarkable successes to China's armies. But Mosby refused with the excuse that he was reluctant to fight a nation that had befriended America during the Revolution.

The consul's last two years in Hong Kong were made easier by the presence of Beverly, who had come over in the winter of '82-'83 as vice-deputy consul. William T. Brooke of Warrenton, ex-Ranger, was deputy.

Mosby's consulship ended with the inauguration of Grover Cleveland. Hearing and supposing he would not be reappointed, he dispatched a letter to Grant asking that he help locate employment with some corporation. Mosby could see little promise in a return to Warrenton. His law practice there had been shattered. His children were living with relatives, including his mother, widowed by the death of his father in '79, and his home had been sold to General Hunton.

July came and Mosby prepared to return to the United States. No reply had been received from Grant. The day before the retiring consul set sail, a message came that his Republican friend was dead.

But even in the cancerous pain of his last days, Grant had not forgotten the Rebel who had bucked the South to bring him political support. One of his last pieces of correspondence was a note to the railway builder and executive, Leland Stanford. When Mosby stepped ashore at San Francisco, carrying among his effects a silver loving cup given him in appreciation by Chinese merchants, he was notified by Stanford an attorneyship with the Southern Pacific railroad awaited him.

Soon he was offered an opportunity to increase his income still further. A lecture bureau of Massachusetts confronted him with a contract to tell from the platform in New England the inside story of his amazing military activities. He accepted and for weeks followed the strenuous schedule of a speaking tour. This led to another offer, and soon he was preparing his talks for publication in the Boston *Herald*. By '87, the newspaper series had been rewritten and book stalls were featuring "Mosby's Reminiscences."

Other volumes came from the Partisan's pen. He gave a defense of his war idol in "Stuart's Cavalry Campaigns," and championed him again later in "Stuart's Cavalry in the Gettysburg Campaign," a dissertation based largely on the official Rebellion Records and one that caused other military leaders to answer him sharply. Further effort as an author resulted in "The Dawn of the Real South" and finally his "Memoirs."

Mosby's position with the Southern Pacific required him to reside in San Francisco. Once settled there, he had to rely mostly on the mails to maintain contact with survivors of his command. He wrote numerous letters, sometimes two and three to Monteiro before he got one in return. Still, the East did not forget him. In the early 90's while on one of his well-spaced visits to his children, he received an unexpected and conspicuous honor. Virginia's famous sculptor, Edward V. Valentine, artist who had prepared the recumbent statue of Lee, made a bust of the raider. In appreciation, Mosby presented him with his plumed campaign hat. This hat, the one he had worn at the Lake home, had been returned to him, years after it was captured, by a niece of the Federal officer in command.

When the equestrian statue of General Lee on Monument Avenue in Richmond was unveiled in '94, Mosby was among the list of special guests invited. He refused the invitation, although his men were there in a body and created considerable attention. One cause for his reluctance to attend was General Early, to whom he had taken considerable dislike since the war.[41]

In January, '95, while on annual leave, the Partisan attended a reunion of the Forty-third Battalion at Alexandria. More than 150 Rangers were present, some gripping the hand of their commander—now sixty-two, gray, and much fuller in body and face than he had been during the war—for the first time since the final meeting at Salem. Several who arrived changed from the broadcloth of the pulpit to the cadet gray of the Confederacy, which led Mosby to comment: "Well, boys, if you fight the devil like you fought the Yankees, there will be something to record Judgment Day." [42]

The reunion reached its climax at a banquet, an affair that ere the end developed into a free-for-all crying fest. An address by Mosby started the tears. In his talk, the lawyer went back to Salem for a theme and was himself so overcome with emotion he never again attended an assembly of his men. The greatest pang was stimulated by these words:

"Your presence here this evening recalls our last parting. I see the line drawn up to hear read the last order I ever gave you. I see the moistened eyes and quivering lips. I hear the command to break ranks. I feel the grasp of the hands and see the tears on the cheeks of men who had dared death so long it had lost its terror. And I know now, as I knew then, that each heart suffered with mine the agony of the Titan in his resignation to fate.

"Modern skepticism has destroyed one of the most beautiful creations of Epic ages, the belief that the spirits of dead warriors meet daily in the halls of Valhalla, and there around the festive board recount the deeds they did in the other world. For this evening, at least, let us adopt the ancient superstition, if superstition it be. It may seem presumptuous in me, but a man who belonged to my command may be forgiven for thinking that, in that assembly of heroes, when the feast of the wild boar is spread, Smith and Turner, Montjoy and Glasscock, Fox and Whitescarver, and all their comrades, will not be unnoticed in the mighty throng." [43]

One more narrow escape from death was in store for Mosby. On a lovely summer day in 1896, while driving with a friend at Charlottesville,[44] he leaned over the dashboard of the buggy to lift the horse's tail from the reins. The animal became frightened and lashed out with one of its mailed hoofs, striking the lawyer a terrific blow in the face. Eyewitnesses lifted him from the dust, a limp figure, bleeding profusely from a gash in his forehead, and took him to the University of Virginia hospital where he lay unconscious for days. Diagnosis revealed his skull was fractured and that his left eye never would be of use again.

As hours of uncertainty mounted, the train from Richmond brought one of the best known surgeons of the South—Dr. Hunter McGuire, Stonewall Jackson's army physician. He entered the sick room and found an interne beside the bed.

"Is he conscious?" asked the surgeon.

"I'll see," replied the interne.

He leaned over the prostrate form, putting his mouth close to the bandaged face.

"What's your name?"

Quickly the victim's lips moved. "None of your damned business."

"He's conscious all right," said McGuire, taking off his coat and rolling up his sleeves.

With careful treatment, the danger period passed. In a few more days, the frail body was beginning to fight its way back to recovery. But never again would Mosby look the same. Always from then his physical appearance was marred by an eye that took no part in his actions and interests. It was the beginning of the years in which his keen eyesight failed and he had to rely on the aid of glasses. Moreover, he became dependent on an afternoon nap and insisted on it under practically all circumstances.

In 1901, in a sudden move, the Southern Pacific railway was reorganized. Among those who lost out in the shakeup of personnel was Mosby, now bucking the world without his Grant.

Again the Partisan's political affiliations came to his rescue. During July, it was announced that President McKinley had appointed him a special agent of the General Land Office. For three years, he worked at this new assignment with headquarters at Sterling, Colorado, spending much of the time on the trail of cattle barons who were fencing land illegally in Nebraska, Colorado and Alabama. Then, in 1904, President Theodore Roosevelt, listening to the pleas of some of Mosby's friends, among them Thomas Nelson Page, the Virginia author, named him an assistant attorney in the Department of Justice.

The years after 1904 were not kind to Mosby. A marked characteristic at this period of his life was a bad disposition, perhaps an aftermath of his days as a military leader. He talked fast and expected his orders to be obeyed just as promptly as if he still were at the head of a battalion. At times he was an irascible, intolerant old man, rude to those who bothered him. One of his sons said "the war ruined a good father." [45]

Back in '63 and '64, he had been apart, above the average walk of life. The same was true during his busy stride as a consul, as railroad attorney, as land agent. But now, in a swivel chair job fitted more to his years, surrounded by men and women who knew his war reputation only by hearsay, he was brought down to earth and crucified by personalities.

He had an abundance of personal dignity. But along with it were pronounced traits and peculiarities which tended to make enemies. He frequently was repellant on first acquaintance, yet interesting and kindly later. A youthful admirer once was introduced to him by an elder. The lawyer stuck out his hand, uttered a gruff "hi" and abruptly turned his back. It made the youngster furious, and his injured pride swelled until an arm was laid across his shoulder later in the day, and there was Mosby, calling the boy by name.[46]

A willingness to hurt others seemed to be an obsession. Frequently he would have his say and walk away from a conversation, or satisfy his appetite and leave the dining table before others seated with him had finished. Some of his actions of this nature may have been rightfully blamed on advanced age. But, in the eyes of the public, particularly young people, they were inexcusable. He was to a rising generation a self-centered old man, best remembered to some by a red bandanna he carried in his pocket. They heard tales of his cunning and wondered if they were true.

Behind all his peculiarities and his social violations, Mosby had one trait that was typical of his years as a leader: until his dying day he maintained a personal and paternal interest in his men. Hearing that one of them was in financial difficulty, he took it on himself to get the fellow's son a responsible job, reminding the young man as he prepared to depart for work that he must send a part of his salary to his father.[47] He frequently shared with others money he himself needed worse. And he spent tireless hours in study to be better able to defend the campaigns of his long-dead friend and hero, Jeb Stuart.

In his late years, Mosby was emotional and poetic in temperament, and lived his best in reminiscence. New inventions upset him, left him resentful toward them in that they disturbed or made more out of date the historical setting of the Civil War. His thinking advanced with his years; his habits and his personal life remained in the 60's. The war period was the hub around which revolved the half-century span of his later

life. As the decades passed and the ranks of his veterans
thinned, he felt more pathetically the separation from his battalion. "I am beginning to feel very lonely in this world now,"
he once remarked. "Nearly all of my friends are gone and I
have made no new ones." [48]

During the last decade of his life, he reminisced much of
the time, misconstruing his own accomplishments and purposes
as a military leader, confusing dates he himself had fixed. On
his anniversaries, Union and Confederate soldiers alike came
to his home in Washington to wish him well. Occasionally, he
went to Garfield Hospital for observation and treatment for a
kidney ailment that had begun to bother him. This and an
inherited deafness that came on in his last years were his sole
physical complaints. He enjoyed always a hearty appetite,
sometimes to the vexation of his Rangers' wives. One Christmas, it was felt by the wife of the Forty-third Battalion's
fighting Surgeon Dunn: a ham and turkey she had carefully
prepared for the holy occasion suddenly disappeared. After
diligent investigation, she pinned the blame on her husband.
Finally he confessed: Mosby had written he would like to have
such delicacies for the holidays.

In 1910, Mosby made a "peaceful entry" into New England
to lecture. The journey was designed to help a boys' cause, as
well as to bolster his own dwindling purse. Shortly before, the
Associated Press had given notice that he had been ousted
from the Justice Department without cause and was in pov-
erty.[49] "I was up against it during the war and did not take it
seriously to heart," the press service quoted him. "I shall endeavor not to do so now." No mention was made then, or ever
in print, of a charge that has whipped about by word of mouth
from year to year—that Mosby was a grafter, leaning heavily
on his friends of Civil War days and those closely associated
with him in Northern Virginia. This much at least was saved
him. His discharge from the government had followed a change
of administration, though it may have been predicated on his
age. He was nearly seventy-seven and his hair was snow white.
But his cheeks were ruddy and his step was quick. He showed
his age only in attenuation and general frailty.[50]

Mosby Shortly after the War

Mosby at the Age of Sixty

The next four years were spent in quiet and periodical work on his memoirs.[51] Once during this period the old fight in him was stirred by a letter that appeared in the London *Times*. Defending residents of Belgium from execution for sniping at Germans in World War I, it pointed out that this harsh punishment was not meted out in the Shenandoah Valley in '64, when crippled farmers who hobbled about their fields in the daytime became active raiders with Mosby at night and sniped at the Federals. Mosby was furious. He wrote a spirited reply in which he recalled that one of his Rangers was Baron von Massow, since commander of the Ninth German Army Corps. "If you were to ask Massow if he ever was a sniper in the Shenandoah Valley, he would answer you from the mouth of a Krupp gun," the letter concluded.[52]

Occasionally in his moments of reminiscence, Mosby remarked: "I pitched my politics in too high a key when I voted for Grant. I ought to have accepted office under him. My family would now be comfortably supplied with money." But those who remembered his staunch political sentiments knew these words did not come from the heart.[53]

As Mosby's work on his memoirs neared an end, a delegation one day brought a token of appreciation from the university that had expelled him in 1853.[54] It consisted of a bronze medal and an embossed address expressing the affection and esteem of his friends and admirers at the University of Virginia. "Endowed with the gift of friendship, which won for you the confidence of both Lee and Grant," it stated, "you have proven yourself a man of war, a man of letters, and a man of affairs worthy the best traditions of your University and your State, to both of which you have been a loyal son."

The address afforded a happy sequel to the chapter of Mosby's life that had made the blackest mark, to the weeks he had spent in the stinking little Charlottesville jail.[55] He accepted the token joyfully, and commented that "my chief regret is that I could not do for my prison what Tasso did for his dungeon at Ferrara—confer immortality upon it." [56]

By the close of 1915, Mosby was confined to his home by

general debility. In three months, he was at Garfield Hospital. In six months, he was dead.

The end came at 9 o'clock the morning of May 30—Decoration Day—of 1916, one year before America entered another and greater war than that which had brought him his fame, a war that would prove the value of his type of military operation. He was conscious almost to the last. In the final moments, when the senseless body of the warrior, nearly six months past its eighty-second year, gave out its last shuddering breath, a daughter uttered above it the baptismal words of the Catholic Church—the church of his wife, the church he had admired, though never as a staunch worshipper. Other members of the family were there as witnesses to the ceremony. All of them knew it was mockery, that baptism administered to an unconscious person does not "take."

The body was moved to Warrenton by train the morning of June 1. On board as bodyguard and pallbearers were Fount Beattie and other Rangers. Along, too, were the Alexandria, Culpeper and Charlottesville units of National Guard. At the destination, joined by the Warrenton Rifles, the uniformed troops formed line beside the station and trod behind a high black hearse to the town hall, where the body lay in state for several hours. During the afternoon, the frail remains were taken up again, and carried this time to the cemetery for burial.

An open grave waited on a rise near a shaft marking the mound under which lay bodies of 500 soldiers. Closer by were the graves of Pauline Clarke, the two sons who died in infancy, and the fresh-turned sod where rested John S., Jr., the war baby, buried the preceding August. A few yards distant, farther down the slope and more in the shade of scattered trees, stood a handsome gray monument erected by comrades in 1907 as a memorial to Montjoy. Cut in stone across its face were words written by Mosby in his general order of December 3, '64, announcing the tragedy that had overtaken the Mississippian: "... his death was a costly sacrifice to victory. He died too early for liberty and his country's cause, but not too early for his own fame."

So John Singleton Mosby, lawyer, soldier, patriot, author, was buried in appropriate company on the brow of a hill at Warrenton, overlooking the green fields through which had romped his phantom legion. They buried him two days after he died, but fifty-two years too late to bring him the glory he deserved.

The Ranger captain's most widespread praise after the war came from the North, from the enemies he had pestered, sometimes from the front, sometimes from behind.[57] Grant said of him in his memoirs, that great military narrative:

"Since the close of the war, I have come to know Colonel Mosby personally and somewhat intimately. He is a different man entirely from what I had supposed.... He is able and thoroughly honest and truthful. There were probably but few men in the South who could have commanded successfully a separate detachment, in the rear of an opposing army and so near the border of hostilities, as long as he did without losing his entire command."[58]

From the standpoint of fame, better would it have been for Corporal Kane's revolver to have cast its bullet a shade higher that night at the Lake home. Then, perhaps, Mosby's name would have stood with such heroes as his beloved Stuart, with Forrest, Morgan, the gallant Pelham and others.

For there was no fleeing from the Scalawags, the radicals, the die-hards; no escaping the boys and young men he angered in his senility. Whether the test came in politics or in everyday social contact, it was his nature to stand by his guns. And in standing by them, he tore away the veil of mystery that had made him famous. The reckless abandon with which he attacked and galloped away as a Partisan could not be repeated as a citizen.

He himself seemed to feel that he had outlived his day. Thirty years after he rode away from his battalion at Salem, he said: "I wish that life's descending shadows had fallen upon me in the midst of friends and the scenes I loved best."[59]

NOTES

CHAPTER 2

1. *Personal Memoirs of P. H. Sheridan* (New York, 1888), p. 499. (Referred to hereafter as *Sheridan's Memoirs.*)

2. *The War of the Rebellion: A Compilation of the Official Records of the Union and Confederate Armies* (Washington, 1880-1901), Ser. I, Vol. XLIII, Pt. I, p. 57. (Referred to hereafter as *O. R.*)

3. *Sheridan's Memoirs,* p. 100.

4. Dr. Douglas Southall Freeman, eminent authority on Confederate history, commented to the author on one occasion that General Lee paid more attention to Mosby's reports than to those of any of his scouts.

5. Letter written from Clifton Forge, Va., by a Virginia woman under the pseudonym "Fairfax." An undated newspaper clipping of it was obtained by the author from Curtis Chappelear of Delaplane, Va.

6. John W. Munson, in his *Reminiscences of a Mosby Guerrilla* (New York, 1906), p. 17. (Referred to hereafter as Munson.) Mosby's son, Beverly C., of Washington, D. C., told the author that he once heard someone ask his father to what he attributed his success. The reply, the son recalled, was that his raiders were mere boys, most of them unmarried and hence without fear or anxiety for the effect their daring would have on their wives and children.

7. The author once asked Beverly Mosby for an opinion as to how his father held his men. He replied: "Men judge each other. My father's men judged him as a man who did what he said he was going to do."

CHAPTER 3

1. Edward Lewis Goodwin, *The Colonial Church in Virginia* (Milwaukee, 1927), p. 289.

2. Copied from the original now in the possession of Beverly C. Mosby.

3. This home is now the residence of Charles McCormick.

4. University of Virginia Registry of 1850.

5. Law Orders of Albemarle County Circuit Court, on file in the courthouse at Charlottesville, Va.

6. *Ibid.*

7. William D. Lewis, *Great American Lawyers* (Philadelphia, 1907-09), VII, 137.

8. Virginia Senate Journal and Documents, 1853-54, p. 134.

9. This incident in Mosby's life has been greatly distorted by other biographers. Invariably the fight between the two students has been attributed to some other cause. The most popular report relates that Mosby was battling for a young lady's honor. This is the explanation given in the introduction to Mosby's memoirs, prepared by his brother-in-law, Charles W. Russell, after the veteran's death.— *The Memoirs of Colonel John S. Mosby* (Boston, 1917.) (Referred to hereafter as *Mosby's Memoirs.*) Earlier this explanation had been included in an article by John S. Patton in the Baltimore *Sun.* The account the author has uncovered in the records of the General Assembly of Virginia appears indisputable. Mosby once corroborated some of its detail with this note written on the margin of a newspaper clipping (*Memoirs,* p. 9): "I did not go to Turpin's house, but he came to my boarding house, and he had sent me a message that he was coming there to 'eat me up.'"

CHAPTER 4

1. Lewis Preston Summers, *History of Southwest Virginia* (Richmond, 1903), p. 679. (Referred to hereafter as Summers.)

2. *Ibid.,* p. 510.

3. Beverly Mosby remembered hearing his mother talk of this after she had been coldly received by Andrew Johnson on a visit to the White House after the war.

4. As related by Beverly Mosby.

5. *Ibid.*

6. Both Mosby and Sperry gave accounts of this meeting in later years. As the editor's account was much more in detail than the other, it has been followed more closely by the author in trying to piece together the conversation between them.

7. Famous English executioner of the seventeenth century.

8. *Munsey's Magazine,* XLIX, 35-41.

CHAPTER 5

1. John S. Mosby, *Mosby's War Reminiscences, and Stuart's Cavalry Campaigns* (Boston 1887), p. 43. (Referred to hereafter as *Reminiscences.*)

2. John S. Mosby Papers, Manuscript Division, Library of Congress.

3. Richmond *Dispatch,* June 17, 1861.

4. *Battles and Leaders of the Civil War* (New York, 1887-88), III, 148-51. (Referred to hereafter as *Battles and Leaders.*)

5. This was brought out by Mosby in his *Memoirs* and since has been confirmed to the author by Beverly Mosby, who recalled that he often had heard his father remark on the fact.

6. Mosby recorded in his *Memoirs* that his last official act as adjutant of his regiment was to carry an order from Jones, promoted by that time to a colonelcy, for the arrest of Swan.

7. Copied in *Mosby's Memoirs.*

CHAPTER 6

1. John S. Mosby Papers, Manuscript Division, Library of Congress.

2. Douglas Southall Freeman, *Lee's Lieutenants* (New York, 1942), I, 279.

3. Some historians take no recognition of Mosby's part in inaugurating the idea of Stuart's ride around McClellan, but there seems ample record to confirm it. Included in this is Mosby's own account to his wife, dated only a day or two after the circuit was made. Moreover, Major John Scott, in his *Partisan Life with Colonel John S. Mosby,* a volume published shortly after the war (New York, 1867), tells of it in some detail. (Referred to hereafter as Scott.)

4. John Esten Cooke observed that "it is possible" the battle of Cedar Mountain was fought in consequence of this information.— *Wearing of the Gray* (New York, 1867), p. 116. This theory is also supported by *O. R.,* in which a message from Lee to Jackson on August 4, 1862, indicates that he did not have the information, while correspondence three days later reveals very plainly that he did. In the meantime, according to his letters home, Mosby had been to see Lee.

5. This officer was Colonel Isaac I. Wistar, leading a California regiment. A few years after the war, the two men met in Philadelphia and were mutually identified. Mosby related in a letter published in newspapers December 20, 1905, that they afterward dined together.

6. John Esten Cooke, member of Stuart's staff, recorded in his *Wearing of the Gray* that the cavalry leader related to him "with great glee" the incident in which Mosby caused an entire brigade to fall back before a tiny party of sharpshooters. There seems to be some variance as to the size of the enemy force. Cooke speaks of it as a brigade, but in a letter to his wife dated November 24, 1862, Mosby describes it as only a regiment.

CHAPTER 7

1. Now the Washington and Old Dominion Railroad.

2. Mosby says in his *Reminiscences* that the reason more of them did not stay was that Fitz Lee had complained because some were from the First Virginia and had forced him to send them back.

3. Later Mosby was joined by Underwood's brothers, Bush and Sam, both good scouts and good fighters.

4. Cooke, *Wearing of the Gray*, p. 385.

5. Confederate prison at Richmond.

6. This was not Mosby's first report to Stuart. Library of Congress records show that he sent the cavalry leader on January 15, 1863, a brief account of his first activities, but the author has been unable to locate the original or a copy of this paper. Search for it was extended to the United States Department of Archives, where such papers ordinarily are filed, but there, too, trace of it was lacking.

CHAPTER 8

1. Now Atoka.

2. *O. R.*, Ser. I, Vol XXV, Pt. I, p. 37.

3. *Ibid.*, Vol. XXI, Pt. I, p. 1114

4. *Mosby's Reminiscences*, p. 47.

5. Washington *Star*, March 2, 1863.

6. In a general court martial convened in Washington March 27, 1863, Gilmer was found guilty of drunkenness and was dismissed from the service. Evidence failed to sustain the cowardice charge. The outcome was reported in General Orders No. 229.

7. Mosby to Stuart, February 4, 1863, *O. R.*, Ser. I, Vol. XXV, Pt. I, p. 5.

8. In an account of the raid on Fairfax Court House prepared for *Belford Magazine* and published in 1892, Mosby gives Ames much credit for the success of the enterprise. He also reveals that he told none of his men except the Yankee deserter about his plans and bared them to him only after they had started.

9. Mosby in a later account identified Barker as Ames' former commander and said the deserter treated the officer civilly and seemed to take pride in introducing him to the raiders.

10. John Stewart Bryan of Richmond, Va., relates in *Joseph Bryan* (Richmond, 1935), a biography of his father, who fought with the Forty-third Battalion, that Mosby, while visiting the Bryan home during the latter part of his life, often told of the Fairfax raid and of how Fitz Lee "came out of his tent and welcomed General

Stoughton...as a long lost brother, took him into the tent to give him a drink, and left me out in the rain."

11. *O. R.*, Ser. I, Vol. XXXVII, Pt. II, p. 664.

12. Washington *Star*, March 16, 1863.

CHAPTER 9

1. From the original now in the possession of the author through the generosity of Mrs. Stuart Mosby Coleman.

2. *O. R.*, Ser. I, Vol. XXXVII, Pt. II, p. 667.

3. *Ibid.*, Vol. XXV, Pt. I, p. 66.

4. One member of the command was Walter W. Gosden, whose son, Freeman Gosden, today is known for his role of Amos Jones in the radio team of Amos and Andy. In Baltimore in 1931, the radio star met Mosby's daughter, Miss Pauline Mosby, who gave him two buttons from her father's military coat.

5. Related to the author by W. K. Milhollen of Bailey's Cross Roads, Va., who lived near Sinclair and often as a youth heard him recall his experience during the war.

6. *O. R.*, Ser. I, Vol. XXXVII, Pt. II, p. 71.

7. *Ibid.*, p. 856.

8. John S. Mosby Papers.

9. *Ibid.* The author was unable to locate Mosby's reply to this request.

10. *Ibid.*

11. *O. R.*, Ser. I, Vol. XXXVII, Pt. II, p. 169.

12. *Ibid.*, p. 77.

13. *Ibid.*, p. 71.

CHAPTER 10

1. Washington *Star*, March 16, 1863.

2. Now Calverton.

3. *Reminiscences*, p. 130.

4. *Ibid.*, p. 129.

5. *O. R.*, Ser. I, Vol. XXXVII, Pt. II, p. 860.

6. *Ibid.*, p. 861.

CHAPTER 11

1. *Reminiscences*, p. 146.

2. Scott, p. 75.

3. Cooke, *Wearing of the Gray*, p. 487.

4. *O. R.*, Ser. I, Vol. XXVII, Pt. III, pp. 65, 72.

5. John Esten Cooke recorded in his *Wearing of the Gray*, p. 123, that Stuart was greatly worried over his inability to get news of the

enemy. "Silent, puzzled and doubtful, the general walked up and down, knitting his brows and reflecting," Cooke wrote. "When the lithe figure of Mosby appeared, Stuart uttered an exclamation of relief and satisfaction. They were speedily in private consultation. . . ."

6. *Reminiscences*, p. 164.
7. *O. R.* Ser. I, Vol. XXVII, Pt. III, p. 194.
8. *Ibid.*, p. 229.
9. *Ibid.*, p. 255.
10. *Ibid.*, Pt. II, p. 687.
11. *Ibid.*

CHAPTER 12

1. *O. R.*, Ser. I, Vol. XXIX, Pt. II, p. 585.
2. A full account of her experiences is given by Roberta Pollock in a letter to a friend, now on file at the Confederate Museum at Richmond, Va., numbered G-419, Metal Case 3. It was written soon after the war and later was indorsed as accurate by Mrs. W. V. Randolph, née Janet H. Weaver, of Warrenton, Va., who was familiar with the details.

CHAPTER 13

1. Now Rixeyville.
2. *O. R.*, Ser. I, Vol. XXXIII, Pt. I, p. 13.

CHAPTER 14

1. This seemed to be the opinion of Stuart and others. John Esten Cooke, of Stuart's staff, wrote on the attack that it was Mosby's "only serious failure."—*Op. cit.*, p. 123.
2. Lee's Confidential Dispatches, p. 131.
3. Richmond *Dispatch*, August 13, 1863.
4. *O. R.*, Ser. I, Vol. XXXIII, p. 1081.
5. John S. Mosby Papers.
6. From the *Personal Memoirs of U. S. Grant*, republished in *Battles and Leaders*, IV, 110. Grant wrote: "Had he [Mosby] seen our train coming, no doubt he would have let his prisoners escape. I was on a special train. If I remember correctly, without any guard."
7. *O. R.*, Ser. I, Vol. XXXIII, p. 259.
8. Other versions of this incident exist. In his *Reminiscences*, prepared in the late 80's, Mosby says he met a woman driving toward Washington in a wagon and that he gave her a lock of his hair

to be conveyed to Lincoln with a message that the raider would come into the city soon to get one of the President's. He added that he afterward noticed in the *Star* that it had been delivered and that Lincoln enjoyed the joke. F. R. Hathaway, writing in the Detroit *Free Press* an article later republished in the *Confederate Veteran*, XVIII, 201, said, on the basis of an interview with Mosby in 1910, that the raider had stopped at a house in near-by Virginia to get a drink of water and had left the hair with a housewife. Because of the lapse of time between the actual incident and these two accounts, the author has based his details on the report given by the *Star* of April 24, 1864, at the time of occurrence.

CHAPTER 15

1. Washington *Star*, May 27, 1864.
2. This quotation, which seems out of character with the customary style of Mosby's correspondence, was taken from Anna Pierpont Siviter's *Recollections of War and Peace* (New York, 1938), a biography of her father, Governor Pierpont.
3. *O. R.*, Ser. I, Vol. XXXVII, Pt. I, p. 358.
4. Washington *Star*, July 9, 1864.
5. *O. R.*, Ser. I, Vol. XXXVII, Pt. I, p. 358.

CHAPTER 16

1. Washington *Star*, July 19, 1864.
2. Jubal A. Early Papers, Library of Congress.
3. James J. Williamson, *Mosby's Rangers* (New York, 1909), p. 189. (Referred to hereafter as Williamson.)
4. *O. R.*, Ser. I, Vol. XXXVII, Pt. II, p. 389.
5. *Sheridan's Memoirs*, I, 462.
6. *O. R.*, Ser. I, Vol. XLIII, Pt. I, p. 742.
7. Scott, p. 272.
8. Quotation from original order as republished in Williamson, p. 430.
9. Testimony of Mann before board of inquiry on wagon train raid.
10. *Ibid.*
11. *Ibid.*
12. Letter of John S. Russell, December, 1899, reproduced in *Mosby's Memoirs*, p. 367.
13. These figures were taken from Mosby's report to Lee. In his account of the raid, Scott places the total at 300 prisoners, 700 mules and horses, and 230 beef cattle, explaining the difference was

due to the fact that Mosby made his report before all the captures had been brought in.

14. *O. R.*, Ser. I, Vol. XLIII, Pt. I, p. 841.

15. *Ibid.*

CHAPTER 17

1. *O. R.*, Ser. I, Vol. XLIII, Pt. I, p. 798.

2. *Ibid.*, p. 792.

3. *Ibid.*, p. 57.

4. *Ibid.*, p. 811.

5. *Ibid.*

6. Name given the area along the upper Potomac after it was consolidated through Grant's insistence.

7. Washington *Star*, August 18, 1864.

8. *O. R.*, Ser. I, Vol. XLIII, Pt. I, p. 822. Records do not reveal the identity of these seven victims. Mosby later denied that they were members of his command. He presumed they were bushwhackers or men of the neighborhood, unfortunate subjects on whom the Federals had wreaked their vengeance.

9. *O. R.*, Ser. I, Vol. XLIII, Pt. II, p. 51.

CHAPTER 18

1. Sheridan to Augur, September 21, 1864. *O. R.*, Ser. I, Vol. XLIII, Pt. II, p. 131.

2. Stevenson to Stanton, September 27, 1864. *Ibid.*, p. 189.

3. Williamson, p. 240.

4. Mrs. Davis-Roy, as reported in *ibid.*, p. 240.

5. Thomas A. Ashby, *The Valley Campaigns* (New York, 1914), p. 293.

6. *Southern Historical Society Papers*, XXV, 239-44.

7. Mrs. Davis-Roy, as reported in Williamson, p. 240.

8. Eyewitness account in Warrenton (Va.) *True Index*, February 15, 1896. Also in *Southern Historical Society Papers*, XXVII, 314-22.

9. This detail was given in an account by S. C. Willis, Worcester, Mass., in a letter to H. L. Cook, Front Royal postmaster, dated March 27, 1902. At the time of the hangings, Willis was a sergeant in the First Rhode Island Cavalry and witnessed the execution of Overby and Carter.

10. Scott, p. 320.

11. *O. R.*, Ser. I, Vol. XLIII, Pt. II, p. 920.

CHAPTER 19

1. *Reminiscences*, p. 81.

2. *O. R.*, Ser. I, Vol. XLIII, Pt. II, p. 152.

3. *Sheridan's Memoirs*, II, 53.

4. In his *Memoirs*, p. 313, Mosby says, "I preferred derailing the train in a cut to running it off an embankment because there would be less danger of the passengers being hurt."

5. *Mosby's Memoirs*, p. 322.

6. *Ibid.*, p. 315.

7. Scott, p. 336.

8. J. W. Slaughter of The Plains possesses a Bible his uncle, John H. Foster of Company A, brought away.

9. Related to the Newark *Daily Advertiser* by a passenger and repeated in the Richmond *Whig*, October 27, 1864.

10. Richmond *Daily Dispatch*, October 18, 1864.

11. *Ibid.*

12. These two paymasters were Majors Edwin L. Moore and David G. Ruggles. Mosby records in his *Memoirs*, p. 321, that they were sent South to prison and that Ruggles died there. As the government held them responsible for loss of funds, application had to be made to Congress for relief. Moore came to see Mosby after the war to get an affidavit certifying that the money had been captured.

13. *Mosby's Memoirs*, p. 316.

14. *O. R.*, Ser. I, Vol. XLIII, Pt. II, p. 373.

15. Records on these dismissals are found in both the United States Archives and the Archives Division of the Virginia State Library.

16. John Stewart Bryan, *Joseph Bryan*, p. 123.

17. Statement of Joseph Bryan to John Stewart Bryan, as related in *ibid.*, p. 132.

18. *O. R.*, Ser. I, Vol. XLIII, Pt. II, p. 509.

19. Williamson, p. 289.

20. *O. R.*, Ser. I, Vol. XLIII, Pt. II, p. 909.

21. W. W. Badger, "My Capture and Escape from Mosby," republished in *U. S. Service Magazine*, III, 548.

22. *Ibid.*

23. Williamson, p. 456.

24. Munson, p. 151.

25. *Southern Historical Society Papers*, XXVII, 319.

26. As related by John Russell to Henry W. Carpenter and published in the Washington *Star*, July 2, 1922, several years before Russell's death.

27. *O. R.*, Ser. I, Vol. XLIII, Pt. II, p. 920.

CHAPTER 20

1. *O. R.*, Ser. I, Vol. XLIII, Pt. II, p. 648.

2. Cole's death caused a furore, then as in later years. Puryear's chief defense was his youth. His companions remembered that immediately after the killing he gave way to the strain and sobbed like a child. Over half a century later, the author sat on many occasions around the hot stove at Gordonsville, Va., hangout for many of the old-timers, and listened to Puryear and others relive their war experiences. Then white-haired, with a silvery moustache and a body as slim as in his youth, the veteran spoke without bitterness, but invariably recalled that Cole had spat in his face.

3. In his *Memoirs,* p. 99, Sheridan says that, during his entire campaign, he was annoyed by guerrilla bands which considerably depleted his line-of-battle strength because of large escorts required by supply trains. The "most redoubtable" of the leaders of these irregulars, he adds, was Mosby.

4. *O. R.*, Ser. I, Vol. XLIII, Pt. II, p. 671.

5. *Ibid.*

6. *Ibid.*, p. 675.

7. *Ibid.*, p. 682.

8. *Ibid.*, p. 679.

9. Munson, p. 9.

10. *Ibid.*

11. *O. R.*, Ser. I, Vol. XLIII, Pt. II, p. 687.

12. Williamson, p. 316.

13. *Ibid.*, p. 322.

14. *Ibid.*

15. Williamson says this was done by Welt Hatcher of Mosby's command.—*Mosby's Rangers*, p. 324.

16. *O. R.*, Ser. I, Vol. XLIII, Pt. II, p. 730.

17. A description of this cave was given by John Lozier of New York, assistant surgeon of the First New York Cavalry, in an undated newspaper clipping preserved in the war scrapbook of Mrs. Elizabeth Iler Fisher of Shreveport, La.

CHAPTER 21

1. Richmond *Whig*, November 22, 1864.

2. *Ibid.*, November 26, 1864.

3. A. Monteiro, *War Reminiscences by a Surgeon of Mosby's Command,* p. 12. (Referred to hereafter as Monteiro.)

4. Dr. W. L. Dunn, young surgeon of Southwest Virginia, who

invariably joined in the battalion's fights instead of waiting in reserve to care for the wounded.

5. *Mosby's Memoirs,* p. 334.

6. *Ibid.,* p. 336.

7. In his report of the incident, Colonel Gamble said a Rebel officer inside "came to the door with his boots off and fired his revolver at our men." As Mosby was cornered and was trying to hide his presence, it does not seem likely that he would have done such a futile thing. Moreover, the accounts of the Lakes and of Tom Love, all eyewitnesses, do not agree with this version. Mosby, too, exaggerates the story somewhat in his *Memoirs,* which were prepared many years later, in the closing decade of his life.

8. Frazer's report, *O. R.,* Ser. I, Vol. XLIII, Pt. II, p. 843.

9. H. L. Hutton of Warrenton, Va., told the author that his uncle, Dr. Samuel H. Halley of Rectortown, was summoned to Mosby's side after the Federals left and also was convinced the raider had no chance of recovery.

10. Account of Federal major-general published in the New York *Herald,* December 31, 1864, and copied in the Richmond *Whig,* January 3, 1865.

11. *O. R.,* Ser. I, Vol. XLIII, Pt. II, p. 831.

12. Republished in the Richmond *Whig,* December 28, 1864.

13. *O. R.,* Ser. I, Vol. XLIII, Pt. II, p. 838.

14. *Ibid.,* p. 844.

CHAPTER 22

1. In his *Memoirs,* p. 342, Mosby wrote: "My own belief was that the wound was mortal; that the bullet was in me; that the intestines had been cut."

2. Mrs. E. S. Renalds of Marshall, Va., daughter of Dona Lake, told the author that she often had heard her mother discuss the incident and that Ludwell Lake thought Mosby ungrateful because of his violent words when Lake sent him off alone with the slave.

3. Monteiro, p. 34.

4. New York *Herald,* December 31, 1864.

5. Richmond *Whig,* January 28, 1865.

6. *Ibid.,* February 1, 1865.

7. *Ibid.,* January 28, 1865.

8. Records, 75th day, House of Representatives session, Confederate States Congress, February 6, 1865.

9. Washington *Star,* February 13, 1865.

10. *Ibid.,* February 1, 1865.

11. Scott, p. 446.

12. *O. R.,* Ser. I, Vol. XLVI, Pt. I, p. 463.

13. *Ibid.*, Vol. XXXIV, Pt. I, p. 46.
14. *Ibid.*, Vol. XLVI, Pt. II, p. 1359.
15. Scott, p. 464.

CHAPTER 23

1. *O. R.*, Ser. I, Vol. XLVI, Pt. II, p. 699. Copy in John S. Mosby Papers.
2. *Ibid.*, Pt. III, p. 685.
3. *Ibid.*, p. 714.
4. *Ibid.*, p. 725.
5. *Ibid.*, p. 765.
6. Monteiro, p. 174.
7. *O. R.*, Ser. I, Vol. XLVI, Pt. III, p. 799.
8. *Ibid.*, p. 804.
9. Channing Smith in the *Confederate Veteran*, XXXV, 327.
10. *O. R.*, Ser. I, Vol. XLVI, Pt. III, p. 817.
11. Williamson, p. 386.
12. *O. R.*, Ser. I, Vol. XLVI, Pt. III, p. 830.
13. *Ibid.*, p. 839.
14. Williamson, p. 386.
15. Monteiro, p. 206.
16. *O. R.*, Ser. I, Vol. XLVI, Pt. III, p. 868.
17. From a poem dedicated to Mosby's men by Armistead Churchill Gordon, Virginia author, poet, historian, and lawyer. It was read at one of the last of the Ranger reunions, held at Fairfax Court House September 11, 1900.
18. *O. R.*, Ser. I, Vol. XLVI, Pt. III, p. 1396. Several copies of Mosby's farewell address exist. One is at the Library of Congress and is believed by the author to be the original because of a change in its wording. Others, all conforming to the altered version, are in the Confederate Museum at Richmond, Va., in the public library at Warrenton, Va., and in the possession of William Chapman's descendants at Greensboro, N. C. This last copy was read by Colonel Chapman to the Rangers who went to Winchester to be paroled at the time the command was disbanded.

CHAPTER 24

1. *O. R.*, Ser. I, Vol. XLIX, Pt. II, p. 442.
2. Letter written by Grant to Halleck from Philadelphia May 4, 1865.
3. *O. R.*, Ser. I, Vol. XLVI, Pt. III, p. 1157.
4. Munson, p. 275.
5. Letter to Mrs. Mosby dated August 27, 1865.

6. An anecdote grew out of this incident after the war. It appears in the Albemarle County Historical Society Papers, and was repeated by Editor Virginius Dabney of the Richmond *Times-Dispatch* in an editorial September 20, 1943. In this account, Mosby is said to have been informed on his arrival at Charlottesville that Federal soldiers were looking for him. Examining his pistols, he sank spur into horse and rode down the middle of Main Street, directly through the Union cavalrymen who were approaching from an opposite direction, and passed on out of town. Asked later why he took such a chance, he replied that he often had found that the boldest way was the best and that, anyway, he didn't believe they would know who he was. Queried next as to what he would have done if he had been recognized, he answered: "Well, I reckon I could have demoralized them and gotten away!"

7. Remark repeated to the author by Mosby's daughter, Mrs. Stuart Mosby Coleman of Warrenton, Va.

8. Mosby wrote his wife in August: "Uncle John made John Hipkins (member of Company H) go to Richmond, as we were anxious to learn what were the designs of the Yankees toward me.... General Lee sent me word ... that he was waiting to see General Grant; he also said he entirely approved of everything I had done."

9. W. G. Waller in *Magazine of American History,* XV, 609.

10. Washington *Star,* June 29, 1865.

11. Cooke, *Wearing of the Gray,* p. 125. Repeated in *Munsey's Magazine,* Vol. XLIX.

12. Washington *Star,* December 18, 1865.

13. Letter to Mrs. Mosby dated January 6, 1865.

CHAPTER 25

1. Washington *Star,* March 27, 1867.

2. Monteiro Letters, No. 4, Confederate Museum, Richmond, Va.

3. William H. Payne Papers, Archives Division, Virginia State Library.

4. *Ibid.*

5. Copied in the Washington *Star,* April 25, 1867.

6. Washington *Star,* October 24, 1867.

7. New York *Post,* November 19, 1867.

8. From undated newspaper clipping now in possession of J. W. Slaughter of The Plains, Va.

9. Southern Historical Society Papers, Chapter 23, of Mosby Notes.

10. *Mosby's Memoirs,* p. 380.

11. *Ibid.*

12. *Ibid.*, p. 382.
13. Alexandria *News,* October 9, 1871.
14. As recalled by Beverly C. Mosby in a letter to the author dated June 11, 1942.
15. *Mosby's Memoirs,* p. 383.
16. *Ibid.*, pp. 384-85.
17. *Ibid.*, p. 392.
18. Notes by Colonel Mosby published in the Warrenton *Virginian,* May 12, 1904.
19. *Mosby's Memoirs,* p. 393.
20. Washington *Star,* August 8, 1872.
21. Political Notes, Washington *Star,* August 9, 1872.
22. Washington *Star,* October 5, 1872.
23. *Ibid.*, November 8, 1872.
24. *Mosby's Memoirs,* pp. 388-89.
25. Washington *Star,* June 10, 1873.
26. Notes by Colonel Mosby published in the Warrenton *Virginian,* May 12, 1904.
27. Warrenton correspondent of the Alexandria *News,* quoted in the Washington *Star,* March 3, 1874.
28. Washington correspondent of the Wytheville (Va.) *Enterprise,* quoted in the Washington *Star,* April 4, 1874.
29. *Ibid.*
30. Correspondence of the Baltimore *Sun* from Vernon Mills, Fauquier County, Va., republished in the Washington *Star,* June 15, 1874.
31. Revealed in a letter of C. M. Smith, written from Upperville, Va., August 20, 1874, and now on file in the William H. Payne Papers.
32. William H. Payne Papers.
33. Unidentified editorial among William H. Payne Papers.
34. Reprinted in the Washington *Star,* September 29, 1874.
35. Letters of Colonel Mosby and John Tyler, Jr., from the New York *Herald,* August 12, 1876. On file in the University of Virginia Library.
36. New York *Herald,* August 12, 1876.
37. Note by Mosby published in the Warrenton *Virginian,* May 12, 1904.
38. Among congratulatory letters received by Mosby was one from General Stoughton, who said he had asked his representative in the United States Senate to vote for confirmation of the appointment.—*Southern Historical Society Papers,* XXVII, 270.
39. Recalled by Beverly Mosby, who told the author he frequently had heard his father refer to this line.
40. *Mosby's Memoirs,* p. 398.

41. On June 5, 1894, Mosby wrote Monteiro from San Francisco: "The fact is that I would have gone, but I supposed the invitation was sent to me as a mere matter of form and that I would be given the cold shoulder if I went, and probably that old fraud—Jubal Early —who assumes to be a sort of administrator of the Confederate Army, would, as he generally does on such occasions, make some insulting allusions to 'men who have deserted since the war'—meaning those who have voted the Republican ticket.... The fact is that old Early himself was the first man after the war who deserted our people. As soon as he heard of Lee's surrender, he took to his heels and ran away to Canada instead of doing as I did—staying with our people—taking all the chances—and helping them to recover self-government."—Monteiro Letters, No. 26.

42. *University of Virginia Alumni News*, IV, 237.

43. Williamson, p. 521; Munson, p. 274.

44. His companion on this ride was Mrs. Dudley DuBose, daughter of William H. Robertson, the Commonwealth's attorney of 1853.

45. Remark of the late John S. Mosby, Jr., repeated to the author by his sister, Miss Pauline Mosby of Warrenton, Va.

46. An experience recalled by Major Robert A. McIntyre of Warrenton in reminiscing for the author on Mosby's years there after the war.

47. *Ibid.*

48. Concluding sentence of a letter written by Mosby from Washington, February 21, 1908.

49. *Confederate Veteran*, XVIII, 429.

50. Dr. Douglas Southall Freeman, who occasionally saw Mosby on his visits to Richmond at this period, told the author that the veteran, even as an old man, possessed a picturesqueness of appearance, a rough, colorful air, that fitted perfectly with his reputation.

51. Mosby had had this volume in mind for many years. In 1895. he wrote Monteiro: "I shall not publish the book I am going to write—'Memoirs of the War in Virginia'—for a year." Delay in this instance was a result of his decision to wait until the Rebellion Records could be revised. The *Memoirs*, edited by his brother-in-law, Charles W. Russell, were published posthumously in 1917.

52. *University of Virginia Alumni News*, III, 182, and the Washington *Star*, April 19, 1915.

53. *Mosby's Memoirs*, p. 63.

54. *University of Virginia Alumni News*, III, 156; *Mosby's Memoirs*, p. 9.

55. A portrait of Mosby now hangs in the University of Virginia Library.

INDEX

330 INDEX

Cole (*cont.*)

8; Blakeley's Grove fight, 176

Cole, Louis, robbed, 218

Cole, Lieutenant, death, 231

Colorado, 304

Colston, William E., wounded, 169

Commandos, 11

Company A, organized, 132-3; sent after Blazer, 230-1; disbanded, 270; mentioned, 133, 154, 197, 245

Company B, organized, 154; sent after Blazer, 230-1; disbanded, 270; mentioned, 190, 245

Company C, organized, 154; leaves for Northern Neck, 252; disbanded, 270; mentioned, 222, 245, 268

Company D, organized, 179; Montjoy killed, 233; Grogan wounded, 248; disbanded, 270; mentioned, 189, 197, 245

Company E, organized, 190; leaves for Northern Neck, 252; disbanded, 270; mentioned, 197, 245

Company F, organized, 203; leaves for Northern Neck, 252; disbanded, 270; mentioned, 245

Company G, organized, 234; leaves for Northern Neck, 252; disbanded, 270; mentioned, 245

Company H, organized, 258; disbanded, 270

Compson, Captain Hartwell B., Chapman's raid, 204-5

Confederate army, 144, 267

Confederate Cavalry, reorganized, 53; mentioned, 36, 62, 65, 71, 95, 109

Confederate Congress, Partisan Ranger Act, 62; repeals Partisan Ranger Act, 174; welcomes Mosby, 253; mentioned, 35, 57, 172, 175

Confederate States of America, nearing end, 230; mentioned, 12, 13, 34, 42, 102, 171

Confederate War Department, approves reorganization, 244; mentioned, 97, 132, 173

Conservative Party, 293

Couch, General D. N., death for spies, 233

Crook, General George, part in windup, 178-9; mentioned, 190

Croquette, Mosby's horses, 285; mentioned, 219

Crowninshield, Colonel C., burning property, 239

Cub Run, 86, 96, 107

Culpeper, Stoughton at, 97; Mosby at, 212, 252; Mosby reported at, 275; mentioned, 64, 73, 100, 101, 109, 135, 136, 139, 276, 293, 296, 308

Cumberland, 233

Cumberland Valley, Gettysburg campaign, 136; mentioned, 233

Custer, General George A., orders homes burned, 201; hangings, 208-11, 222, 226, 228, 284; Mosby's retaliation, 223-8; mentioned, 227, 238, 254

Dabney, Lieutenant Chiswell, at Verdiersville, 65-6

Dandy, Mosby's horses, 285

Daniel, Colonel J. J., 43

Danville, 257

Darnestown, 264

Davis, Alexander F. (Yankee); Mosby's hat, 249; mentioned, 82

Davis, Jefferson, 34, 41, 43, 46, 57, 103, 104, 108, 109, 114, 173, 273

Dawn of the Real South, publication of, 301

D Company, organized, 179; Montjoy killed, 233; Grogan wounded, 248; disbanded, 270; mentioned, 189, 197, 245

Dear, Charley, kills Federal, 218; captures payroll, 218

De Barros, Francis Xavier Monteiro, 20, 244

DeButts, John, at Warrenton Junction, 120

DeForest, Colonel Othneil, trailing Mosby, 135

Democratic Party, indorses Greeley, 286; nominates Tilden, 298; mentioned, 30, 293, 294, 297

Department of Justice, 304

Department of Washington, 115

Devin, General Thomas C., burning property, 235

Dewdrop, Mosby's horses, 285

Difficult Run, 110, 135

Dixie Artillery, 112, 123

Dobb's farm, 59

Douglas, Stephen A., 43

Dover, Mosby at, 90

Lazelle, Colonel H. M., anti-Ranger plan, 190-1; embarrassed, 192; strengthens picket posts, 202; plan copied, 203

Lee, Agnes, at Richmond, 284

Lee, General Fitzhugh, Mosby's dislike for, 57; Stoughton delivered to, 97; at Stuart's headquarters, 146; sets out for Gettysburg, 149; mentioned, 53, 57, 58, 61, 65, 66, 71, 95, 100, 103, 207

Lee, *Light Horse Harry*, Partisan, 254

Lee, General Robert E., takes command, 58; heeds Mosby's information, 64; advance on Pope, 65; first Maryland campaign, 67; commends Mosby, 80, 97, 103, 108, 202, 214; praises Mosby in general orders, 85; Mosby's commission, 114; Chancellorsville, 117; Gettysburg, 122-3; military elections, 131, 133; Gettysburg advance, 135; at Winchester, 141; communications uncovered, 144; orders cavalry into Maryland, 145; sent proposed Gettysburg route, 146; letter of *ifs*, 148; urges Stuart to hurry, 149; approve Stuart's route, 150; winter dispositions, 154; army dwindling, 172; criticises Mosby, 173; saves Forty-third Battalion, 174; Mosby's promotion, 175; urges coöperation, 181; V. M. I. cadets, 182; feints, 185; home of, 188; Mosby visits, 212, 243-4, 254, 284; windup, 213; letter on hangings, 222; approves retaliation, 223; Mosby letter, 230; William Chapman visits, 252; enemy closes on, 257; message to Mosby, 258; lines broken, 259; surrender, 260, 262; surrender terms, 261; advises Smith, 263-4; terms extended, 267; Mosby parole, 274; statue, 302; mentioned, 12, 20, 37, 59, 60, 61, 62, 66, 68, 104, 121, 130, 136, 137, 139, 146, 179, 186, 290, 307

Lee, General W. H. F., sets out for Gettysburg, 149

Lee County, 38

Leesburg, Montjoy killed near, 233; Mosby reported at, 262; Mosby arrested at, 278; Mosby defies Federals at, 279; Mosby at, 281; mentioned, 72, 81, 110, 132, 134, 189, 197

Letcher, Governor John, 37, 38, 43

Lewinsville, 51, 52

Lewis, Senator John F., quotes Mosby, 286

Liberal Republican Party, 286

Li Hung Chang, seeks Mosby's support, 300

Limerick, Ireland, 175

Lincoln, Abraham, summons Stahel, 115; Mosby's hair, 179-80; defending Washington, 189; objection to Sheridan, 191; assassination, 261, 263, 264, 266, 267; Rangers regret assassination, 265; peace conference, 275; mentioned, 34, 39, 82, 84, 100, 144, 174, 178

Lincoln, Va., 257

Little River, 88

Little River Turnpike, significance to Rangers, 106; mentioned, 73, 74, 87, 90, 91, 92, 102, 122, 132, 138, 140, 147, 237

Locksley Hall, 299

London Times, angers Mosby, 307

Longstreet, General James, transferred to Gordonsville, 64; Gettysburg advance, 135-6; at Winchester, 141; approves Stuart's route, 150; at Petersburg, 212; mentioned, 62, 65, 69, 112

Loudoun County, visited by Stuart, 68; Gettysburg advance, 149; property destroyed, 199-200; Sheridan's depredations, 232; Sheridan's ultimatum, 236; Federal scout, 257; mentioned, 38, 76, 80, 106, 110, 115, 140, 165, 189, 192, 218, 241, 252, 261, 270, 297

Loudoun Heights, camp attacked at, 164-70, 221; mentioned, 166, 170, 171

Loudoun Rangers, organized, 81; routed, 186, 219; kill Montjoy, 233; captured, 259

Loudoun Valley, Sheridan's depredations, 231; burning property, 235; damage, 239; deserters in, 255; mentioned, 240, 243, 244, 252, 269

Love, Lucian, executed, 209

Love, Tom, accompanies Mosby, 245-6; captured, 248

visits, 287, 288, 291, 297, 298; Mosby welcome at, 290-1; mentioned, 115, 294

White House, Va., 58, 59

Whitescarver, George H., joins Mosby, 84; capturing Stoughton, 94; captures couriers, 95; at Warrenton, 116; lieutenant, 133; death, 134; mentioned, 271, 303

White's Ford, 189

Whiting, C. F., captures officer, 224-5

Wild, John, first Rangers, 72; at Miskel farm, 112; at Warrenton Junction, 120

Willard Hotel, Mosby at, 281, 282

Williams, Franklin, captures guard, 84; capturing Stoughton, 94; returns Stoughton's watch, 95; at Warrenton, 116

Williamsburg, Ranger raid on, 263

Williamsport, trains fording at, 145

Willis, A. C., hanged, 222

Wiltshire, Jim, guards payroll, 218

Winchester, Gettysburg advance, 135; Early at, 192; property destruction, 200; Sheridan returns to, 220; Hancock at, 262; Mosby reported at, 272; mentioned, 44, 45, 72, 136, 181, 190, 193, 196, 206, 223, 226, 227, 229, 250

Wise, General Henry A., 43

Wise's Brigade, 244

Wistar, General Isaac I., 67

Woodbury, Lieutenant Charles A., killed, 113

Woods, Peter, 42

Woodstock, 182

World War I, 307

Wright, General Horatio G., 297

Wyatt, Dick, 42

Wyndham, Colonel Percy, Mosby angers, 76; newspapers praise, 83; calls Mosby thief, 86; newspapers criticise, 89; wanted by Stuart, 109; successor, 114; replaced, 115; mentioned, 74, 77, 78, 79, 85, 90, 93, 94, 95

Yancey, William L., 30, 31, 33

Yellow Tavern, Stuart wounded at, 182

York River, 58

York River railroad, 59

Yorktown, 57, 58

Zouaves, 54